Catholicism in Motion

The Church in American Society

JAMES D. DAVIDSON

Liguori/Triumph
LIGUORI, MISSOURI

Imprimi Potest:
Thomas D. Picton, C.Ss.R.
Provincial, Denver Province
The Redemptorists

BX
140.3
D38
2005

Published by Liguori/Triumph
An imprint of Liguori Publications
Liguori, Missouri
www.liguori.org

Library of Congress Cataloging-in-Publication Data

Davidson, James D.
    Catholicism in motion : the church in American society / James D. Davidson.—
1st. Ed.
        p.   cm.
    Includes bibliographical references and index.
    ISBN 0-7648-1345-5 (pbk.)
    1. Catholic Church—United States. 2. United States—Church history. I. Title.

BX1406.3.D38   2005
282'.73—dc22   2005022970

Excerpts from the English translation of the *Catechism of the Catholic Church* for the United States of America, copyright © 1994, United States Catholic Conference, Inc.—Libreria Editrice Vaticana; English translation of the *Catechism of the Catholic Church: Modifications from the Editio Typica*, copyright © 1997, United States Catholic Conference, Inc.—Libreria Editrice Vaticana. Used with permission.

Liguori Publications, a nonprofit corporation, is an apostolate of the Redemptorists. To learn more about the Redemptorists, visit *Redemptorists.com.*

Printed in the United States of America
09 08 07 06 05   5 4 3 2 1
First edition

To my wife, Anna,
our son, Jay, and
our daughter, Theresa.

Contents

Part II: Organizational Issues in the Church

Chapter 4: Parishes, Schools, and Other Catholic Institutions 63

Chapter 5: Challenges With Authority, Sexual Abuse,
       and Other Problems 81

List of Tables

Introduction

Since 1999, I have written two columns a month for twelve diocesan newspapers. The columns have summarized social theories and the latest research on American Catholics and American Catholicism. *Catholicism in Motion* contains ninety-eight columns that explore Catholicism's changing place in American life, organizational changes in the Church, and the changing beliefs and practices of American Catholics.

I have written this book for three reasons. First, research has been more than a career for me; it is something I feel called to do. It has been my ministry, my way of contributing to the Church. In addition to sharing my research with academic colleagues, I want to share it with Catholic clergy and laypeople through books, articles in Catholic periodicals, columns in diocesan newspapers, and presentations at church gatherings. Putting a selection of my newspaper columns into a book provides an excellent opportunity to make the latest research accessible to an even wider audience.

Second, I want to share my research with the widest possible audience, because I believe research is an important resource for the Church. Research adds to our knowledge of the many ways society affects the Church and the many ways the Church impacts society. It not only helps us describe trends in the Church, it also helps us examine the roots and ramifications of these trends. It also tells us what Catholics actually believe, how they actually practice their faith, and why they think and act the way they do.

Finally, research has important implications for both clergy and laity. When it confirms our a priori assumptions, it reassures us that our instincts are sound and lends legitimacy to the attitudes and actions that flow from our presuppositions. When research challenges our taken-for-granted assumptions, it invites us to consider new ideas and new courses of action. Whether its effects are to affirm ongoing patterns or encourage alternative courses of action, research usually contributes to the well-being of the Church.

My columns have addressed three rather distinct (but not totally separable) levels of analysis. As a result, *Catholicism in Motion* is divided into three parts, each containing several chapters. Part 1 emphasizes the societal, or macro, level of analysis. It explores Catholicism's changing place in American society. Chapter 1 considers the historical context of Protestant-Catholic tensions in America. It also examines the extent to which Catholics have risen from the bottom to the top of the American economic ladder, their movement from the margins to the middle of American society, and competing models of Catholic life that have emerged over the course of U.S. history. In addition, it provides a profile of American Catholics today, considers the size and changing racial/ethnic composition of the Catholic population, and documents the geographical relocation of American Catholics. Chapter 2 explores religion's role in American society and culture. Are American's really more spiritual but less religious than they used to be? Does religion affect Americans' social interactions? Chapter 3 raises a number of questions about the connection between religion, the economy, and American politics. For example, how much impact does religion have on the economy? How do the Church's social teachings affect our thinking about social and economic inequality? How has religion affected America's political culture, Americans' access to the nation's highest political offices, and the way Catholics vote?

Part 2 stresses the organizational, or meso, level of analysis. It focuses on a variety of opportunities and challenges facing the Catholic Church today. Chapter 4 introduces four different approaches social scientists use to study organizations in general and religious groups in particular. It also invites readers to consider the areas in which the "golden years" of Catholic organizations are behind us as well as the areas in which they lie before us. These sections are followed by analyses of changes in Catholic parishes and Catholic schools and a study of Catholics' financial contributions to these key institutions (Does having a Catholic school increase financial contributions to a parish?). Chapter 5 examines bishops' authority (Is it declining and, if so, why?), the recent sexual abuse scandal (How are laypeople perceiving and reacting to it?), and other problems facing the Church (Which ones do laypeople consider most serious?). Chapter 6 addresses leadership issues. One concern is the growing shortage of priests and its many implications (Is it unique to the Catholic Church? How are laypeople coping with it?). Another has to do with the emergence of the permanent diaconate and the increasing number of deacons (How is this new leadership role working out so far?). The chapter ends with research on the growing number of lay ministers, the attributes they bring to the Church, the challenges they face, and their spiritual practices.

Part 3 stresses the individual, or micro, level of analysis. It examines American Catholics' beliefs and practices. Chapter 7 reviews social theories that might help readers understand the reasons why Catholics think and act the way they do. Chapter 8 looks at Catholic identity, commitment to the Church, and the relationship—including the gap—between the two. It also explores the effects that identity and commitment have on Catholics' attitudes and actions outside the Church. Chapter 9 focuses on trends in Catholics' beliefs and practices. It contains the latest findings that point to declining rates of participation in the sacraments, especially Eucharist, reconciliation, and marriage. It also examines the importance Catholics attach to Church teachings (Which ones do laypeople consider most and least important?) and the extent to which they comply with them (How many Catholics believe in Christ's presence in the Eucharist and agree with the Church's pro-life stance on abortion?). The book ends with articles on factors that affect Catholics' beliefs and practices (see chapter 10). One article shows that Catholic parents have changed the way they raise their children. Others demonstrate that Catholics' beliefs and practices are affected by generation (How different are pre-Vatican II and post-Vatican II Catholics?), race and ethnicity (How different are Anglos and Hispanics?), religious roots (Are converts better Catholics?), and gender (Are Catholic men and women from different planets?).

Each chapter starts with an introduction, which offers a brief summary that explains why I have put these columns together in a single chapter, although they often were written months, even years, apart. At the end of each chapter, there is a short series of questions inviting Catholics to explore the implications the chapter has for them personally and/or for their parishes and dioceses.

How the Book Came About

In the mid-1990s, I directed a research project that eventually led to my co-authored book *The Search for Common Ground: What Unites and Divides Catholic Americans*.[1] That book was widely read by people in both the academic community and the Church. It received very positive reviews in academic journals and the 1998 Research Award from the National Conference for Catechetical Leadership. It also led to many invitations to speak at national, regional, and local meetings of Church leaders. Reflecting on this very positive response, I was pleased—and somewhat surprised—to find that Catholic audiences were so eager to learn about the latest research and explore its implications for their parishes and diocesan programs.

One day, while driving home from a meeting in Indianapolis, I thought about writing a regular column for diocesan newspapers. It would not be an opinion column. Instead, it would provide clergy and laypeople with information that might be useful in their personal lives and especially in their church activities. The next day, I called Tom Russell—editor of my diocesan newspaper, *The Catholic Moment*—to see what he thought about the idea. He liked it and encouraged me to proceed. We agreed that a couple of columns a month would be plenty of work for me and would provide enough material for the editors of diocesan papers.

I contacted the editors of papers in dioceses where I had recently spoken. Several of them agreed to give the column a try. I sent out my first two columns at the end of February 1999, and I have sent out two every month since then. Some of the research I have reported in the columns includes my ongoing studies of U.S. Catholics. These include a 1993 national study that eventuated in my 1996 book *Laity: American and Catholic* (with William D'Antonio, Dean Hoge, and Ruth Wallace),[2] the 1995 national survey that was the basis of *The Search for Common Ground* (with Andrea Williams, Richard Lamanna, Jan Stenftenagel, Kathleen Maas Weigert, William Whalen, and Patricia Wittberg, S.C.), the 1999 national survey that was reported in my 2001 book *American Catholics: Gender, Generation, and Commitment* (with D'Antonio, Hoge, and Katherine Meyer),[3] the 1999 study that was the foundation of my 2003 book *Lay Ministers and Their Spiritual Practices* (with Thomas Walters, Bede Cisco, O.S.B., Katherine Meyer, and Charles Zech),[4] and the 2003 national survey Dean Hoge and I did for the University of Notre Dame (and which was reported in the November 19, 2004, issue of *Commonweal* magazine).[5] Other columns have been based on other research conducted by other people.

The columns have appeared in the following diocesan papers: *The Catholic Moment* (Diocese of Lafayette-in-Indiana), *The Florida Catholic* (which covers all Florida dioceses), *The Catholic Review* (Archdiocese of Baltimore), *The Criterion* (Archdiocese of Indianapolis), *The Dialog* (Diocese of Wilmington), *The Catholic Accent* (Diocese of Greensburg), *The Tidings* (Archdiocese of Los Angeles), *The Observer* (Diocese of Rockford), *Today's Catholic* (Diocese of Fort Wayne-South Bend), *The Intermountain Catholic* (Diocese of Salt Lake), *The Message* (Diocese of Evansville), and *The Messenger* (Diocese of Belleville). *The Catholic Review* and the Diocese of Greensburg also have used the column on their Web sites.

By 2002, I wondered if there would be any value in putting some of my columns in a book that would reach clergy and laypeople in dioceses where my columns do not appear. I sorted the columns into topical categories and experimented with these categories in summer school classes at the University of Dayton and at Sacred Heart University. The response was very positive. I decided to accumulate more columns, select what I consider to be my best columns (you cannot hit a home run every time), make a few editorial and substantive improvements, and send the collection to Liguori Publications, which agreed to publish this volume. I offered the new collection to a summer school class of Catholic school principals at Sacred Heart University in July 2004. Once again, the response was very positive. It also led to a sharpening of the book's focus and a consolidation of its chapters. In the fall of 2004, I used the revised manuscript in an undergraduate course at Purdue University. That experience led to some final changes.

Most columns are exactly the way they appeared when I sent them to the editors of the diocesan papers. Of course, the editors have printed some columns and not others, so this book contains some columns that never appeared in diocesan papers. Because editors also are expected to edit the columns and fit them into the space that is available, there are likely to be some differences in the way the columns appeared in their papers and the way they appear in this book. In a very few cases, I have made editorial corrections or substantive changes to increase the continuity between columns that were written at very different times but now appear right next to, or very near, one another. I also have updated a few columns. In most cases (such as the column on trends in Catholic schools), the update has meant adding data that has become available since the article was originally written. In a few cases (such as the column on presidential appointments to the Supreme Court), it has involved additional interpretation of events that have occurred since the column first appeared.

Another feature is the addition of endnotes. We have identified points in each column where the reader might want more detailed bibliographical information than can be included in a standard newspaper column. At these points, numeric superscripts have been added to the text. Each number is tied to a separate entry in the Notes section at the end of the book. Readers who want to consult original sources or seek additional information will appreciate this feature.

Acknowledgments

Many people have contributed to this book, often without realizing their impact. My wife, Anna, and our children, Jay and Terry, have provided so much personal support and experience with the issues discussed in my columns that I have dedicated the book to them. Lilly Endowment Inc.'s fingerprints are all over the research reported in this book. I am especially grateful to Robert Lynn, Fred Hofheinz, and Sister Jeanne Knoerle—all of whom have contributed to my research. To all of my collaborators and coauthors, once again I say thanks. I am especially grateful to Thomas Russell and all of the other editors who have published my columns in their diocesan papers. Daniel Michaels, acquisition editor with Liguori Publications, has been a wise counselor as we have transformed a collection of newspaper columns into a book. Sister Angela Ann Zukowski, MHSH, at the University of Dayton and Ms. Patricia Murphy and Father Barry Meehan, SJ, at Sacred Heart University have offered me wonderful opportunities to explore my ideas with clergy and lay leaders in their highly successful programs. The students in my classes at Dayton, Sacred Heart, and Purdue have stimulated my thinking and given me great hope for the future of the Catholic Church.

JAMES D. DAVIDSON
WEST LAFAYETTE, INDIANA
SEPTEMBER 2005

Part I

Catholicism in America

Chapter 1

History and Profile of American Catholics

This chapter begins by inviting readers to think about the extent to which religion has been a positive force contributing to the well-being of our society or a negative force that has divided Americans. Recognizing that religion has had at least some divisive consequences, other parts of this chapter show that in America's colonial period, Catholics were a small, mostly European, and lower-status religious out-group. Overcoming many obstacles, Catholics have become a relatively large, increasingly non-European, highly educated, and prosperous people of many colors and cultures who also have moved from the margins to the middle of American life and culture. In the course of these changes, Catholics have fluctuated between a Roman model, which sees the Church as being in tension with the society, and an American model, which sees the two as compatible. Today's Catholic population is larger than official Church statistics suggest. Largely as a result of the immigration of Hispanic and Asian Catholics, it will continue to grow. However, its presence in the Northeast is likely to decline as its presence in the Southeast and Southwest increases.

What Is Your View of Religion's Role in Society?

Like social researchers, we all have theories about religion's role in society. We all make assumptions about the essence of religion, the nature of society, and the relationship between the two. Although we do not dwell on these theories all of the time, they still frame our thoughts and actions. They shape our reactions to books, newspaper stories, and television reports about religion. They explain why we agree with some friends and family members more than others when religion comes up in conversations. They also account for our support of, or opposition to, specific practices in our parishes and dioceses.

3

Given the importance of our theories, perhaps we should reflect on them for a few minutes. I invite you to think about two theories, which sociologists call *functionalism* and *conflict theory*. Proponents of functionalist theory think of society as a social system consisting of many interdependent parts called social institutions. These institutions include marriage, education, economy, politics, and religion. Each institution has a role to play and, in performing its function, it contributes to the well-being of society. The parts of this system work well together, because at the core of society is a set of widely shared values, beliefs, and priorities. In other words, there is a core culture that allows society to run in an orderly fashion.

Conflict theorists, on the other hand, picture society as being in a constant state of disorder. The main reason for this turmoil is that at society's core there are classes of people who are pitted against one another in a struggle to maximize their own self-interests. As one group (the "haves") gets the upper hand over the others (the "have-nots"), it tries to control as many spheres of life as it can, especially the economy and politics but also religion. Once it does, it creates social policies that work to its advantage and to the disadvantage of others. Never fully embracing these policies, the have-nots struggle to subvert or overcome them. The struggle between the haves and have-nots produces social instability.

These theories offer two very different views of religion's role in society. Functionalism sees religion as an important social institution. According to functionalists, religion answers questions about the meaning and purpose of life. It promotes norms, values, and skills that allow people to live together in an orderly fashion. It provides people with an identity ("a child of God") and a sense of belonging (being Catholic). In other words, religion contributes to the well-being of society and its individual members. It is highly functional.

Conflict theory offers a very different view of religion. It proposes that religion is relatively inconsequential, especially in comparison to the economy and government. However, just as the haves seek control of the economy and government, they also seek control of religious organizations and influence over religious leaders. In this way, they are able to promote religious ideas that justify their power, privilege, and prestige and keep the have-nots from rebelling against them. From a conflict point of view, religion is a divisive and oppressive force in society. Its effects are more negative than positive.

Which of these theories comes closest to your way of thinking about religion's role in society?

TABLE 1.1 Range of Responses to Functionalism and Conflict Theory

Accept functionalist view, reject conflict theory	Accept most of functionalism and some parts of conflict theory	Accept most of conflict theory and some parts of functionalism	Accept conflict theory, reject functionalism

Do you identify with the functionalist view and reject the conflict perspective? Do you tend toward the functionalist view but acknowledge that there is some truth to what conflict theorists say? Do you tend toward conflict theory but concede that functionalism is not entirely wrong? Or, do you fully embrace conflict theory and disagree with the functionalist perspective? Your response might explain your reactions to media reports about religion, your conversations with friends and family members about religion, and your willingness to support some Church policies more than others.

The Origins of Religious Stratification in America

Religious stratification occurs when religious affiliation affects access to resources such as education, jobs, income, the right to own land, and the right to vote. It exists when members of some religions accumulate more power, privilege, and prestige than members of other religious traditions.

Religious stratification emerged during America's colonial period. Sixty-one percent of the men signing the Declaration of Independence in 1776 were Episcopalian; 23 percent were Congregationalist. Only one was a Catholic, and only one was a Baptist. Forty-eight percent of the men attending the Constitutional Convention in 1787 were Episcopalian, and 20 percent were Congregationalist. Only two were Catholic, and none were Baptist. Almost half of Boston's fifty leading families during the seventeenth and eighteenth centuries were Congregationalists. Anglicans were overrepresented among wealthy individuals in New York City in the 1750s and they dominated economic relations in Southern colonies. Catholics, Baptists, Jews, and other religious groups ranked much lower in both economic and political influence.

How did religious stratification become part and parcel of America's social fabric at the time of the nation's birth? In a recent paper addressing this question, Ralph Pyle (of Michigan State University) and I pointed to the importance of three factors: prejudice, competition, and differential power.[1]

Religious prejudice is a predisposition to think of one's group as superior and members of other faiths as inferior. It stresses the virtues of one's group and the vices of others. Anti-Catholicism and other forms of religious prejudice were widespread in the colonies. For example, government officials in Maryland in the eighteenth century talked about "Popish priests and zealous Papists" who "seduce, delude, and persuade diverse people of his Majesty's good Protestant subjects to the Romish faith." John Adams wrote to Thomas Jefferson saying that Catholicism was "Hindu and cabalistic." Patriot Samuel Adams said the Stamp Act (which imposed British taxes) was a less serious threat to colonial liberation than popery.

Competition involves contentious relationships between religious groups striving to achieve the same scarce goals, such as land, political office, religious adherents, civic freedoms, recognition by the state, cultural influence, and jobs. Religious groups try to increase their access to these resources and limit others' access to them. The more valuable the resources, the more intense the conflict. The more intense the conflict, the greater the likelihood that religious stratification will result. Religious competition was widespread in the colonies. For example, the 1609 Virginia Charter specified that Catholics could not settle in the colony and numerous acts were passed by the General Assembly to enforce conformity to Church of England rules and doctrines. In Pennsylvania, Catholics were excluded from office and, by 1743, were excluded from naturalization. In Massachusetts, a 1647 law designed to prevent Jesuit priests from entering the colony decreed that any priests who might come into the colony were to be banished and, if they returned, put to death.

Religious prejudice and competition do not lead to religious stratification unless religious groups are of such unequal power that some are able to impose their will on others. Larger, more organized groups with more resources are able to impose their will on smaller, less organized groups with fewer resources. Anglicanism (now called Episcopalians) was the established religion in Virginia, North Carolina, South Carolina, Georgia, Maryland, and New York. Congregationalism (now called the United Church of Christ) was the established religion in Massachusetts, Connecticut, and New Hampshire. These colonies, often with help from the English crown, passed laws favoring members of the established churches and discriminating against members of other groups, including Catholics.

No one of these factors (prejudice, competition, differential power) is enough to create religious stratification. All three are needed. All three existed in the colonies and, together, they produced a pattern of religious inequality that had consequences for years to come.

In-Group Virtues and Out-Group Vices

Think for a moment about the hostilities between Protestants and Catholics during the Colonial Period of American history. Now, think about the tensions between Protestants and Catholics in Northern Ireland.

The fact that these situations involve different places and different points in time means there are important differences in these relationships. However, the fact that Protestants are the in-group and Catholics are the out-group in both situations means there also are important similarities in these relationships. Let me explain.

In his book, *Social Theory and Social Structure*, Columbia University sociologist Robert K. Merton offers a general theory of the relationship between in-groups (which have disproportionate amounts of power and influence) and out-groups (which have less).[2] Merton argues that in-groups tend to see themselves as superior and out-groups as inferior. Regardless of the facts bearing on the case, in-groups believe their own members are capable of acting in virtuous ways, but members of out-groups are not. Defining the situation in this manner, in-groups believe they are entitled to more social rewards and benefits than members of out-groups. In accordance with this self-fulfilling prophecy, in-groups accumulate more than their fair share of power, privilege, and prestige; out-groups have less than their fair share of these scarce resources.

What happens, then, when members of the out-group engage in virtuous behavior? What if members of out-groups exhibit the same qualities as members of in-groups (for example, they too are successful in the workplace, careful with their money, and socially responsible)? What do members of in-groups do then? According to Merton, they "resent any personal achievement not warranted by social position." Under these circumstances, Merton says, "the very same behavior undergoes a complete change of evaluation in its transition from the in-group...to the out-group." In other words, in-groups quickly convert in-group virtues into out-group vices. In Merton's words: "Is the in-group hero frugal, thrifty, and sparing? Then the out-group villain is stingy, miserly and penny-pinching." If the in-group hero is "smart, shrewd, and intelligent," the out-group villain is "cunning, crafty, and too clever by far." According to Merton, "moral virtues remain virtues only so long as they are jealously confined to the proper in-group. The right activity by the wrong people becomes a thing of contempt, not of honor."

The process of converting in-group virtues into out-group vices accomplishes two things for in-groups: they are able to "retain their distinction, their prestige, and their power…and enforce the mediocrity of others." Merton contends that such circumstances are only possible when social institutions (such as families, churches, schools, businesses, and governments) support the in-group's behavior. As long as institutional supports are in place, out-groups will not be able to prove that they are as virtuous as the in-groups. The only solution is to challenge institutional practices that sustain in-group privileges and perpetuate out-group powerlessness.

Merton's theory can be applied to a variety of settings where an in-group of one race, ethnicity, and/or gender is dominant over an out-group with different characteristics. It also sheds light on historical conflicts between the "established" churches (for example, Congregationalists and Episcopalians) and the "dissenters" (for example, Catholics and Baptists) in the American colonies. It also helps us understand the religious hostilities between Protestants and Catholics in Northern Ireland. Finally, it suggests that the only real solution to these—and other religious—conflicts is to address the social policies and practices that allow dominant groups to convert in-group virtues into out-group vices.

The First Amendment and Religion's Place in Society

The First Amendment to the U.S. Constitution says: "Congress shall make no law respecting an establishment of religion, or prohibiting the free exercise thereof." The first part of the amendment has come to be called "the establishment clause." The second part is known as "the free exercise clause."

Over the years, there has been a lot of discussion about what the nation's founders meant when they drafted this amendment. What were they trying to avoid, and what did they want to accomplish? What did they have in mind when they referred to "an establishment of religion"? What did they mean by the "free exercise" of religion?

The founders were fully aware that nine of the thirteen colonies had established religions. In three New England colonies (Massachusetts, New Hampshire, and Connecticut), the Congregational church was the established religion. In six others (New York, Maryland, Virginia, North Carolina, South

Carolina, and Georgia), Anglicanism (known as the Episcopal Church after 1776) was the established religion. Only four colonies (New Jersey, Pennsylvania, Delaware, and Rhode Island) did not have religious establishments.

There were numerous benefits for members of the established religion, and many costs for all other religious groups, including Catholics, who were a distinct minority in the colonies. For one thing, members of established religions could claim legal residence; members of other religious groups could not. Members of established religions also could run for and hold political office; people in other religious groups could not. Government meetings were often held in establishment congregations, never in other churches.

Members of other religions paid taxes and tithes that were used to pay the salaries of establishment clergy and to support establishment congregations. Members of other groups who followed their religious consciences could be, and often were, whipped, jailed, or hanged. So-called "dissenters" were sometimes expelled, which is what happened to Roger Williams who was driven out of Massachusetts for insisting that church and state should be separate (He retreated to what had come to be called "Rogue's Island.").[3]

Certainly, some founders understood the unfairness of established religions in the colonies. It also was true, however, that no one religious group had enough political clout to become the established religion for the new country. If one's own group could not be the established religion, one did not want any other group to have the advantages that came with being the established religion. The solution, found in the establishment clause, was to prevent any group from becoming the established religion.

If religious groups could not be the established religion, they wanted assurances that the new government would not interfere with their beliefs and traditions (the way establishment religions had mistreated other religions). The free exercise clause offered that assurance.

Competing Models of Catholicism in America

If you are looking for a good cultural history of Catholicism in America, you ought to read Jay P. Dolan's book *In Search of an American Catholicism*.[4] Dolan outlines two models or images of Catholicism and the Church's place in American society. He also shows how cultural conditions have contributed to movements back and forth between the two models over the course of U.S. history. He achieves these goals with clear thinking, convincing historical data, and a very readable writing style.

First, the models. Dolan calls one the "American," or "liberal," model. The other he calls the "traditional European monarchical," "conservative," or "Roman" model.

Dolan insists that these two orientations should not be viewed in "either-or" terms, but rather in "both-and" terms. It is not that one is right and the other is wrong. They coexist at all times, usually in considerable tension. Here's how they differ.

The American model assumes Catholicism is compatible with American culture, while the Roman model assumes they are incompatible. The liberal (American) model emphasizes lay participation and democratic decision making, while the traditional (Roman) model stresses papal and episcopal authority. The liberal model offers a positive view of human nature and modern society, while the conservative model emphasizes human and societal sinfulness. The American model stresses the need for Catholics to assimilate into American culture, while the Roman model offers a more separatist view of Catholics' place in society. The American model assumes benign relations with other religious groups, while the Roman model is very concerned about anti-Catholicism and nativist opposition to Catholicism.

The American model stresses loyalty to the new land, while the Roman model emphasizes loyalty to one's ethnic ancestry and homeland. The liberal approach promotes a spirit of toleration toward other faiths, while the conservative model stresses an animosity between faiths. The American model embraces the separation of church and state, while the Roman model believes the state should act in accord with church teachings. The liberal model celebrates reason and persuasion, while the conservative model emphasizes the need for compliance, even coercion if that is called for. The American model stresses personal piety, while the Roman model emphasizes the Church's role in mediating human beings' relationship with God. The liberal model offers a modern view of women's role in society, including the labor force, while the conservative model promotes the traditional role of women in the family and the home.

Dolan says American Catholic history shifts back and forth between these two orientations. During the republican era of 1780–1820, the Enlightenment's emphasis on reason and the American experiment with democracy gave impetus to the American model of church. In the mid-1800s and continuing into the 1920s, immigration increased, as did anti-Catholicism. As a result, the liberal model receded and the traditional, Roman model gained the upper hand. From 1920 to 1950, the Tridentine model prevailed, but by the 1950s, its cultural foundations were being challenged by a number of social conditions. Chief among these were the increasing percentage of American-born Catholics, the upward mobility and suburbanization of the Catholic population, declining levels of anti-Catholicism, and the beginning of the modern-day women's movement. These forces joined with the Second Vatican Council to produce a renewed interest in the liberal model. However, the papacy of Pope John Paul II and a new wave of immigration have combined to challenge the liberal approach and restore key components of the traditional model.

Dolan's book offers us a useful way of thinking about American Catholic history. His analysis gives us an excellent way to understand long-term trends and recent developments in the Church.

Dramatic Improvements in the Status of American Catholics

The upward mobility of American Catholics is one of the great stories of the twentieth century. At the beginning of the century, Catholics were among the nation's poorest religious groups. Today, they are among the most prosperous.

As America entered the twentieth century, Episcopalians, Presbyterians, and Congregationalists were the nation's most prominent religious groups. They had the best educations, occupied the loftiest positions in the labor force, and possessed a disproportionate share of the nation's wealth. A study of the religious affiliations of entries in the *Who's Who in America*, a well-known listing of prominent Americans, shows that these groups were highly overrepresented in the upper echelon of our society relative to their numbers in the total population. Though the country had no established religion in any legal sense, these groups comprised an informal "Protestant Establishment."

The U.S. Catholic population ballooned from only 650,000 in 1836 to 16 million by 1920, due mainly to immigration from places such as Ireland, Italy, and Poland. These European immigrants had very little education and took blue-collar jobs that produced only meager incomes. Catholics were at the bottom of the socioeconomic ladder. Very few Catholics occupied leadership positions at the top of American social institutions. There were only one-tenth as many Catholics in the *Who's Who in America* as one might expect given the size of the Catholic population in the early 1930s.

As time passed, Catholics worked their way up the social ladder. By the middle of the century, they had penetrated America's middle class. Gallup surveys in the early 1960s showed that Catholics averaged eleven years of education (the same as the national average). About four in ten Catholics were in white-collar jobs (again, right at the national average). Catholics' median family income was about $6,000 (again comparable to median income for the nation as a whole). Catholics now ranked higher than Baptists and most other evangelical groups, were about equal to Methodists and Lutherans (which were solid, middle-class denominations), but still lagged behind Presbyterians and Episcopalians.

Since midcentury, two things have happened. There has been a new wave of Catholic immigration, this time mainly from Mexico, Central and South America, and Asia. While some new immigrants have been prosperous on arrival, more have arrived with only modest means. Groups such as Mexicans, Puerto Ricans, and Filipinos now form the nucleus of the Catholic working class. Meanwhile, the descendants of the earlier wave of European immigration have continued to gain in social status. Irish, Italian, and Polish Catholics are now among the nation's most highly educated, most occupationally privileged, and most prosperous churchgoers.

The net effect is that Catholics are now firmly planted in the nation's upper middle class. Of Catholics who have completed their schooling, about 30 percent are college graduates or have gone on to postgraduate work. Another 30 percent have gone to technical schools or attended college without graduating. Among Catholics who have spent most of their lives in the labor force, over 60 percent are (or, if retired, were) in white-collar jobs. One-third are (or were) executives, business managers, or professionals (such as teachers, lawyers, nurses, and doctors). Nearly 40 percent of Catholics have family incomes of $50,000 or more. Another 30 percent have family incomes between $30,000 and $49,999. Though Catholics still have not caught up to Episcopalians and Presbyterians in the *Who's Who*, we now have almost as many entries (23 percent) as one would expect, given the fact that about 25 percent of all Americans are Catholic.

At the beginning of the century, Catholics lagged far behind elite Protestant denominations in social status. Even while absorbing a whole new wave of immigrants, they have taken their place among the nation's most prosperous religious groups. Though Episcopalians and Presbyterians still have a bit of a socioeconomic edge, Catholics now rank near the top of American society and are continuing to close the gap in terms of power, privilege, and prestige.

Catholics Still Underrepresented but Nearing Parity in *Who's Who*

Who's Who in America is the best-known and most highly regarded listing of persons who have achieved prominence in American society. It includes some people because of the important positions they hold, such as the president of the United States and members of the U.S. Senate. It includes others because of their accomplishments in their chosen fields, such as Michael Jordan and Oprah Winfrey.

By comparing the religious affiliations of persons listed in *Who's Who* over time, we can tell how much the status of America's religious groups has, or has not, changed. Are Catholics anymore prominent in American life today than they were, let us say, back in the 1930s? How prominent are Catholics today, compared to Episcopalians, Presbyterians, Lutherans, Baptists, and Jews?

Ralph Pyle, David Reyes, and I have examined these questions by comparing the rate at which various religious groups appeared in the 1930–31 and 1992–93 editions of *Who's Who*. We calculated the frequency with which members of each group appeared in each edition, and each group's representation relative to its size in the total U.S. population. We also compared the religious affiliations of the "power elite" (people in occupations such as business, banking, and government) and the "cultural elite" (people in fields such as entertainment, education, and writers).

In the 1930s, members of the old "Protestant Establishment"—Episcopalians, Presbyterians, and Congregationalists—comprised 53 percent of all *Who's Who* entries.[5] Episcopalians comprised 22 percent of all entries; Presbyterians, 20 percent; and Congregationalists, 11 percent. Other groups, in descending order, included Methodists, 14 percent; Baptists, 9 percent; Unitarian-Universalists, 6 percent; Catholics, 4 percent; and Jews, 1 percent.

By the 1990s, the old Protestant Establishment had lost a bit of ground, comprising 35 percent of all entries. Episcopalians were 18 percent of all entries; Presbyterians, 14 percent; and members of the United Church of Christ (formerly Congregationalists), 3 percent. Catholics, Jews, and Lutherans had gained, while Methodists and Baptists had slipped in stature. In rank order, Catholics were 23 percent; Jews, 12 percent; Methodists, 10 percent; Lutherans, 6 percent; Baptists, 5 percent; and UnitarianUniversalists, 2 percent.

These results have led some analysts to claim that the old Protestant

Establishment is a thing of the past, and that Catholics and members of other religious groups have penetrated society's upper echelons. However, a somewhat different picture emerges when we compare the religious affiliations of *Who's Who* entries with the religious affiliations of the American population in each time period.

In the 1930s, there were twenty-one times more Unitarian-Univeralists in *Who's Who* than there were in the U.S. population; six times more Episcopalians; six times more Congregationalists; five times more Quakers; and three times more Presbyterians. All other groups, including Catholics, were underrepresented. There were 87 percent fewer Catholics in *Who's Who* than one would expect, based on the number of Catholics in America at the time.

In the 1990s, the Protestant Establishment persists, though its influence has waned a bit. There are still ten times as many Unitarian-Universalists in *Who's Who* as one might expect; seven times as many Episcopalians; six times as many Quakers; three times as many Presbyterians; and three times as many members of the United Church of Christ. There also are now six times as many Jews in *Who's Who* (12 percent) as one might expect, based on the fact that Jews are only about 2 percent of the U.S. population.

Catholics, who are about 25 percent of the U.S. population, occupy 23 percent of the entries in *Who's Who*. Thus, they are still underrepresented but are gaining ground in the *Who's Who*. They have gained among both the power elite and the cultural elite. Overall, Catholics are still underrepresented among the nation's elite, but are likely to achieve parity in the very near future.

How Many Catholics Are There in the United States?

Here's a question for you. How many Catholics are there in the United States? More precisely, how many Roman Catholics live in the 50 states (not counting Catholics in the Eastern rite or people living in Puerto Rico, Guam, and the Virgin Islands)? Is the answer: 61 million, 71 million, or 81 million?

According to the 2002 edition of the *Official Catholic Directory*,[6] the answer is 61 million. But, wait. How does the *Directory* arrive at a figure like 61 million, and what does that number mean? Does it refer to Catholics who agree with Church teachings, people who attend Mass regularly, registered parishioners, or people who identify themselves as Catholic?

Every year, the *Directory* asks Church leaders to report the number of

Catholics in their parishes and dioceses. The *Directory* does not require leaders to use a specific theological or behavioral criterion when making their estimates. For example, it does not say to report only those Catholics who attend Mass weekly, use Sunday envelopes, participate in parish activities, or accept Church teachings. It leaves it up to diocesan and parish leaders to use whatever criteria they think are best.

Not long ago, colleagues and I asked leaders in five dioceses what criteria they use. In one diocese, leaders said they report the number of Catholics who are registered parishioners. In another, they said they consider two factors: the number of registered parishioners and the average number of people attending Mass in October (known as a pew census). In a third diocese, leaders said they rely most heavily on parish registration lists, but also take other things into account (such as the October pew census and pastors' estimates). In two other dioceses, leaders simply said they use a variety of methods.

Thus, church leaders use multiple methods but are most likely to report the number of people who have enough connection to local parishes to be on parish rolls and/or to be counted when parish leaders do a pew census. Therefore, the *Directory*'s figure of 61 million could reflect one of two things. It could indicate the number of Catholics who are registered parishioners (a narrow interpretation). Or, it could signify the number of registered parishioners and other Catholics who, even though not registered parishioners, attend Mass often enough to be included in an October head count (a broader interpretation). There is no way of knowing for sure which interpretation is most accurate.

In two recent national studies, colleagues and I have found that only two-thirds of Americans who say they are Catholic are registered parishioners. Another 16 percent or so say they are not registered parishioners, but that there is "a parish they attend more often than any other." The rest, another 16 percent or so, have no connection to a local parish.[7]

Thus, we have two options. We could assume the *Directory*'s figure indicates the number of registered parishioners and other Catholics who, although not on parish rolls, attend Mass often enough to be included in an October head count (the broader interpretation). Based on this assumption, we would have to add about 10 million people to account for the people who say they are Catholic but have no connection to a parish. Doing that produces an estimate of 71 million American Catholics. On the other hand, we could assume the *Directory*'s figure reflects only the number of registered parishioners (the narrow interpretation). Making this assumption, we would have to add about 20 million people to account for the Americans who identify themselves as Catholic but are not on parish rolls. Using this approach, the estimate is that there are about 81 million Catholics in the United States.

In either case, the *Directory*'s figure of 61 million U.S. Catholics almost certainly underestimates the total number of Catholics in this country. Depending on which assumption one makes, the real number is closer to 71 or 81 million.

A Racial Profile of American Catholics

You might think it is easy to draw a racial profile of American Catholics, but it is not. The main reason is that, when researchers try to estimate the number of Catholics who are white, Hispanic, African American, Asian, or Native American, they use different methods and get different results.

Some researchers use a formula that combines census data, findings from national surveys, and official Church statistics. They use census data to determine the number of Americans who belong to particular racial groups. Then, because census takers cannot ask questions about religion, these researchers consult national surveys to find out how many people in each racial group think of themselves as Catholic. Next, they turn to the *Official Catholic Directory* to learn how many Catholics there are in this country. The final step is to divide the number of people in each racial group who think of themselves as Catholic by the total number of Catholics. This procedure indicates that somewhere between half and three-quarters of American Catholics are white; 25 to 38 percent are Hispanic; and 5 to 8 percent are African American, Asian, or Native American.

This profile is problematic, however. Census data are about as accurate as one could hope for, but survey estimates of how many people in each racial group identify themselves as Catholic vary widely. For example, estimates of how many Hispanics think of themselves as Catholic vary between 55 and 80 percent. Also, the total number of Catholics reported in the *Official Catholic Directory* reflects the number of registered parishioners and/or people who have used parish services enough to be included on parish records, not the number of people who identify with the Church. It also is inflated by the fact that it includes over three million people living in territorial sees outside of the U.S. mainland (such as Puerto Rico and Guam). Thus, the numerator (Catholic identity) varies widely and is not comparable to the denominator (total Catholics).

Other researchers use national surveys, which are based on telephone interviews with Catholics in a cross-section of American households. Pollsters ask respondents about a wide range of issues, including their race and religious affiliation. Depending on which survey one reads, 80 to 85 percent of Catholics are white; 10 to 16 percent are Hispanic; 2 to 3 percent are African American; 1 to 2 percent are Asian; and about 1 percent are Native American.

This approach has many advantages, but it also has limitations. For one thing, pollsters are not as likely to reach racial minorities by phone. In urban areas, for example, 96 percent of white and Asian households have telephones, compared to 90 percent of Native Americans and only 86 percent of African American and Hispanic households. Racial differences are even greater in rural areas. Second, because most national surveys are conducted in English, pollsters are unable to interview people who speak other languages. Bilingual surveys report 2 to 4 percent more Hispanics than English-only surveys do. Finally, although all U.S. households average 2.8 people, household size varies by race. White households average 2.6 people, and African American households average 2.8. However, American Indian households average 3.2 people, and Hispanic and Asian households average 3.5. Thus, telephone surveys lead to an undercount of racial minorities.

Is there any way, then, to draw an accurate racial profile? I believe there is. I would not recommend the method that uses census data, national surveys, and official Church statistics. I also would rule out English-only surveys. Instead, I would start with bilingual national surveys of 1,000 or more Catholics. These studies show that, give or take three percentage points, approximately 78 percent of Catholics are white; 16 percent are Hispanic; 3 percent, African American; 2 percent, Asian; and 1 percent, Native American. Then, using figures cited above, I would make adjustments for telephone access and household size. With these adjustments, I estimate that, plus or minus three points, 71 percent of Catholics are white; 22 percent are Hispanic; 3 percent, African American; 3 percent, Asian; and 1 percent, Native American.

TABLE 1.2 Catholics by Race

Race	Percent *
White	71
Hispanic	22
African American	3
Asian	3
Native American	1

* Plus or minus 3 percent.

Catholics Are Largest Religious Group Among New Immigrants

Since President Lyndon Johnson reopened the doors of immigration in 1965, millions of new immigrants have been admitted to permanent residence in the U.S. In a paper presented at the annual meeting of the American Sociological Association in Chicago in August 2002, researchers Guillermina Jasso, Douglas S. Massey, Mark R. Rosenzweig, and James P. Smith presented the latest research on the religious characteristics of these new immigrants.[8] Their findings are based on interviews with 985 new immigrants and national survey data on the religious characteristics of native-born Americans. Three findings are of special interest to Catholics.

First, Catholics are the largest religious group among new immigrants: 42 percent are Catholic, 19 percent are Protestant, 15 percent have no religion, 8 percent are Muslim, 4 percent are Orthodox, 4 percent are Buddhist, 3 percent are Hindu, 3 percent are Jewish, and 2 percent indicated "other" or gave no response.

This religious profile is quite different from the religious profile of native-born Americans. Catholics, Muslims, Buddhists, Hindus, and people with no religion are overrepresented among new immigrants. Catholics are 23 percent of the native-born population, but 42 percent of new immigrants. Muslims, Buddhists, and Hindus are only 4 percent of the native-born population, but 17 percent of new immigrants. Those who have no religion are 12 percent of the native-born population, but 15 percent of new immigrants. On the other hand, Protestants are 59 percent of the native-born population, but only 19 percent of new immigrants.

Second, new Catholic immigrants come to this country from many different homelands. The homelands with the highest percentage of new immigrants who are Catholic are Poland (92 percent), Peru (87 percent), the Dominican Republic (86 percent), the Philippines (82 percent), and Mexico (78 percent). However, the number of new immigrants coming from Poland, Peru, and the Dominican Republic is relatively small, compared to the number coming from Mexico and the Philippines. As a result, Mexico produces the largest percentage of all new Catholic immigrants (28 percent). It is followed by the Philippines (13 percent), Poland (7 percent), the Dominican Republic (6 percent), and Vietnam (6 percent).

Third, new Catholic immigrants have comparatively little education (11.7 years compared to 13.5 years for all new immigrants). Among men, Catholics and Hindus rank at the bottom, averaging only 12.1 and 12.2 years of schooling respectively. Buddhist men rank the highest with 16.4, and Muslim men rank second with 15.1. Among women, Muslims rank the lowest with only 10.8 years of schooling, but Catholic women are next lowest with only 11.4. On the other hand, Hindu women are the most educated with 15.4 years of schooling. They are followed by Orthodox women with 15.0 and women with no religious preference, who have 14.8 years of education.

These findings have at least three important implications for Catholics. First, the percentage of the U.S. population that is Catholic is likely to increase in the years ahead. If so, Catholics' presence in and contributions to American society are likely to grow. Second, the fact that new Catholic immigrants come from many different homelands means that ethnic diversity will continue to be a characteristic of American Catholicism. Although Mexico is the largest single source of new Catholic immigrants, Church leaders need to appreciate the linguistic and cultural differences among the new immigrants. Finally, Catholic social teachings call for a preferential option for the poor. As a result of the current wave of immigration, a growing number of the nation's poor will be Catholic.

Catholic Population Trends in the Fifty States

According to the 2002 edition of the *Official Catholic Directory*, sixteen states are at least 25 percent Catholic, 20 states are 10 to 24 percent Catholic, and fourteen states are less than 10 percent Catholic. A comparison of the 1960 and 2002 editions of the *OCD* also indicates that the percentage of the total population that is Catholic has remained quite stable in twenty-three states, declined in thirteen states, and increased in fourteen others. Combining the current size of the Catholic population and the trends since 1960, we can identify nine population dynamics.

TABLE 1.3 Current Size of Catholic Population and Trends Since 1960

	Stable (n=23)	Declining (n=13)	Increasing (n=14)	Total
Large (n=16)	16% RI, MA, NJ	8% CT, NH, VT	8% CA, TX, NV	32%
Medium (n=20)	22% FL, AZ, IN	14% NM, ME, MD	4% DE, NE	42%
Small (n=14)	8% AL, WV, OK	4% WY, AK	16% VA, NC, SC	28%
Total	46%	26%	28%	

Eight states (16 percent) have Catholic populations that are large and relatively stable. These states—mostly in the Northeast and upper Midwest—include Rhode Island (61 percent Catholic), Massachusetts (50 percent), New Jersey (43 percent), Illinois (31 percent), Wisconsin (30 percent), Pennsylvania (30 percent), Minnesota (26 percent), and North Dakota (26 percent). In these states, the percentage of the population that is Catholic today is within three points of what it was in 1960.

Eleven states (22 percent) have medium-sized and relatively stable Catholic populations. Florida, for example, was 14 percent Catholic in 1960, and it remains 14 percent Catholic to this day. Arizona was 17 percent Catholic; it is still 16 percent Catholic. Catholics were 15 percent Indiana's population in 1960; they are still 13 percent. The other states include Michigan, Washington, South Dakota, Ohio, Oregon, Kansas, Kentucky, and Iowa.

Four states (8 percent) have small, stable Catholic populations. These states include Alabama, West Virginia, Utah, and Oklahoma. In all four cases, the Catholic population is between 3 and 5 percent and has changed very little since 1960.

Four states (8 percent) have large Catholic populations that are shrinking percentage wise. Three of these states are in the Northeast. Connecticut was 52 percent Catholic in 1960, but is only 38 percent Catholic today. New Hampshire was 38 percent Catholic in 1960; now it is only 27 percent Catholic. Vermont was 32 percent Catholic; now it is 24 percent. Louisiana, which was 37 percent Catholic in 1960, is only 30 percent Catholic today.

Seven states (14 percent) have medium-sized Catholic populations that are declining as a percentage of the total population. The two states with the steepest declines are New Mexico (down from 41 percent Catholic to only 24 percent) and Maine (down from 28 percent to 17 percent). The others, scattered throughout the country, include Maryland, Colorado, Montana, Missouri, and Hawaii.

Only two states (4 percent) have small Catholic populations that are declining. Wyoming is down from 15 percent Catholic to only 9 percent. Alaska also has dropped from 15 percent to 9 percent.

Four states (8 percent)—three of which are in the Southwest—have large Catholic populations that are growing. California, which was 20 percent Catholic in 1960, is now 30 percent Catholic. Texas was 19 percent Catholic; now its Catholic population is up to 26 percent. Nevada has gone from 19 percent Catholic to 26 percent Catholic. New York was 36 percent Catholic in 1960; today it is 40 percent Catholic.

Two states (4 percent) have medium-sized Catholic populations that are increasing as a percentage of the total population. Delaware was 12 percent Catholic; now it is 18 percent Catholic. Nebraska has gone from 18 to 22 percent Catholic.

Eight states (16 percent)—seven in the Southeast—have small but growing Catholic populations. Virginia, for example, has gone from 4 percent Catholic in 1960 to 8 percent Catholic today. North Carolina, which was only 1 percent Catholic in 1960, is now 4 percent Catholic. In South Carolina, the Catholic population has increased from 1 percent to 3 percent. Georgia's Catholic population has risen from 2 percent to 5 percent. The other states are Mississippi, Arkansas, Tennessee, and Idaho.

Questions for Reflection

1. To what extent do you think of religion as contributing to the well-being of our society, or as a source of conflict and social problems? Explain.
2. Use the theory of religious stratification and Merton's theory of in-group virtues and out-group vices to describe the religious history of the region, state, and community where you live.
3. Of the two models of Church described by Dolan, which one do you like the most: the Roman or American model? Why?
4. Consider the improvements that have taken place in Catholics' social standing. What implications do you think these improvements have for the laity's role in the Church and Catholics' role in American society?

5. One section in this chapter suggests that the number of Americans who identify themselves as Catholic is considerably larger than the number of Catholics who are counted in official Church statistics. Do you know any people who, if asked, would identify themselves as Catholic but have little or no relationship with a parish? Who are these Catholics, and what—if anything—could be done to bring them into closer contact with a local parish?

6. The racial, ethnic, and geographic characteristics of American Catholics are changing. Describe these changes and explore their implications for the Church, especially the church in your diocese.

7. Given the increasing racial, ethnic, and cultural diversity among American Catholics, what might be done to preserve the distinctive identities of each subgroup while building bridges between groups?

Chapter 2

The Social and Cultural Context

This chapter begins by introducing the debate between scholars who believe that modern society is increasingly secular and those who claim religion is still a vital part of American culture. Subsequent sections provide information to demonstrate that, while there has been some uncoupling of spirituality and religiosity in recent years, Catholics still tend to think of themselves as both spiritual and religious. Although America's postmodern culture poses many challenges for the Church, it also offers many opportunities for Church leaders who understand its emphases on personal experience, active participation, visual images, and connectedness. The final three sections of this chapter show that religious affiliation is socially visible and affects Americans' social interactions.

Is Society Increasingly Secular?

For years, social scientists have believed that, as a result of modernization, our society would become increasingly secular. As science provided more answers to questions about our universe, there would be less need for religious explanations. With the shift from an agrarian economy to an industrial economy, modern society would be able to satisfy our human needs, thus reducing our dependence on a supernatural being. Finally, as government took over functions that used to be performed by churches, religion's role in society would shrink. In short, with modernization, reason would reduce the need for faith, prosperity would reduce dependence on God, and reliance on the state would reduce the need for churches.

Proponents of secularization theory have cited evidence pointing to the declining significance of religion and the increasing secularity of modern society. They have noted that membership in many churches is declining and that the percentage of Americans saying they have no religious preference has doubled in the last decade. For the most part, prayer has been removed from our public schools. Nativity scenes have been removed from courthouse squares.

However, a number of scholars are rethinking secularization theory.[1] For one thing, they suggest that the term *secularization* has so many meanings (that religious symbols, doctrines, and institutions have lost prestige, or that religion increasingly is confined to personal and family life) that it is no longer useful. They also question whether it is possible to make a clear distinction between the sacred and the secular, believing instead that the two are inevitably intertwined. Third, they question the assumption that there once was a time (for example, the Old Testament era, medieval Europe, colonial America) when society was wrapped in a sacred canopy and people were more religious than they are today. Fourth, they argue that, even though modern society meets many of our material needs, it does not meet our spiritual needs.

Fifth, critics of secularization theory point to evidence that seems to conflict with it. They note that church membership, religious belief, and religious practice are more common today than they were in medieval Europe and colonial America (for example, two-thirds of Americans now belong to a church, compared to only about 17 percent of American colonists). While membership in mainline Protestant churches is declining, membership in the Catholic Church and evangelical churches is increasing. Over 90 percent of Americans still believe in God. Scientists are among the most religious, not the least religious, members of university faculties. Instead of being strictly private, religion affects the nation's economy and leads some people to view their work as a calling. It also puts issues such as abortion and economic justice on the political agenda and affects the way many people vote in presidential elections.

Finally, critics assert that at least some secularization theorists might have their own reasons for promoting the idea that religion is declining in significance. For example, some academicians might deny the significance of faith so they can bolster confidence in science. Some Marxist scholars might hope that secularization is occurring because they see religion as an opiate that stands in the way of a class revolution and the establishment of a classless society. Some feminist thinkers might like secularization theory because they see religion as an instrument men use to oppress women. Outside the academy, some business leaders might believe in secularization because they would like to minimize religious and moral questions about unethical business practices. Also, some religious leaders might proclaim that secularism is on the increase, so they can rally churchgoers against an outside foe and, in the process, increase solidarity within their churches.

As this debate over secularization theory proceeds, Catholic clergy and lay leaders might want to consider programs in which parishioners could explore the arguments on both sides, examine the evidence bearing on this debate, and consider the motives of those who support and question secularization theory.

Number of Religious "Nones" Is Increasing: Why?

When pollsters ask Americans about their religion, they usually ask: "What is your religious preference? Is it Protestant, Catholic, Jewish, some other religion or no religion?" People who say "no religion" are called "nones."

Between 1972 and 1991, about 7 percent of Americans were nones. Since 1992, the percent of nones has doubled, going from 7 percent to 14 percent. For people raised in Protestant churches, the percentage claiming no religious preference has jumped from 5 to 11 percent. For Catholics, it has increased from 8 to 11 percent.

Why has the percentage of people claiming no religion increased so dramatically? What does it tell us about American society in general and American religion in particular? Sociologists Michael Hout and Claude Fischer of the University of California at Berkeley explored three possible interpretations.[2]

One possibility is that the increased percentage of nones signals a marked increase in the secularization of our society (or, stated differently, a sudden decrease in religious belief and practice). However, after examining data on a number of beliefs and practices, Hout and Fischer conclude that there has been no sudden loss of faith among Americans. What about people with no religious preference? Two-thirds believe in God or a higher power; 59 percent say they "believe that God watches over them"; 32 percent "believe in a God that concerns himself with each human being personally." Also, "over half believe in life after death, and about a third believe in heaven and hell." Nones seldom attend worship services, but 93 percent pray sometimes and 20 percent pray every day. About 40 percent are "at least moderately spiritual." In Hout and Fischer's words, nones "are believers of some sort, and many are quite conventional. Relatively few are secular, agnostic, or atheist; most actually pray. Their most distinguishing feature is their avoidance of churches."

Then, what explains the increase in nones? Some of the increase is related to birth cohorts. Among Americans born between 1900 and 1929, there are very few nones, and there has been virtually no increase in the percent claiming no religious preference. The percentage of nones has increased from 5 to 9 among people who were born between 1930 and 1944. It has jumped even more (from 10 to 15 percent) among people born between 1945 and 1959. The biggest increase (from 12 to 18 percent) has been among young adults, who were born between 1960 and 1974. On this basis, Hout and Fischer conclude that "the cultural turmoil of the 1960s" explains some of the increase. But, it does not explain all of it.

Hout and Fischer also test the hypothesis that churches' involvement in partisan politics "might have caused people who dissent from the conservative agenda of vocal Christian leaders to stop identifying with those religions." Their evidence supports this hypothesis. Among political liberals, 11 percent are nones, compared to 7 percent of moderates who lean toward liberal, only 4 percent of moderates who lean toward conservative, and only 2 percent of political conservatives. They also find that nones have "an aversion to the politics of the 1990s—a politics that made religious identity seem like an endorsement of conservative views." Hout and Fischer conclude: "The disaffinity of liberals and moderates for the social agenda of the Religious Right led the ones who had weak religious attachments to disavow organized religion."

This study has two implications for Church leaders. First, leaders should be careful not to view the increase in nones as a sign of increased secularization. It is not. Second, they should view these results as a warning. Church leaders who use partisan politics to promote a conservative religious agenda will cause some young adults, especially those who are only tenuously connected to organized religion, to dissociate themselves from the Church.

Are People More Spiritual but Less Religious?

Let's begin by defining *spirituality* as a feeling or experience of being connected with God. It is an awareness of God's presence in one's life. Next, let's define *religiosity* as the extent of a person's involvement in a church. It has to do with religious practices such as Mass attendance.

In the 1950s, most people, including most social researchers, assumed there was a strong positive correlation between spirituality and religiosity. In other words, believing that God was present in one's life would lead one to participate in a church, and participating in a church would strengthen one's relationship with God.

Then the nation experienced a cultural revolution. This revolution began with the social movements and turmoil of the 1960s, but was extended into the 1970s by the political crisis known as Watergate. In the course of this revolution, the nation grew increasingly skeptical of virtually all social institutions, including government, the economy, marriage, education, and religion. People increasingly questioned the need for these institutions and the importance of complying with the rules and regulations they promoted. As people distanced themselves from social institutions, they came to rely on their own sense of what is right or wrong. Most observers agree that this cultural emphasis on the rights and responsibilities of the individual continues to this day.

In the context of this revolution, the close relationship between spirituality and religiosity was called into question. People increasingly felt it was possible to be spiritual without being religious. One could have a personal relationship with God without participating in a church, and one could be active in a church without being spiritual. Some people went so far as to claim that these two phenomena are negatively related. In this view, the more spiritual one is, the less likely one is to participate in a religious group, and the more one participates in a religious group, the less spiritual one is likely to be.

The relationship between spirituality and religiosity has been the focus of much recent research and several recent publications. These include my book *The Search for Common Ground*,[3] Wade Clark Roof's *Spiritual Marketplace*,[4] Dean Hoge's *Young Adult Catholics*,[5] Robert Fuller's *Spiritual but Not Religious*,[6] and Penny Marler and C. Kirk Hadaway's article "'Being religious' or 'Being Spiritual' in America: A Zero-Sum Proposition?"[7]

These studies yield three conclusions. First, there continues to be a positive relationship between spirituality and religiosity. Marler and Hadaway report that at least three out of four Americans, and as many as 88 percent of Catholics, think of themselves as both spiritual and religious. My 1995 national survey also shows that Catholic parishioners are more likely than nonparishioners to report that God has forgiven their sins, cared for them in times of need, and answered their prayers.

Second, about one-fifth of Americans think of themselves as spiritual but not religious. This finding is consistent with data showing that about 90 percent of Americans believe in God, while only two-thirds belong to a religious group. It also is consistent with my 1995 data showing that about two-thirds of Catholics report that God has taken care of them in times of need or has answered their prayers, while less than half attend Mass on a regular basis.

Finally, reflecting the cultural revolution of the last thirty to forty years, the percentage of people who think of themselves as both spiritual and religious is declining, while the percent saying they are spiritual but not religious is increasing. Likewise, my national surveys show that levels of spirituality have slipped only slightly among American Catholics, while the frequency of Mass attendance has declined more sharply, reaching a new low of only 20 percent among young adults in 1999.

Four Traits of Postmodern Culture

In his recent book *Post-Modern Pilgrims*, Leonard Sweet says postmodern culture is an *EPIC* culture: Experiential, Participatory, Image-driven, and Connected.[8] In my view, Sweet's analysis is full of insights and implications for ministering to and with today's young-adult Catholics. Let me share some of his insights and some of their implications for Church leaders.

Experiential. According to Sweet, the modern culture that many older adults grew up in put a great deal of emphasis on cognition and reason. In contrast to this emphasis on rationality, he says, "experience is the currency of postmodern economics....Postmoderns want to experience what life is, especially experience life for themselves." In Sweet's words, postmoderns "literally 'feel' their way through life." If Sweet is right, and I think he is, one implication is that "total experience is the new watchword in postmodern worship. New World preachers don't 'write sermons.' They create total experiences." In doing so, they reach out to "Postmoderns [who] are... hungry for experiences, especially experiences of God."

Participatory. Sweet says that in the modern culture of many older adults, people assumed that decisions would be made for them. In the "radical democracy" of postmodern culture, he says, "vertical authorities like priests and professors have been replaced by peers throughout the world who share common interests....Postmoderns have to explore (hands on) before they can integrate." They "are not simply going to transmit the tradition or the culture they've been taught. They won't take it unless they can transform it and customize it. Making a culture their own doesn't mean passing on a treasure that they've inherited, but inventing and engineering their own heirloom out of the treasures of the past." Among other implications, these insights suggest that "[t]eachers are no longer the sage on the stage." Likewise, clergy are no longer the prophets in the pulpit. "Postmoderns want interactive, immersive, 'in your face' participation in the mysteries of God."

Image-driven. According to Sweet, "The modern world [of older adults] was word-based. Its theologians tried to create an intellectual faith, placing reason and order at the heart of religion." In striking contrast, he says, "Propositions are lost on postmodern ears, but metaphor they will hear; images they will see and understand." One implication is that "[v]isual language…is no longer an option. We are a print-saturated, word-based church in the midst of visual technologies that are creating a whole new visual culture." Church leaders need to appreciate "the importance of shifting worship from the exegesis of words to the exegesis of images."

Connected. The postmodern culture of young adults yearns "for connectedness, for communities not of blood or nation but communities of choice." To make his point, Sweet quotes Louise Conant, associate rector at Christ Church in Cambridge, Massachusetts. She says that in the past "people came together in church on Sunday morning to celebrate the community that they had the rest of the week," but now they "come to church on Sunday morning to find the community that they don't have the rest of the week." In Sweet's own words: "Relationships are at the heart of postmodern culture." One of many implications is that "[p]ostmoderns have had it with religion. They're sick and tired of religion. They're convinced the world needs less of religion, not more. They want no part of obedience to sets of propositions and rules required by some 'officialdom' somewhere. Postmoderns want participation in a deeply personal but at the same time communal experience of the divine and the transformation of life that issues from that identification with God." Sweet concludes that "the church exists to incarnate connectedness and to inculcate greater consciousness of connectedness."

Not all of today's young adults embrace this EPIC culture. After all, there are variations within any generation. But, according to the young adults I have consulted, Sweet accurately describes many of their cultural tendencies. If so, his insights and their implications should be explored by parish and diocesan leaders.

A Person's Religion Is More Visible Than You Might Think

I often hear people say religious favoritism and discrimination are not common. When asked why not, they claim that a person's religion is not visible (the way race and gender are), so religion is not a very reliable or useful criterion when it comes to allocating rewards and/or punishments. I question that claim. A person's religious affiliation is more visible than many people think.

Some people freely and publicly reveal their religious preference. I think, for example, of Jewish comedians such as Alan King, Woody Allen, and Billy Crystal, all of whom are very up front about the fact that they are Jewish. They even build their Jewish heritage into their performances. The same thing is true for many people in other religious traditions. Everybody knows that Andrew Greeley is Catholic, because he is quite willing to reveal his religious identity. My bishop once observed that everyone knows that I am Catholic for the same reason.

Ethnicity is another clue. If you learn that a person is Italian, it is a good bet that he or she is Catholic. Likewise, it's a good bet someone from Ireland is Catholic, a man from Israel is Jewish, a woman from India is a Hindu, and a person from Saudi Arabia is Muslim. Not in every case, but in most.

A person's name also is a good indication of his or her religion. Odds are that Mary Margaret O'Neil is Catholic, Sidney Greenberg is Jewish, and Mohammed Abdul Fasad is Muslim. Studies show that people act on the basis of such assumptions. Several years ago, a researcher sent letters to numerous resort hotels requesting reservations. He signed half of the letters "Mr. Lockwood" and the other half "Mr. Greenberg." Guess what? Over 90 percent of the resorts wrote back to Mr. Lockwood offering him a room, while only half wrote back to Mr. Greenberg and only one-third granted his request for a reservation.

The region of the country and state where one lives is another clue to one's religious background. People from Massachusetts and Rhode Island are probably Catholic. Folks from Utah are likely to be Mormon. There's a better than even chance residents of Mississippi and Alabama are Baptists.

A person's educational background is another highly visible clue. If someone's resumé indicates he or she is a graduate of St. Mary's grade school, Loyola High School, and the University of Notre Dame, it is a good bet the person is Catholic. Someone who attended Bob Jones University or Oral

Roberts University is likely to be a conservative Protestant. Graduating from Yeshiva University suggests one might be Jewish.

Public records also provide information for people who want to know your religion. When wedding announcements in local newspapers say a wedding will be held at St. Thomas Aquinas Church, or First United Methodist Church, or Temple Israel, it is not hard to figure out the religion of the bride. *Who's Who in America* is a great source of information about the religious affiliations of the nation's elite.

Local knowledge is yet another source of information about a person's religion. People ask questions, such as "Where does so-and-so go to church?" They also observe things, such as who comes out of which local church on Sunday morning, who one's friends are, and to which social clubs people belong. If they see you leaving St. Ann's Parish, know you are friends with Mike Fitzpatrick, and find out you belong to the Knights of Columbus, they have good reasons to assume you are Catholic.

No one of these clues is a perfect predictor of one's religion (Not everyone in Massachusetts is Catholic, and some people in Utah are not Mormons.). However, with only two or three pieces of readily accessible information, one can almost certainly identify another person's religion. If Mary Margaret O'Neil is Irish, grew up in Massachusetts, went to Notre Dame, was married at St. Thomas Aquinas Church, is often seen coming out of Holy Family Parish on Sunday mornings, and is good friends with Margaret Sweeney, it is not hard to tell what her religion is!

Is It True? Do Birds of a Feather Really Flock Together?

There is an old proverb: "Birds of a feather flock together." According to the proverb, people prefer being with people who are like themselves. They tend to interact with people of the same race, ethnicity, and religion. They like to be with people who share their attitudes, values, and outlook on life. Is there any truth to this old proverb? Do birds of a feather really flock together? If so, what causes people to gravitate toward others who are like themselves? Finally, what implications do the answers to these questions have for Church leaders?

Sociologists Miller McPherson, Lynn Smith-Lovin, and James M. Cook reviewed the research literature on "homophily," which they defined as "the principle that a contact between similar people occurs at a higher rate than among dissimilar people."[9] Status homophily is based on similarity in "informal, formal, or ascribed status" (such as race, ethnicity, religion, and gender). Value homophily "is based on values, attitudes, and beliefs."

According to the researchers, "patterns of homophily are remarkably robust" in behaviors ranging from very personal relationships, such as marriage, to less intimate ones, such as acquaintanceships. Regarding status homophily, the researchers report that "homophily in race and ethnicity creates the strongest divides in our personal environments, with age, religion, education, occupation, and gender following in roughly that order." People are most likely to cluster along racial and ethnic lines and least likely to do so on the basis of gender (although men and women have gender homophilous relationships in many settings, they are "linked together in households and kinship networks").

Religion is not as potent as race and ethnicity, but it has more impact on our relationships than gender. Controlling for group size, which also affects people's interactions, Protestants exhibit relatively low levels homopohily, "while Catholics, those with no religion and 'other' religions, and Jews show higher levels of homophily (in that order)." Also, "[t]ies between people with the same religion are more likely to be close ties of giving emergency help, loaning money, giving trusted advice or even therapeutic counseling, while the less intense ties of hobby and work-talk often show less religious homophily."

With regard to value homophily, McPherson, Smith-Lovin, and Cook conclude that "attitude, belief, and value similarity lead to attraction and interaction." Thus, within or between religious groups, people gravitate toward others who share their religious worldview and develop fewer relationships with people whose religious outlooks are different.

The researchers also show that relationships involving different races, religions, ages, and values are not as likely to last as ones involving similarities along these same dimensions. While "similarity breeds connection," it also is true that "ties between nonsimilar individuals…dissolve at a higher rate."

What causes birds of a feather to flock together? Part of the answer is geographic: "We are more likely to have contact with those who are closer to us in geographic location than those who are distant." Family ties are another consideration because "family connections are the biosocial web than connect us to those who are similar [for example, in religion] and different [for example, in gender]." Organizational settings, such as school, work, and church, also increase the likelihood that we will interact with others who are like us. The roles we play, such as employer, parent, and

Sunday school teacher, also foster relations with others in similar roles. People also tend to select friends and associates who they perceive to be similar to themselves.

These findings invite Church leaders to consider several questions. To what extent do people in parishes voluntarily cluster on the basis of factors such as race, age, occupation, and attitudes? In what ways do parish policies and programs encourage birds of a feather to flock together along these lines? And, under what conditions should such homophily be encouraged or discouraged?

Why Some Religious Groups Get Along Better Than Others

If you look at the relationships between religious groups in your community, you will find that some groups get along very well. They cooperate with one another in ecumenical ventures. They cosponsor activities and invite their members to participate. They pool their financial resources to support joint programs and activities. Their clergy cooperate on interfaith marriages. They exchange pulpits on special occasions. Church leaders speak highly of one another.

Other groups do not get along as well. They seldom if ever interact. Indeed, they seem to avoid one another. They refuse to combine forces on joint ventures. They do not send representatives to the same organizations. They do not pool their financial resources. When they do interact, there is considerable tension. They are suspicious of one another's motives. They disagree with one another's stances on public policies. They criticize one another's theology and forms of worship. Each side blames the other one for the divisions between them.

These positive and negative relationships are not random. They are quite predictable. They are based on at least two factors, one vertical, the other, horizontal. The vertical dimension has to do with the groups' socioeconomic status (that is, the average levels of education, occupation, income, wealth, and power of their members). Mainline Protestants (such as Episcopalians, Presbyterians, and the United Church of Christ), Catholics, and Mormons rank relatively high in socioeconomic status. Others, such as the Disciples of Christ, American Baptists, Jehovah's Witnesses, and the Assemblies of God, rank lower in status.

The horizontal dimension has to do with the groups' worldviews. Worldviews are very complex, but I find it useful to think of them as falling along a liberal-conservative continuum. The conservative end of the continuum includes groups (such as Mormons and Jehovah's Witnesses) that adhere to fundamentalist or evangelical theologies and stress compliance with traditional beliefs, practices, and ways of life. The liberal end of the continuum includes mainline Protestants and Disciples of Christ, who have more progressive or symbolic interpretations of Scripture, permit more diversity in belief and practice, and tend to embrace change. Catholics and American Baptists fall near the middle of this continuum.

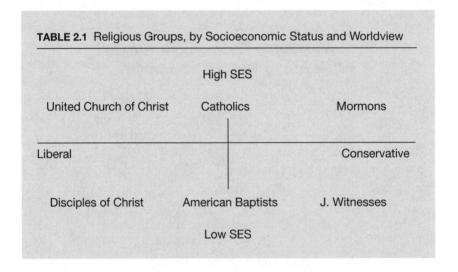

TABLE 2.1 Religious Groups, by Socioeconomic Status and Worldview

When groups are similar in terms of both status and worldview, they are likely to get along quite well. Thus, high-status, liberal Protestant denominations, such as the United Church of Christ, Episcopalians, and Presbyterians are likely to cooperate with one another. So are low-status, conservative groups, such as Jehovah's Witnesses and the Assemblies of God. When groups are similar on one dimension but different on the other, such as Catholics and the United Church of Christ, or Catholics and American Baptists, relations are not likely to be as positive; nor are they likely to be distinctly negative. When groups are different on both dimensions, they are likely to experience negative relationships. Thus, high-status, liberal groups, such as the United Church of Christ, are not likely to get along with low-status, conservative Protestants, such as Jehovah's Witnesses. Likewise, high-status, conservative groups, such as Mormons, are not likely to get along with low-status, liberal groups, such as the Disciples of Christ.

Questions for Reflection

1. To what extent do you agree or disagree with the idea that modern society is increasingly secular? Specify and evaluate the evidence related to your answer.

2. What do you make of claims made by many people these days that they are "spiritual but not religious"? Why do they say this and what do they mean by it? Is it true?

3. Does Sweet's discussion of EPIC culture help to explain the thoughts and actions of young adults in your parish and diocese? What does his thesis suggest your parish and diocese might do differently to reach today's postmodern pilgrims?

4. To what extent, and in what way, is your religious affiliation known to others in your neighborhood, workplace, and community?

5. Do your religious affiliation and religious values enter into your selection of intimate friends and casual acquaintances? If so, how?

6. To what extent, and in what ways, do individuals and religious groups in your community interact on the basis of their religious affiliations?

Chapter 3

Religion, the Economy, and Politics

Religion in general and the Catholic Church in particular have more impact on the economy than many people think. The American economy is marked by a growing gap between the rich and poor, with the poor being a much larger percentage of our society than the government's measure of poverty indicates. Despite claims of a separation between church and state, there is close connection between religion and politics. This relationship is explored in sections on religion and politics in the 1950s. It also is evident in the tendency for members of the "Protestant Establishment" to become America's presidents, members of the cabinet, and justices on the Supreme Court. Religion also affects the way Americans have voted in recent presidential elections.

The Church Has an Enormous Economic Impact

You've probably read newspaper stories touting the vast amounts of money businesses, state fairs, airports, conventions, Super Bowls, and other sporting events pump into the economy. But, have you ever thought about the Catholic Church's economic impact? Two studies indicate that it is enormous.

Margaret Cole, Father Anthony Pogorelc, and I recently studied the Church's economic impact in Tippecanoe County, Indiana.[1] There were twenty-three Catholic organizations in the county, including the chancery and a diocese office of pastoral ministry, six parishes, five parochial schools, five social service groups, four fraternal and prayer groups, and until 1998, a hospital owned by a religious order of Catholic sisters. Four organizations were not included in the study because they were very small and had no budgets. One other organization refused to cooperate, but it also was very small and would have very little effect on our estimate of the Church's overall economic impact.

We collected information on organizational expenditures, including salaries and benefits for all personnel, financial contributions to community-based charities, construction of facilities, equipment, maintenance and utilities, and other operating expenses. Using standard economic practices, we multiplied the Church's total direct expenditures by a regional factor of 2.3 to take into account the indirect effect resulting from the recycling of money that the Church spends. We did not include salaries doctors make at the hospital, the economic expenditures of individual Catholics living in Tippecanoe County, and the economic value of the time Catholics donate to civic and religious organizations as volunteers.

The Church's direct economic impact was $82,500,000. With the multiplier effect, its total impact was $191,500,000. That amounted to $10,600,000 per organization, $131,000 per employee, $8,300 per parishioner, and $18,600 per Mass attendee. Not counting the hospital, these figures were $1,100,000 per organization, $107,000 per employee, $840 per parishioner, and $1,900 per Mass attendee.

The Church's impact is even greater in larger dioceses. When Archbishop Rembert G. Weakland studied the Church's economic impact in the Milwaukee area, he described the results as "staggering."

The Archdiocese of Milwaukee covers 10 counties, includes 620,000 Catholics, and operates 284 parishes. These parishes employ over 3,000 people. The archdiocese contains 147 Catholic schools (which enroll over 33,000 students), 12 parochial high schools (which serve over 7,000 students), and 4 Catholic colleges and 1 university (which enroll over 23,000 students). It also has 22 religious orders and 2 major seminaries. It claims 25 healthcare centers and homes for the aged, along with 15 Catholic hospitals, all of which are run by religious orders. These healthcare facilities serve over a million and a half people a year. The archdiocese lists 35 social and community service organizations, such as Catholic Social Services and the St. Vincent de Paul Society.

The archdiocese employs about 30,000 people, making it the second largest employer in the area (second only to the government). Its total expenditures are $1.25 billion. Factoring in the regional multiplier of 2.5, the archdiocese has a total economic impact of $3.1 billion. Its impact amounts to $2.1 million per Catholic organization, $41,666 per employee, and $20,161 per Catholic parishioner.

If Church leaders in other dioceses were to conduct similar economic impact studies, they too would learn how big a contribution Catholic organizations make to the economy in their area. By publicizing this impact, they would increase awareness that, in addition to being an important spiritual and moral force, the Church also is an enormous economic influence. Appreciation of the Church's economic impact almost certainly would increase Church leaders' opportunities to participate in civic planning processes and public policy discussions. These new forms of civic participation would give clergy and lay leaders even more opportunities to contribute to the quality of life in their dioceses and communities.

Religion's Economic Impact
Far Greater Than Many Realize

As noted above, churches, parochial schools, church-affiliated hospitals, and other religious organizations pump vast sums of money into the economies of their local communities. By constructing and repairing buildings, hiring staff, paying wages and benefits, and purchasing products such as song books and religious education materials, religious groups have both direct and indirect effects on the economic well-being of the towns and cities where they are located.

But, the routine expenses of local religious groups are only part of religion's huge impact on the nation's economy. The religious sphere also generates billions of dollars in other, more extraordinary, ways. Consider the economic impact of religion conventions, pilgrimages and crusades, shrines and cathedrals, and religious holidays.

Convention and visitors bureaus (CVBs) devote lots of time and energy to luring large corporate conventions to their cities, but they also work hard to attract smaller conventions, which they call SMERFs (that is, *So*cial, *M*ilitary, *E*ducational, *R*eligious, and *F*raternal groups). Sometimes, religion conventions are actually quite large. For example, attendance at the 2004 annual meeting of the National Catholic Education Association in Boston was about 14,000. In 2000, when the Southern Baptists held their national convention in Orlando, 12,000 people attended. Other gatherings are a little smaller, but still attract significant numbers of registrants. When the Religious Conference Managers Association (RCMA) went to Tampa in 2002, about 1,400 people from all over the country attended. When the National Conference for Catechetical Leadership (NCCL) meets, about 750 people attend.

CVBs know how much money each visitor is likely to spend per day for lodging, food, drinks, transportation, gifts, and other items. By using multipliers, they also can estimate the indirect, or ripple, effect these expenditures are likely to have. Let us use a middle-range estimate of $250 per day for visitor expenses at a four-day meeting, with a modest multiplier of 1.8. Under these conditions, an NCEA convention would have a total economic impact of about $25 million on its host city. If 12,000 Baptists went to a meeting, they would generate about $22 million. An RCMA conference would yield at least $2.5 million, and an NCCL meeting would have an economic impact of about $1.3 million.

Religious pilgrimages and crusades also bring tourists—and tourist dollars—into cities. The 2003 Billy Graham Crusade in San Diego drew 270,000 people over the course of four days. His Oklahoma City crusade attracted 120,000. When Pope John Paul II visited Denver for World Youth Day in 1993, a half million people (180,000 of whom were from the U.S.) were in attendance. Using the same formula we used for conventions, these events would have total effects of $216 million to $900 million in revenues.

Visitors to shrines and cathedrals also have a major impact on the economies of places, such as Belleville, Illinois (where the National Shrine of Our Lady of the Snows attracts 1.1 million visitors a year) and Washington DC (where the Catholic Shrine of the Immaculate Conception at Catholic University draws 750,000 visitors each year).

Of course, we cannot overlook religious holidays, such as Christmas and Hanukkah. Although the holiday shopping season of late-November and December accounts for less than 10 percent of the year, it accounts for one-third to one-half of annual retail sales and, according to one reliable source, "up to 65 percent of retail profits." In 2002, Christmas holiday shoppers spent an estimated $800 billion. Holidays such as Easter and St. Patrick's Day also pump millions of dollars into the nation's economy.

Who says we live in a secular society and that religion doesn't have any impact anymore!

Gap Between Rich and Poor Still Growing

In 1986, the American Catholic bishops published *Economic Justice for All*, a pastoral letter in which they raised serious moral questions about the growing gap between rich and poor Americans.[2] They asked American Catholics to think critically about trends in wealth and income. Concerned about the harmful consequences these trends might have for the poorest Americans—including many American Catholics—they also challenged Catholics to work for economic justice. Many Catholics, and organizations such as the Catholic Campaign for Human Development, have responded to the bishops' call.

However, recent research indicates that the economic inequalities the bishops described in 1986 continue to grow. Income and wealth are increasingly concentrated among a relatively small percentage of people at the top of America's economic ladder. Meanwhile, the economic resources of other Americans, especially people on or near the bottom rung of the economic ladder, are declining.

Income refers to money (wages, salaries, interest, and dividends) derived from work, social security, welfare, pensions, savings accounts, and other financial investments. In his book, *Social Inequality*, Martin Marger reports that in 1997 the median family income was $44,568.[3] Half of American families earned more than $44,568; the other half earned less.

Now imagine the U.S. population being divided into vertically-arranged quintiles based on family income. Marger shows that the top 20 percent of American families possesses 47 percent of the nation's income. The second 20 percent has 23 percent of the country's income. The third 20 percent has 16 percent. The fourth 20 percent controls 10 percent. The bottom 20 percent possesses only 4 percent.

Income inequality was quite stable, even declined a bit, between 1950 and 1970, but it has increased ever since. The income possessed by the top 20 percent of families has jumped from 41 percent in 1970 to 47 percent in 1997 (The percent owned by the top 5 percent has risen from 16 to 21 percent.). Meanwhile, the portion of the nation's income controlled by the middle 60 percent has shrunk from 54 percent in 1970 to 49 percent in 1997. The share owned by the bottom 20 percent has declined from 5 percent to 4 percent.

Wealth refers to economic value of assets, such as stocks, bonds, real estate, and business equity. Inequalities based on wealth are even greater than income inequalities. In his book, *Social Stratification and Inequality*, Harold Kerbo reports that in 1995, the top 20 percent of families had 85 percent of the nation's wealth.[4] The second 20 percent had only 11 percent. The third 20 percent had only 4 percent. The fourth fifth had just 1 percent. And the bottom fifth owed more than it had.

TABLE 3.1 Wealth 1989–95 (percent)

Families	1989	1995
Top 20%	79	85
Second 20%	14	11
Third 20%	6	4
Fourth 20%	1	1
Bottom 20%	-0.4	-1

Thus, while the top 20 percent of families has 47 percent of the income, it also has 85 percent of the wealth. The bottom 20 percent, which has less than 1 percent of the nation's income, has an even smaller share of the nation's wealth (data from 1997 indicated a similar distribution of wealth).

While wealth inequality went down a bit in the 1960s and early 1970s, it too has increased since then. In 1969, the top 1 percent of the population had 24 percent of the wealth; today it has 36 percent. In 1989, the top 20 percent of families had 79 percent of the wealth; now it has 85 percent. Meanwhile, share of wealth possessed by all other quintiles has declined.

The bishops were prophetic in calling attention to the growing gap between the rich and poor, but the gap continues to grow. For better or worse, increased economic inequality is one of the defining characteristics of the last thirty years. It also is one of the most serious challenges facing American Catholics as we launch the new millennium.

A Critique of the Government's Poverty Line

In their 1986 pastoral letter *Economic Justice for All*, the American bishops urged Catholics to think of poverty as a matter of economic justice, not just a matter of minimal subsistence. Defining poverty as "a lack of sufficient material resources required for a decent life," the bishops challenged us to think of poverty as a condition that deprives many Americans of the resources they need to live productive lives, provide for their families, and participate in the life of their communities.[5]

If we think of poverty in these terms, we might be dismayed to learn how the U.S. government measures poverty, what its poverty line means in real-life terms, and that its figures probably underestimate the actual amount of poverty in our society. Let me explain.

In the late 1950s, the government wanted to determine how much poverty there was in America. It adopted a formula consisting of two components: the cost of food and all other expenses (such as clothing, rent/mortgage, transportation, education, medical bills, and entertainment). When faced with a choice between four USDA food plans ("liberal," "moderate," "low-cost," and an "economy" plan meant for "temporary or emergency use when funds are low"), the government chose the economy plan and calculated the cost of the items in that food plan. Using USDA's estimate that families of three or more people spend about one-third of their income on food, the government multiplied the cost of the economy food plan by three (to cover the cost of other family expenses). The result was a dollar figure that was known as the poverty threshold. The same formula has been used ever since. Each year the threshold is adjusted to take into account increases in the cost of living. Thresholds are computed for unrelated individuals and families of different sizes.

In 2000, the poverty line for an individual was $8,794; for a family of four, it was $17,603. Here's what these amounts mean in real-life terms. A poor individual living on $8,794 has about $24 a day to live on. Using the government's one-third/two-thirds formula, that amounts to $8 per day to eat and $16 a day for all other expenses. A poor family of four living on $17,603 has about $48 per day to live on ($16 per day for food, $32 for everything else). In 2003, the poverty line was $9,393 for an individual and $18,810 for a family of four (about $52 per day).

Based on these figures, the government estimates that about 31 million individuals (11 percent of all Americans) are poor. About 6 million families, or 9 percent of all families, are poor. All percentages are considerably higher for African Americans and Hispanics than for whites and Asians.

In my view, there is a sizable gap between the Church's social teachings and the government's approach to poverty. The government's approach does not see poverty in relation to the overall distribution of the nation's social and economic resources (for example, relative to the median income for individuals or families). Instead, it defines poverty in purely absolute terms (as the total number of dollars needed for minimal subsistence). Instead of using a food plan that would provide an adequate diet over time, it relies on an economy plan that was meant for temporary or emergency purposes only. Although the average American family might spend one-third of its income on food, the average poor family spends a larger percentage of its income on food (In effect, it must "borrow" from the nonfood portion of its budgets to feed its members.). Using pretax income, instead of aftertax income, as its standard, the poverty line does not make allowances for the dent taxes put in low-income family incomes. Finally, although the government's measure adjusts for increases in the cost of living, it does not adjust for increases in the standard of living.

Thus, the government's official measure of poverty has several serious limitations. It is quite likely that other measures reflecting Catholic social principles would show there is considerably more poverty in our society than government figures indicate.

Catholics Helped Put "Under God" in the Pledge of Allegiance

When Francis Bellamy drafted the Pledge of Allegiance in 1892, he wrote: "I pledge allegiance to my Flag and the Republic for which it stands: one nation, indivisible, with liberty and justice for all." Bellamy soon inserted the word "to" in front of "the Republic." In 1923 and 1924, the American Legion and the Daughters of the American Revolution succeeded in changing "my Flag" to "the Flag of the United States of America."

The wording of the pledge remained unchanged from 1924 to 1954, when it was changed to: "I pledge allegiance to the Flag of the United States of America and to the Republic for which it stands, one nation, *under God*, with liberty and justice for all." Why were the words "under God" added to the pledge in 1954, and who brought about that change?

To answer these questions, we have to understand the political climate of the 1950s and the patriotism of American Catholics, especially the Knights of Columbus.[6] In the 1950s, the United States was engaged in a cold war with the Soviet Union, which—in the words of one U.S. Congressman—espoused "the pagan doctrine of communism." Catholics also were trying to overcome decades of anti-Catholicism by demonstrating their complete support of the United States in its fight against communism.

In April 1951, the Supreme Council of the Knights of Columbus adopted a resolution adding "under God" to the pledge when it was recited at K of C meetings. In April and May 1952, K of C councils in Florida, Michigan, New York, and South Dakota voted to petition the Congress to add "under God" to the pledge. In August 1952, the Supreme Council agreed to send letters urging the same thing to President Dwight Eisenhower, Vice President Richard Nixon, and the Speaker of the House. In September 1952, the National Fraternal Congress (whose president was K of C leader Luke Hart) agreed to do the same. On April 20, 1953, Democratic Congressman Louis Rabaut of Michigan introduced House Joint Resolution 243 to change the pledge to read "one nation, under God, indivisible, with liberty and justice for all." In August 1953, the K of C extended the letter-writing campaign to include all members of the Senate and the House.

On February 7, 1954, Rev. George M. Docherty, pastor of the New York Avenue Presbyterian Church in Washington DC preached on the topic. With President Eisenhower in attendance, Docherty said something was missing from the pledge. In his words: "[T]hat which was missing was the characteristic and definitive factor in the American way of life. Indeed, apart from the mention of the phrase, 'the United States of America,' it could be the pledge of any republic. In fact, I could hear little Moscovites repeat a similar pledge to their hammer-and-sickle flag in Moscow with equal solemnity. Russia is also a republic that claims to have overthrown the tyranny of kingship. Russia also claims to be indivisible."[7]

On May 5, 1954, Rabaut echoed Docherty's words in the House of Representatives when he explained the history of the pledge and the reasons why he had introduced his resolution a year earlier. So did other congressmen as they rose to support it on June 7, 1954. Congressman Charles A. Wolverton also noted that "the Members of Congress have received innumerable petitions, letters and telegrams from individuals from all over this land of ours endorsing [Rabaut's] amendment, and likewise resolutions of approval from religious, fraternal and patriotic organizations."[8]

Rabaut's resolution was passed on June 7 and signed into law by President Eisenhower on Flag Day, June 14, 1954. In August, Eisenhower wrote to the K of C saying: "We are particularly thankful to you for your part in the movement to have the words 'under God' added to our Pledge of Allegiance. These words will remind Americans that despite our great physical strength we must remain humble. They will help us to keep constantly in our minds and hearts the spiritual and moral principles which alone give dignity to man, and upon which our way of life is founded. For the contributions which your organization has made to this cause, we must be genuinely grateful."[9]

When and Why Was "In God We Trust" Put on Our Money?

Although many Americans believe the motto "In God We Trust" has always been on our money, that is not true. It was added to the nation's coins in the midst of the Civil War of the 1860s and our paper money during the Cold War of the 1950s. Here is what happened in each case.

In the mid-1800s, a number of American Protestants viewed the Civil War as God's revenge on the United States for not including any reference to the Almighty in the U.S. Constitution. Calling themselves the Christian Amendment Movement (later the National Reform Association), some of these churchgoers launched an effort to rewrite the preamble to the Constitution. Although this amendment failed, another one of the movement's efforts was more successful: to acknowledge God on the nation's coins.

Greatly disturbed by the Civil War, Rev. Mark R. Watkinson of Pennsylvania wrote to Secretary of the Treasury Salmon P. Chase on November 13, 1861, urging him to acknowledge the Almighty on the nation's money. A week later, Secretary Chase wrote the following to James Pollack, Director of the Mint in Philadelphia:

> "No nation can be strong except in the strength of God, or safe except in His defense. The trust of our people in God should be declared on our national coins.
>
> You will cause a device to be prepared without unnecessary delay with a motto expressing in the fewest and tersest words possible this national recognition."[10]

Pollack did so, and on December 9, 1863, Chase approved Pollack's designs, including the motto "In God We Trust." In the Mint Act of [April 22] 1864, Congress authorized a two-cent piece, with the inscription "In God We Trust" appearing on the front. On March 3, 1865, Congress declared that "In God We Trust" was to appear on all gold and silver coins.

Ninety years later, the country was involved in a cold war with the Soviet Union. Americans wanted to emphasize the differences between America's religious heritage and "godless communism." In 1953, Matthew Rothert, a Presbyterian and president of a furniture company in Arkansas, attended church with his wife's family in Chicago. During the collection, Rothert realized that "In God We Trust" was on U.S. coins but not on U.S. paper money. In November of that year, he wrote to President Eisenhower, Secretary of the Treasury George W. Humphrey, and many other political leaders proposing that "In God We Trust" be added to all of the nation's currency.

Rothert's idea was introduced on the House floor as H.R. 619 on June 7, 1955. Speaking on behalf of the bill, Congressman Charles E. Bennett of Florida said: "In these days when imperialistic and materialistic communism seeks to attack and destroy freedom, we should continuously look for ways to strengthen the foundations of our freedom. At the base of our freedom is our faith in God and the desire of Americans to live by His will and His guidance. As long as this country trusts in God, it will prevail. To serve as a constant reminder of this truth, it is highly desirable that our currency and coins should bear these inspiring words 'In God We Trust.'" The bill passed the same day. On June 29, the same bill was introduced in the Senate, where it also passed. On July 11, 1955, Eisenhower signed Public Law 140 declaring that the "inscription In God We Trust shall appear on all United States currency and coins." A year later, on July 30, 1956, "In God We Trust" became the national motto. The first paper currency carrying new motto entered circulation on October 1, 1957. By 1966, "In God We Trust" was on all paper money.

Thus, in the 1860s and again in the 1950s, assertive Christian constituents and responsive political leaders believed that publicly acknowledging our trust in God would fortify the society in perilous times. As a result of their actions, "In God We Trust" was added to our coins when the country was sharply divided in a civil war, and to our paper money when the nation was pitted against a foreign enemy in a cold war.

The Real Reason Churches Cannot Endorse Political Candidates

The Catholic Church cannot endorse or oppose political candidates. It can speak about political issues, such as economic justice and abortion, but dioceses and parishes cannot align themselves with or against particular candidates.

When I ask people why the Church cannot endorse or oppose candidates, they usually say it has to do with the First Amendment or, using Thomas Jefferson's phrase, the "wall of separation between church and state."

They are wrong. There is nothing in the First Amendment that prevents churches from endorsing or opposing political candidates. The courts have never used the separation of church and state as an argument to block churches' involvement in partisan politics.

Churches have always had a constitutional right to support or campaign against political candidates. And, sometimes, they have done just that. For example, several Protestant organizations actively, and quite legally, opposed the candidacy of Al Smith when he was the first Catholic to campaign for president in 1928.

What, then, prevents churches from endorsing or opposing political candidates? The ban on electioneering has to do with the fact that churches are tax-exempt organizations. Like all other 501(c) 3 organizations, churches must abide by IRS rules. Since 1954, these rules have included a prohibition on electioneering. Tax-exempt groups that publicly support or oppose political candidates can lose their tax-exempt status. They could be taxed on their income, and their benefactors no longer could deduct their contributions from their personal income taxes.

Why did the ban on electioneering suddenly appear in 1954? It was introduced into the 1954 tax reform package by Lyndon Johnson, who wanted to thwart tax-exempt, anticommunist groups that supported his political adversaries. It had nothing to do with churches or constitutional issues relating to the separation of church and state. Churches simply shared the same tax-exempt status as the political organizations that Johnson was really after.[11]

The Religious Affiliations of U.S. Presidents

Most Catholics know that John F. Kennedy was the first and only Catholic to be president of the United States. But, do you know the religious affiliation of the nation's other presidents? How many and which presidents have belonged to the Episcopal and Presbyterian churches? How many, and which ones, have been United Methodist or Baptist? What about other groups, such as Unitarians and Quakers; how many presidents have belonged to these religions?

Most of the nation's forty-three presidents have been lifelong members of one church. However, some have grown up in one faith but converted to another or drifted away from religion during their adult lives. Two famous examples are Thomas Jefferson, who was raised Episcopalian but later claimed no specific denomination, and George W. Bush, who also grew up Episcopalian but has embraced the United Methodist affiliation of his wife, Laura. I will concentrate on the religious affiliation that presidents claimed during their adult years.

TABLE 3.2 Presidents by Religious Affiliation

Religious Group	Number of Presidents	Percent
Episcopal	11	26
Presbyterian	8	19
Methodist	4	9
Baptist	4	9
Unitarian	4	9
Disciple of Christ	3	7
No Group	3	7
Dutch Reformed	2	5
Quaker	2	5
Cong/UCC	1	2
Catholic	1	2

Forty-seven percent of all U.S. presidents have belonged to three relatively small but highly influential Protestant denominations: Episcopal, Presbyterian, and Congregational (now the United Church of Christ). There have been eleven Episcopal presidents, far more than any other single faith group. Indeed, the Episcopal Church alone accounts for 26 percent of all presidents (including George Washington, James Madison, James Monroe, William Henry Harrison, Franklin Delano Roosevelt, Gerald Ford, and George H. W. Bush). Presbyterians rank second, with 19 percent of all presidents, including Andrew Jackson, James Buchanan, Grover Cleveland, Benjamin Harrison, Woodrow Wilson, and Dwight Eisenhower. There has been one Congregational/UCC president: Calvin Coolidge.

Another 30 percent of U.S. presidents have belonged to other Protestant denominations. Nine percent have been Methodist (Ulysses Grant, Rutherford B. Hayes, William McKinley, and George W. Bush). Nine percent have been Baptist (Warren Harding, Harry Truman, Jimmy Carter, and Bill Clinton). Seven percent have been members of the Disciples of Christ (James Garfield, Lyndon B. Johnson, and Ronald Reagan) and 5 percent have been Dutch Reformed (Martin Van Buren and Theodore Roosevelt).

Twenty-three percent of U.S. presidents have belonged to other religious groups or have claimed no particular church. Nine percent have been Unitarians (John Adams, John Quincy Adams, Millard Fillmore, and William Howard Taft). Seven percent have had no specific denomination (Thomas

Jefferson, Abraham Lincoln, and Andrew Johnson). Five percent have been Quakers (Herbert Hoover and Richard Nixon). John F. Kennedy is the lone Catholic.

When we examine the religious affiliations of the first fourteen presidents, the next fifteen, and the most recent fourteen, we find that there have been some important changes over time. Episcopalians, Presbyterians, and Congregational/UCCs accounted for 64 percent of the nation's first fourteen presidents, 40 percent of the next fifteen, and 38 percent of the latest fourteen. Thus, their access to the presidency declined in the 1800s but has leveled off since then. It still far exceeds their percentage of the total U.S. population. Other Protestants accounted for only 7 percent of the first fourteen presidents, but 40 percent of the next fifteen, and 43 percent of the last fourteen. In other words, their access to the presidency increased during the nineteenth century and has remained relatively constant since then. It too exceeds their numbers in the total population. Other groups, including people with no religious preference, accounted for 29 percent of the first fourteen presidents, 20 percent of the next fifteen, and 21 percent of the last fourteen. Their access to the presidency has not changed dramatically and is small relative to their memberships. Catholics, for example, currently comprise about one-fourth of the U.S. population, but only one of the last fourteen presidents has been Catholic.

Religion a Factor in Presidents' Appointments to the Cabinet

Rachel Kraus, Scott Morrissey, and I are studying the religious affiliations of U.S. presidents and the people they appoint to their cabinets.[12] Four findings indicate that religious affiliation has important implications for one's access to these high political offices.

First, a disproportionate number of presidents (47 percent) and cabinet officers (45 percent) have belonged to the three denominations that have come to be called "the Protestant Establishment." Twenty-six percent of presidents have been Episcopalians, 19 percent have been Presbyterians, and 2 percent have been Congregationalists (more recently known as the United Church of Christ). Nineteen percent of cabinet officers have been Episcopalians, 21 percent have been Presbyterians, and 5 percent have been Congregationalists/UCCs.

Second, one of the reasons the Protestant Establishment is so prominent among cabinet appointees is that presidents belonging to the Establishment have been more inclined to appoint members of the Establishment to the cabinet than they have been to appoint members of other religious groups. Establishment presidents have appointed members of the Establishment to their cabinets 47 percent of the time. They have appointed members of other Protestant denominations (such as Baptists and Methodists) only 29 percent of the time, and other groups (such as Unitarian-Universalists, Catholics, and Jews) only 23 percent of the time.

Third, presidents who do not belong to the Protestant Establishment also have been more inclined to appoint members of the Establishment than members of their own religious groups to cabinet posts. For example, when Unitarian and Quaker presidents have made their cabinet selections, they have chosen members of the Protestant Establishment 65 percent of the time and members of all other religious groups only about one-third of the time. When non-Establishment Protestants (such as Baptists and Methodists) have chosen cabinet officers, they have selected members of the Protestant Establishment 36 percent of the time and non-Establishment Protestants only 30 percent of the time. Members of other religious groups (such as Unitarians and Catholics) account for the rest of their cabinet appointments.

Fourth, when presidents have appointed non-Protestants to their cabinets, they have selected only a limited number of religious outsiders and, when these appointees left office, replaced them with other members of the same religious group. The effect has been the creation of outsider seats in the cabinet. Some of the best examples of this phenomenon have involved Catholics. In 1933, President Franklin Delano Roosevelt (an Episcopalian) chose James A. Farley (a Catholic) to be his Postmaster General. When Farley left office in 1940, Roosevelt chose another Catholic, Frank C. Walker who, in turn, was replaced by a Catholic in 1945 when President Harry Truman (a Baptist) selected Robert E. Hannegan to be his Postmaster General. Truman also appointed J. Howard McGrath as Attorney General in 1949. When McGrath left that post in 1952, Truman appointed another Catholic, James P. McSweeney. President Eisenhower (a Presbyterian) appointed Martin Patrick Durkin (a Catholic) to be Secretary of Labor in 1953. Within a year, Durkin was replaced by another Catholic, James P. Mitchell. Finally, President Lyndon Johnson (who belonged to the Disciples of Christ) appointed a Catholic, John A. Gronouski, Postmaster General in 1965 and replaced him with another Catholic, Lawrence F. O'Brien.

Thus, religious affiliation has been a factor in people's access to the presidency and the cabinet. Relative to its numbers in the total population, the Protestant Establishment has had more than its fair share of presidents.

Moreover, presidents' cabinet appointments have tended to perpetuate the prominence of the Protestant Establishment, but in some cases, have introduced change in the religious makeup of our nation's political elites through the creation of outsider seats in the cabinet, such as the Catholic seats I have described.

The Religion of U.S. Presidents and Their Appointees to the Supreme Court

Nearly half of all U.S. presidents have belonged to just three mainline Protestant denominations, which often have called the Protestant Establishment. Episcopalians alone account for 26 percent of our presidents; Presbyterians, 19 percent; and Congregationalists, 2 percent. Another 14 percent of presidents have belonged to two other groups that achieved prominence in the colonial period: Unitarians (9 percent) and Quakers (5 percent). Thirty percent of presidents have belonged to "other Protestant" groups: Methodists (9 percent), Baptists (9 percent), Disciples of Christ (7 percent), and the Dutch Reformed Church (5 percent). The remaining 9 percent of presidents have had no religious preference (7 percent) or have been Catholic (2 percent).

Is there is any connection between the presidents' religious affiliations and the religious affiliations of the people they appoint to the Supreme Court? Do presidents choose members of their own faith or similar faiths? Do they use appointments to build relations with constituencies, including churches, they do not belong to? Or, does religious affiliation have nothing to do with presidents' appointments to the Court?

Sociologists Rachel Kraus, Scott Morrissey, and I are exploring these questions. So far, we have reached three conclusions.[13] First, the religious profile of justices is very similar to the profile of presidents. Half of Supreme Court justices have come from the three Protestant Establishment groups. Thirty-one percent of justices have been Episcopalians, 18 percent have been Presbyterians, and 2 percent have been Congregationalists. Unitarians (8 percent) and Quakers (1 percent) account another 9 percent. One-fourth have belonged to "other Protestant" denominations (5 percent Methodist, 3 percent Baptist, 1 percent Lutheran, 1 percent Disciples of Christ, and 15 percent unspecified Protestant groups). The rest (17 percent) have had other religious outlooks: Catholicism (9 percent), Judaism (7 percent), or no religious preference (1 percent).

Second, presidents belonging to the Protestant Establishment are most inclined to appoint their own kind to the Court. Forty-five percent of their appointees have been Episcopalian, Presbyterian, or Congregationalist. Thirty-two percent have been "other Protestants," 13 percent have been "others," and only 9 percent have been Unitarians or Quakers. Our first president, George Washington, an Episcopalian, made eight appointments, including five Episcopalians. Our forty-first president, George H. W. Bush, also an Episcopalian, made two: one Episcopalian, the other Catholic.

Third, all other religious groups are more inclined to appoint members of the Protestant Establishment than members of their own religious traditions. Sixty-three percent of the time Unitarian and Quaker presidents have appointed members of the Protestant Establishment, 31 percent of the time they have appointed "other Protestants," 6 percent of the time they have appointed "others," and they have never appointed members of their own faith tradition to the Court. For example, Richard Nixon, a Quaker, made four appointments: two Presbyterians, one Lutheran, and one Methodist. Presidents belonging to "other Protestant" denominations have appointed members of the Protestant Establishment 48 percent of the time, "others" 28 percent of the time, "other Protestants" only 14 percent of the time, and other colonial elites only 10 percent of the time. For example, President Lyndon Johnson, who belonged to the Disciples of Christ, appointed one Episcopalian and one Jew. Finally, presidents in "other" religious groups have appointed members of the Protestant Establishment 60 percent of the time, other colonial elites 20 percent of the time, and "others" 20 percent of the time (They have never appointed "other Protestants" to the Court.). Abraham Lincoln, who had no religious preference, appointed two members of the Protestant Establishment, a Unitarian, a Quaker, and a "none." John F. Kennedy appointed an Episcopalian and a Jew.

President George W. Bush grew up in the Episcopal Church but has since converted to the United Methodist Church, his wife Laura's faith. Given his Protestant affiliation, and with three Catholics already on the court, Bush's choice of John Roberts (a Catholic) to be chief justice is both surprising and historic. It marks the first time in U.S. history when two-thirds of the justices are Catholic (44 percent) or Jewish (22 percent), and only one-third is Protestant.

How Catholics Vote

American Catholics represent one of the largest constituencies of voters in the United States. No one can predict exactly what candidates will tell Catholics, or how Catholics will respond. However, we can get some sense of how Catholics are likely to vote by looking at how they have voted over the last half century.

University of Maine political scientist Mark Brewer reviewed Catholics' voting habits from twelve presidential elections.[14] Brewer used data collected by the highly regarded National Election Studies Center at the University of Michigan.

TABLE 3.3 Catholic Votes for President, 1952–1996

Year	Democrat	Republican	Other
1952	52 (Stevenson)	48 (Eisenhower)	—
1956	46 (Stevenson)	54 (Eisenhower)	—
1960	82 (Kennedy)	18 (Nixon)	—
1964	79 (Johnson)	21 (Goldwater)	—
1968	56 (Humphrey)	37 (Nixon)	7
1972	39 (McGovern)	59 (Nixon)	2
1976	57 (Carter)	41 (Ford)	2
1980	41 (Carter)	50 (Reagan)	9
1984	46 (Mondale)	54 (Reagan)	<1
1988	52 (Dukakis)	47 (Bush)	1
1992	50 (Clinton)	30 (Bush)	21
1996	55 (Clinton)	37 (Dole)	8

Half or more of Catholics voted for the Democratic candidate in eight of the twelve elections: 1952, 1960, 1964, 1968, 1976, 1988, 1992, and 1996. Democrats won five and lost three of these elections. Catholics were most inclined to vote Democrat when John Kennedy ran against Richard Nixon in 1960, and when Kennedy's former vice-president Lyndon Johnson ran against Barry Goldwater in 1964.

Half or more of Catholics voted for the Republican candidate in four elections: 1956, 1972, 1980, and 1984. Republicans won all four elections. Catholics were most likely to vote Republican when Richard Nixon defeated George McGovern in 1972, Ronald Reagan beat Walter Mondale in 1984, and Eisenhower won over Adlai E. Stevenson in 1956.

Catholics have never given third-party candidates a majority of their votes. However, as many as 21 percent of Catholics voted for "other" candidates in 1992—mostly for Ross Perot.

Over these twelve elections, Catholics have given Democrats an average of 55 percent of their votes. They have given Republicans an average of 41 percent of their votes. When there have been third-party candidates, they have received an average of 6 percent of the Catholic vote.

Some researchers have argued that Catholics are drifting away from the Democratic Party.[15] They offer two explanations: that Catholics are leaving the Democratic Party as it has endorsed liberal, especially pro-choice, social positions, and that Catholics are increasingly turning toward the Republican Party as they move up the nation's economic ladder.

Brewer shows that there is no support for the first of these arguments. Catholics are a bit more liberal than the rest of the U.S. population on most social issues, and despite the Church's opposition to abortion, Catholic laypeople are as pro-choice as other Americans.

According to Brewer, there is more validity to the second argument. Though Catholics in the lower- and middle-income brackets still strongly favor Democratic candidates, there has been some shift toward the Republican Party among Catholics in the upper-income bracket. However, upper-income Catholics are still more likely to vote Democratic than Protestants of the same socioeconomic status.

Two presidential elections have taken place since this column was written. In 2000, Catholics favored Albert Gore over George W. Bush 50 percent to 47 percent. In 2004, Bush appealed to Catholics almost as much as Eisenhower in 1956, Nixon in 1972, and Reagan in 1980 and 1984, garnering 52 percent of the Catholic vote versus 47 percent for John Kerry.

George W. Bush and the Catholic Vote

Religious affiliation affects the way people vote. Of America's major religious groups, Protestants are most likely to vote Republican. For example, in the 2000 presidential election, 56 percent of Protestants voted for George W. Bush, 42 percent voted for Al Gore, and 2 percent voted for Ralph Nader. Jews, people with "other" religious affiliations (such as Muslims and Buddhists), and Catholics are more likely to vote Democrat. In 2000, 79 percent of Jews voted for Gore, 19 percent for Bush, and 1 percent for Nader. Sixty-two percent of "others" voted for Gore, 28 percent for Bush,

7 percent for Nader, and 1 percent for Buchanan. Sixty-one percent of people with no religious affiliation voted for Gore, 30 percent for Bush, and 7 percent for Nader. Fifty percent of Catholics voted for Gore, 47 percent for Bush, 2 percent for Nader, and 1 percent for Pat Buchanan.

Since religious affiliation affects the way people vote, the religious composition of the electorate affects election outcomes. The larger the percentage of the electorate that is Protestant, the easier it is for Republicans to win the White House. The larger the percentage of the electorate that is Jewish, "other," "none," and Catholic, the easier it is for Democrats to win. What, then, is the trend in the religious composition of the electorate? Are Protestants a growing or shrinking percentage of the people who vote? What about Jews, "others," "nones," and Catholics? Are they a growing or shrinking percentage of the electorate? Answers to these questions can be found in data recently reported by the University of Michigan's politically neutral and highly reliable National Election Study.[16]

TABLE 3.4 Religious Composition of Electorate, 1952–2000

Religion	1952	1960	1968	1976	1984	1992	2000
Protestant	72%	74%	72%	65%	62%	59%	54%
Catholic	22	20	22	25	26	24	26
Jewish	3	3	3	2	2	2	4
Other/None	3	2	4	8	10	15	15

Protestants are declining as a percentage of the total electorate. In 1952, 1960, and 1968, 72 to 74 percent of the people voting were Protestant. By 1976, Protestants were 65 percent of the electorate. By 1984, only 62 percent of the electorate was Protestant. In 1990, Protestants were only 59 percent of the electorate and, in the 2000 presidential election, they were only 54 percent. Meanwhile, the electoral influence of Catholics, Jews, "others," and "nones" is increasing. Catholics' electoral power has increased a bit (from 20 to 22 percent in the 1950s and 1960s to 24 to 26 percent in the 1990s). Jewish electoral influence has remained relatively small (between 2 and 3 percent) and essentially unchanged. The biggest increase has been among people with "other" religious affiliations and people with none. These groups have climbed from only 3 percent of the electorate in 1952 to 15 percent in 2000.

In short, Protestants are shrinking as a percentage of the electorate, and the political influence of non-Protestant groups is increasing. For the Republican Party to win the White House in 2004, they had to attract voters from other religious groups. They focused on Catholics, because they are the largest of the other religious groups, and they are more likely to vote Republican than Jews, "others," and "nones."

According to an article by Thomas B. Edsall in the *Washington Post*, this effort had begun by April 2001. Edsall reports that "President Bush and top advisers have been assiduously cultivating Catholic voters."[17] According to Edsall, "Bush...has met privately with at least three high Catholic Church officials—1) Then Archbishop Justin Rigali of St. Louis [now Cardinal in Philadelphia], 2) Bishop Donald Wuerl of Pittsburgh, and 3) Cardinal Theodore McCarrick of Washington DC—and has adopted Catholic themes in speeches; his staff has instituted a weekly conference call with an informal group of Catholics advisers; and the Republican National Committee is setting up a Catholic Task Force." Bush's goal was to attract religiously active Catholics to the Republican Party. His tactics were effective, as he went on to win the 2004 presidential election carrying 52 percent of the Catholic vote (5 percent more than the previous election).

Red States, Blue States: It's About Religion

By now we are all familiar with the distinction between red states (where a majority of voters choose the Republican presidential candidate) and blue states (which go for the Democrat). In the 2004 election, the final tally showed 31 red states and 20 blue states (including the District of Columbia). But, why were some states red, while others were blue? Did religion have anything to do with it?

To examine this issue, I consulted Barry Kosmin and Egon Mayer's American Religious Identification Survey (2001), a national sample of 50,281 American households in forty-eight states and the District of Columbia (Hawaii and Alaska were not included).[18] The ARIS survey provides a detailed breakdown of religious identification by state.

The results point to five conclusions. First, the higher the percentage of the population that identifies as Protestant or Mormon, the greater the likelihood that the state voted Republican. Second, the higher the percentage of Catholics, the more likely the state was to be blue. Third, the larger the percentage of people who identify as Jews, the more likely the state was to vote Democrat. Fourth, the larger the percentage of a state's population that identifies with other religions or "no religion," the more likely that state was to be blue.

Fifth, when these findings are combined, the result is that states with the largest Protestant and Mormon populations were red, and the ones with the largest percentage of Catholics, Jews, others, and "nones" were blue. Of the thirteen states that are 60+ percent Protestant or Mormon, every one was red (such as Utah). Of the twenty-eight states that are 40–59 percent Protestant or Mormon, sixteen (57 percent) were red (such as Indiana). Twelve (43 percent) were blue (such as Maryland). Finally, of the eight states where Catholics, Jews, others, and "nones" are the clear majority, seven (87.5 percent) were blue (such as California). Only one (12.5 percent) went red (New Mexico).

TABLE 3.5 Election Results by Religious Identification

Religious Identification	Red States	Blue States	Total
60+% Prot/Mormon	AL, AR, GA, KY, MS, NC, OK, SC, SD, TN UT, VA, WV (100%)		100%
40–59% Prot/Mormon	AZ, CO, FL, IA, ID, IN, KS, LA, MO, MT, ND, NE, NV, OH, TX, WY (57%)	CT, DC, DE, IL, MD, ME, MI, MN, OR, PA, WA, WI (43%)	100%
<40% Prot/Mormon	NM (12.5%)	CA, MA, NH, NJ, NY, RI, VT (87.5%)	100%

But, how does a state's religious composition affect its tendency to be red or blue? A complete answer to that question requires consideration of many factors that I cannot address in this space. However, at least one of them is the fact that religious identification affects the way people vote. According to national exit polls, 59 percent of Protestants voted for Bush. Unlike the last two elections, when Catholics favored the Democratic candidates, this time 52 percent of Catholics voted for Bush, only 47 percent preferred Kerry. As in the past, Jews favored the Democrat, this time by a 74 percent to 25 percent margin. Also, as they have in the past, "others" and people with no religion favored the Democratic candidate (74 percent and 67 percent, respectively).

It is not yet known to what extent this national pattern was repeated in every state. For example, we do not know if Catholics in every state voted for Bush, or if there are some states where a majority of Catholics preferred Kerry. Let us assume the national pattern occurred in most, but not all, states. If so, one reason every one of the mostly-Protestant and Mormon states went red is that the Protestant/Mormon majority voted Republican and got some help from others, including Catholics. States with greater mixtures of religious groups tended to go red when Protestants and Mormons got help from others, such as Catholics in Montana, Wyoming, Colorado, Arizona, Texas, Louisiana, and Florida. Other states with mixed populations went blue when Protestants and Mormons did not get as much support, such as in Illinois and Oregon. All but one of the states where Protestants and Mormons are a distinct minority went blue, because a majority of Jews, others, "nones," and quite probably Catholics voted Democratic.

The religious composition of states certainly is not the only variable affecting the state-by-state outcome of the election. Other factors (such as racial and ethnic composition, economic class, and the urban-rural character of states) also must be taken into account. But, one cannot fully understand the results of the 2004 election unless one takes religion into account.

Questions for Reflection

1. Considering religion's impact on national and local economies, what more could the Church do to improve the quality of life in our country and in your area?
2. If the gap between the rich and poor is growing, and there is more poverty in America than government figures indicate, what more should Catholics do to solve these problems?
3. Major changes took place in the relationship between religion and politics in the Cold War period of the 1950s (For example, the government limited religious groups' participation in partisan politics, but religious groups helped put references to God into the Pledge of Allegiance and onto our money.). Do similar conditions exist in our post-9/11 society, and should we expect similar developments in the relationship between religion and politics?

4. Should the Catholic Church abandon its tax-exempt status so it can openly endorse and oppose political candidates? Explain your answer.
5. Does evidence from recent elections support the claim that Catholics are leaving the Democrat Party in favor of the Republican Party?
6. Did President Bush's effort to recruit Catholic voters work in 2004? If so, why? If not, why not?

Part II

Organizational Issues in the Church

Chapter 4

Parishes, Schools, and Other Catholic Institutions

Social theory and research offer Catholics four ways of thinking about the Church. One approach stresses the Church's bureaucratic structure, another emphasizes the characteristics of its people, a third calls attention to the political dimensions of church life, and a fourth highlights the Church's cultural attributes. In some areas of Church life, the "golden years" seem to be behind us, while in other areas the best years are yet to come. Catholics report that they are more satisfied with their parishes' impact on their spiritual lives than with their impact on other aspects of parishioners' daily lives. Catholic parishes are more racially integrated than most Protestant congregations, but there is an increasing number of Latino faith communities in the U.S. Two sections explore parishes' involvement in issues of social inequality and the conditions under which parishes might be more engaged in such issues. Another section records the dramatic changes that are taking place in Catholic elementary schools, high schools, and colleges. The chapter ends by providing suggestions for what might be done to increase Catholics' financial support of their parishes and schools.

Four Views of Church: Which Do You Favor?

Lee Bolman and Terrence Deal are authors of a wonderful book entitled *Reframing Organizations*.[1] They outline four approaches that social researchers use to study organizations: structural, human resource, political, and symbolic. But social researchers are not the only people who use these approaches. Clergy and laypeople also use them when analyzing Catholic dioceses, parishes, schools, hospitals, and newspapers.

People who like the structural approach stress the hierarchical or bureaucratic nature of the Church, with its chain of command reaching down from the pope to the people in the pews. They emphasize the role that dioceses, parishes, and schools play in the delivery of essential services, such as sacraments. They insist on quality control and efficiency in each area, and that all departments, or ministries, work together. When problems arise, they want to restructure the organization (for example, realign authority, reduce duplication).

People who prefer the human-resource approach think of the Church as a family, as people who love one another and want to help them grow. They stress the importance of the talents people have to offer, and how Church members can nurture and benefit from one another's gifts. They call attention to the need to recruit, train, and support good people. When things go wrong, they stress the need to replace personnel and/or refocus individuals through continuing education, sabbaticals, or counseling.

People who use the political approach see the Church as an arena in which groups with conflicting values and interests compete for scarce resources, especially power (the ability to get one's way), privilege (money), and prestige (respect). From this point of view, groups want to control the Church's agenda and its budget so they can create policies reflecting their own goals and objectives (and prevent other groups from doing the same thing). Problems arise when there is political gridlock and nothing gets done. The solution: negotiations leading to a more equitable sharing of resources.

People who like the symbolic approach think of the Church in cultural, artistic, or theatrical terms. They stress the Scriptures, the historical events, and recent developments that comprise the Church's "script." They emphasize the importance of good liturgies and homilies that tell the Church's story. They insist on words, music, and motions that give meaning to life and inspire people. When things go wrong, the audience is bored or does not bother to attend. The solution, according to people with this view, is to rewrite the script (use new language, music, and liturgies to tell the Church's story).

These four approaches are not mutually exclusive; they simply emphasize different facets of Church life. None of us uses one approach to the exclusion of all the others. However, we tend to favor one or two approaches over the others. Which approach do you use most often? What are your second and third choices? Which approach are you least likely to use?

I find that many, though not all, bishops and pastors tend to use the structural approach. Vocation directors and catechists usually prefer the human-resource approach. Persons who want to defend or expand their stake in the system (for example, large contributors, marginalized groups) tend to use the political model. Liturgists and choir directors are inclined to use the symbolic approach.

This might explain why Church leaders often have such different interpretations of issues facing their dioceses and parishes, why they often seem to talk past one another, and why they often cannot reach agreement on topics that, at first blush, would seem quite easy to resolve. It also might explain why people in the pews have such different reactions to what they see at Mass or hear at adult-education programs, and why some people complain about a specific policy while others think it is great. Knowing that faithful people have different—and quite legitimate—views of Church life might increase our ability to respect and understand one another. If so, it also might foster collegiality and community among the people of God.

The Golden Age of American Catholicism, Statistically Speaking

Some people say the golden age of American Catholicism was in the 1940s, when four Catholic movies (*The Bells of St. Mary's, Going My Way, Song of Bernadette,* and *The Keys of the Kingdom*) received thirty-four Oscar nominations. Others contend the Church reached its peak during the post-World War II years of the 1950s, when local parishes were bursting at the seams with young families. Noting the continuing growth of the Catholic population, some believe we are living in the golden age right now.

So, what is the correct answer? Clearly, there are many different ways of defining the golden age, and every definition produces a different conclusion. Without denying the value of other approaches, I wondered what the answer would be if we used official Church statistics to locate the golden years. Using the *Official Catholic Directory* and other sources, I collated data on twenty-seven aspects of church life for five-year intervals between 1930 and 2000, then added the data for 2002 to be as current as possible.

TABLE 4.1 Religious Categories by Peak Years

Category	Peak Year	Number	2002
Diocesan high schools	1930	2,123	824
Diocesan seminaries	1940	202	70
Private high schools	1950	1,394	552
Infant baptisms	1960	1,344,576	1,005,490
Catholic hospitals	1960/5	808	585
Diocesan seminarians	1965	17,494	3,251
Religious seminaries	1965	479	143
Religious seminarians	1965	22,230	1,271
Sisters	1965	179,954	74,698
Brothers	1965	12,271	5,568
Colleges/universities	1965	304	237
Diocesan high school students	1965	698,032	386,764
Elementary schools	1965	10,503	6,773
Elementary schools students	1965	4,476,881	1,872,848
Private high school students	1965	487,415	299,887
Religious teachers	1965	110,182	10,039
High school students in rel edu	1970	1,368,817	767,739
Elementary students in rel edu	1970	4,081,929	3,582,943
Marriages	1970	417,271	241,727
Diocesan priests	1970	37,272	29,715
Religious priests	1975	22,904	14,772
Parishes	1995	19,723	19,484
Lay teachers	2002	—	161,775
Deacons	2002	—	14,106
College students	2002	—	749,512
Hospital patients	2002	—	84,000,000
Catholic population	2002	—	66,407,105

The 1930s, 1940s, and 1950s were institution-building years in which the Church—with less than half of its current membership—had more diocesan high schools (2,123), diocesan seminaries (202), and private high schools (1,394) than it has ever had. Institution building continued into the 1960s, when new highs were established for the number of Catholic hospitals (808), religious order seminaries (479), Catholic colleges and universities (304), and parochial elementary schools (10,503). During that decade, the Church also set eight new records for the number of people involved in one aspect of Church life or another. These new highs—all of which occurred in 1965—

were for infant baptisms (1.3 million), diocesan seminarians (17,494), religious order seminarians (22,230), sisters (179,954), brothers (12,271), diocesan high-school students (698,032), elementary-school students (4.4 million), private high-school students (487,415), and teachers who were men or women religious (110,182). None of these benchmarks has been duplicated since then.

No new highs were established for institution building in the 1970s, but five new ones were set for participation. Records were set for high-school students in religious education (1.3 million), elementary-school students in religious education (4 million), marriages (417,271), diocesan priests (37,272), and religious order priests (22,904). Again, none of these records has ever been matched.

Although no new records were achieved in the 1980s, several have been set since then. The number of parishes peaked in the 1990s (19,971 in 1992), but has since declined. Meanwhile, 2002 brought record numbers of lay teachers in Catholic schools (161,775), permanent deacons (14,106), students at Catholic colleges and universities (749,512), patients at Catholic hospitals (84 million), and Catholics (66 million).

To date at least, the 1960s seem like the golden era, with 1965 being the peak year. However, there are some indications that the Church's best years might lie ahead. Even in the context of the numerous challenges facing the Church, recent highs indicate that the Church continues to grow, especially in terms of the number of people who are seriously engaged in its mission. The Church's golden years might very well be in the future, not in the past.

Parish Report Card: An A-, Three Bs, and a C+

Have you ever considered what the Church's report card would look like? I am not talking about the grades that Catholic schoolteachers and religious education instructors give their students. No, I am talking about the grades laypeople give their parishes. What do laypeople think about the homilies in their parishes? How do they rate the music they hear at weekend Masses?

In a recent national survey, registered parishioners and people who are not on parish rolls but attend a nearby parish were asked to rate their parishes on five dimensions: friendliness, quality of homilies, quality of music, meeting spiritual needs, and helping with decisions related to work and family life. Respondents could rate their parishes as excellent (A), good (B), fair (C), and poor (F) on each issue.[2]

Overall, the parish report card is pretty good. It includes one A-, three Bs, and a C+.

TABLE 4.2 Parish Report Card	
Friendliness	A-
Homilies	B
Meeting spiritual needs	B
Music	B
Making decisions in families and at work	C+

Laypeople rate their parishes highest (A-) on friendliness. Forty-three percent say their parishes are excellent in terms of the friendliness of the people; 36 percent say their parishes are good on this dimension. Sixteen percent rate them as only fair or poor.

Catholics give homilies a grade of B. One-third of laypeople report that homilies are excellent. Forty-five percent say they are good. Twenty percent rate homilies as only fair or poor.

Parishes also get a B in meeting parishioners' spiritual needs. Thirty-one percent say their parishes are excellent in this area. Forty-three percent rate their parishes as good in meeting members' spiritual needs. Twenty-four percent say they are only fair or poor on this dimension.

Music also earns a grade of B. Thirty-one percent of laypeople say music in their parishes is excellent, and another 41 percent say it is good. Twenty-six percent are more critical, rating music as only fair (20 percent) or poor (6 percent).

Parishes rate lowest (C+) on helping parishioners make daily decisions in their families and at their workplaces. Only 22 percent rate their parishes as excellent in meeting these needs. One-third say their parishes are good in this area. Almost one-third rate their parishes as only fair (25 percent) or poor (6 percent) on this dimension.

On average, then, parishioners seem satisfied with their parishes. They are especially happy with the friendliness of the people they see at church, and they seem more satisfied with homilies and music than their harshest critics would have us believe. Yet, there is room for improvement in all areas. The greatest challenge is to find ways of linking parishes to the daily decisions parishioners face in their family lives and at work.

Catholic Parishes Are More Integrated Than Other Local Churches

It is often said that 11:00 AM to noon on Sunday is the most racially segregated hour of the week. This saying suggests that, when Americans go to church, whites go to white churches, African Americans go to African-American churches, and Hispanics go to Hispanic churches.

Is this an accurate portrait of Sunday morning in America? How segregated are America's churches? Are some more segregated than others? Are Catholic parishes any more, or less, segregated than Protestant congregations? Sociologist Kevin Dougherty has examined these questions using data from a national study of 625 local churches equally divided among the Roman Catholic Church, the Assemblies of God, the Southern Baptist Convention, the Evangelical Lutheran Church of America, and the Presbyterian Church USA.[3]

Dougherty concludes that Sunday morning is, indeed, a highly segregated time of the week. He reports that 43 percent of the churches in his study are completely segregated. Others are somewhat more integrated. But, "even in churches where multiple racial groups are present," Dougherty writes, "these groups do not remotely approximate equal proportions nor do they match racial proportions of the United States."

Why are some local churches more integrated than others? Dougherty examines a number of possible influences, including external factors having to do with the places where churches are located, and internal factors having to do with their religious traditions and organizational characteristics. His analysis pointed to the following conclusions.

1. Churches located in the West are more racially integrated than churches in other regions of the country. Churches located in the Midwest and the South are the most segregated.
2. The larger the community, the more integrated churches are. Churches in cities with populations of 50,000 or more are the most integrated.
3. Catholic parishes and pentecostal Protestant congregations belonging to the Assemblies of God are more integrated than local churches associated with the other three religious traditions. Catholic parishes are the most integrated of all.
4. Churches that sponsor small-faith communities are somewhat more integrated than ones that do not. Although this factor does not explain as much of the variation as other influences do, it makes a small contribution to racial integration.

5. Although church members' income levels have no significant effect, their educational levels do. Educationally diverse congregations are more racially integrated than ones that are educationally homogeneous.
6. External factors (region of the country and community size) have more impact than internal factors (religious group, small-faith communities, and educational levels).

Thus, opportunities for interracial contact are greater in some regions and localities than others, and these opportunities have important effects on the racial makeup of local churches. Although these opportunities are necessary, they are not sufficient conditions for integration. Even in regions and localities that offer significant opportunities for interracial contact, the worship experiences, teachings, and social dynamics in some local churches are more conducive to racial integration than in others.

In short, 11:00 AM to noon on Sunday is a very segregated hour, but it is more segregated for some churches than others. It is most segregated for educationally homogeneous mainline Protestant churches that have no small groups and are located in small towns in the Midwest and the South. It is most integrated for educationally diverse Catholic and Pentecostal churches that do sponsor small groups and are located in large metropolitan areas of the West.

New Study Describes
Latino Faith Communities

Hispanics are the fastest growing portion of the American population in general and the American Catholic population in particular. There were about 15 million Hispanics in the United States in 1980. By 2000, approximately 35 million Latinos live in this country. Estimates are that about two-thirds of Hispanics are Catholic. Thus, it is fair to say that there are now 20 to 25 million Hispanic Catholics in this country, and that number is climbing every day.

One consequence of this remarkable growth has been the rapid development of Latino faith communities. Researchers at the Program for the Analysis of Religion among Latinas/os (PARAL) recently completed a study of these communities.[4] The PARAL researchers defined faith communities as "Latinos/Hispanics formally organized for worship and service." Thus, the faith communities in PARAL's study included parishes and Hispanic groups within parishes. The researchers contacted 1,054 Catholic communities and received responses from 496 of them (a respectable 48 percent return rate). Here are some of the key things they learned about these communities and the people who lead them.

Among leaders of the Latino faith communities, over 90 percent are Catholic priests or women religious (sisters). Forty percent were born in the U.S., 24 percent are non-Spanish Europeans (for example, Irish), and 15 percent are originally from Mexico. Most are fifty to fifty-four years of age. Fifty-six percent have a master's degree, and another 22 percent have either a professional degree or a doctorate. Sixty percent have taken courses in theology/ministry, 55 percent have graduated from a seminary, 41 percent have taken courses on Latino culture, 34 percent have studied Spanish in Latin America, and 28 percent have been missionaries in Latin America. Seventy-two percent work full time for their faith communities. Typically, leaders' salaries are in the $15,000 to $25,000 range. Sixty-four percent of leaders say the Church has been "very supportive" of their communities.

Latino faith communities focus considerable attention on the recent immigrant status of Hispanic Catholics, their family situations, and their economic circumstances. The most widespread professional programs include youth conferences (55 percent), leadership training (45 percent), activities for senior citizens (40 percent), classes for people wanting to learn English (38 percent), and child-care programs (35 percent). The most common non-professional programs relate to clothing and food (70 percent), disasters (52 percent), and excursions (50 percent). About a third of faith communities also sponsor sports groups and scout groups. Programs about AIDS victims, the homeless, political candidates, and people in need of job training are far less common.

TABLE 4.3 Percent of Latino Faith Communities Offering These Services

Professional services	
Youth conferences	55
Leadership training	45
Senior citizens programs	40
English classes	38
Daycare/Preschool	35
Nonprofessional services	
Clothing/food	70
Disaster victims	52
Excursions	50

The most common homily topics have to do with family life and economic hardship. In order of their frequency, these topics include family unity (77 percent), gender equality (55 percent), domestic violence (53 percent), and poverty (42 percent). There are relatively few homilies on political issues, electoral procedures, immigration, and homosexuality.

Worship services, ethnic celebrations, and outreach programs ordinarily take place within a faith community, but about half of faith communities report that they also conduct such programs in collaboration with other faith communities.

Does Your Parish Perpetuate Inequality, or Promote Equality?

Research has shown that religion plays a dual role in relation to social inequality in our society. Religion perpetuates inequalities in power, privilege, and prestige, but it also promotes a more equal distribution of these valued resources. Religion sanctifies inequality at the same time that it condemns it. It justifies the accumulation of wealth in the midst of poverty, and it calls for a more equitable distribution of the nation's economic resources.

How can religion do both things at once? The main reason is that the religious arena includes many religious groups. There are literally thousands of churches, denominations, sects, cults, congregations, temples, parishes, ecumenical groups, and special purpose organizations. These groups have very different theologies and action agendas.

Imagine a continuum. At one end are groups that perpetuate inequality. These groups promulgate "good fortune" theologies. Their members assume that social inequality is inevitable and functional for society. They attribute poverty to the personal sins of the poor, who they believe should turn their lives over to Christ. They stress the vertical dimension of faith such as our relationship with God. They extol the virtues of the nation's leaders and question the lifestyles of those of who are poor and powerless.

These groups also conduct worship services that legitimate an unequal distribution of wealth and income. Sermons seldom, if ever, address issues of social justice. These groups have no staff persons specifically assigned to social ministries addressing the causes and consequences of inequality. They allocate very little staff time to outreach programs, which rank low in their priorities. They invest little or no money in social-ministry programs. Very few of their members are actively involved in programs oriented toward social justice. In one sense, these groups do little or nothing to prevent inequalities that arise in the economic and political sectors of society. In another sense, they actively contribute to inequality.

At the other end of the continuum are groups that promote equality. These groups promote "social justice" theologies. Their members question the inevitability of inequality, thinking that it results from the coercive practices of the rich and powerful. They can imagine a society in which there is a more equitable distribution of money and material goods. They insist on building a more just and equal world. They emphasize the horizontal dimension of faith, such as our love of neighbor and need to do good for others.

These groups conduct worship services that frequently call for a more equitable distribution of the nation's resources. Sermons often challenge the lifestyles of the privileged classes and affirm the lives of those who are less fortunate. These groups have full-time staff persons in the area of social ministry. They devote significant amounts of staff time to social outreach, and sponsor numerous programs related to social concerns. They make sizable expenditures in the area of social ministry. Many of their members are actively involved in outreach programs. Some of these programs serve the needs of needy individuals (charity); others are aimed at reforming society (social justice).

Where do Protestant congregations and Catholic parishes fall along this continuum? In a recent study of thirty-one affluent churches, Alan Mock, C. Lincoln Johnson, and I found that the groups were more likely to perpetuate inequality than to promote equality.[5] Members scored higher on our measures of good-fortune theology than they did on our measures of social-justice theology. Only one of thirty-one affluent congregations employed a full-time social minister. Church staffs allocated less than 10 percent of their time to social ministry. On average, the churches sponsored four social ministry programs. They spent about 4 percent of their budgets on social programs specifically addressing the needs of the poor. Members were more likely to donate money (43 percent) than time (16 percent) to their church's social-concerns programs.

These results offer some comparative basis for assessing the extent to which churches tend to perpetuate inequality or promote equality.

When Are Affluent Churches Most Involved in Social Ministry?

Some parishes have a disproportionately large number of well-to-do members. In terms of occupational status, their members tend to be professionals and business owners or managers. In terms of economic status, their members' incomes and wealth are well above the national average. The prevailing image of such affluent parishes is that they are not very involved in social ministry.

According to this image, the leaders and members of affluent churches have nothing to gain—and much to lose—from sponsoring programs that provide services to the needy or address the underlying causes of social injustice. It is said that affluent churches place high priority on "safe" programs oriented toward serving their members and low priority on "risky" or potentially controversial programs aimed at the causes and consequences of social inequality.

While there is some truth to this image, it also is true that some affluent churches are more actively involved in social ministry than others. As Alan Mock, C. Lincoln Johnson, and I documented in a study of thirty-one affluent congregations, some privileged parishes allocate significant portions of their budgets to social outreach, sponsor or cosponsor numerous social concerns programs, and mobilize a sizable number of members to participate in these programs.[6]

Under what conditions are affluent churches most likely to be involved in social ministry? Our analysis showed they are most socially active when

- they belong to theologically liberal Protestant traditions—such as the Presbyterian Church or the United Church of Christ—or they belong to the Catholic Church;

- pastors stress religion's prophetic role in society at least as much as its role in nurturing personal faith and saving individual souls;
- pastors stress the close relationship between faith and concern for others (with faith being both a cause and a consequence of social concern);
- lay leaders believe that working for social justice and caring for others are essential components of their faith;
- women are members of church boards of directors.

We also found that affluent churches are most socially active when these conditions are combined with four others:

- parishioners perceive their pastors as strong leaders;
- they also perceive parish officers and board members as effective leaders;
- there is a heightened sense of community in the parish (as indicated by members' concern for one another and their belief that their parish has a mission that sets it apart from other ones);
- members are generous in their financial contributions to their parish.

Social ministry does not happen easily in affluent churches, but it can—and does—happen. It is most likely to happen when religious traditions and local pastors stress the connection between personal faith and the Church's prophetic role in society, women and justice-oriented laypeople occupy leadership roles in the parish, and pastors and lay leaders are effective in building solidarity in the parish and mobilizing the financial resources needed to support all parish endeavors, including social ministry.

Dramatic Changes in Catholic Schools, Students, and Teachers

A number of questions can be asked regarding recent trends in Catholic education. Is the number of Catholic schools increasing, decreasing, or holding steady? Has enrollment in these institutions changed much over the last forty years? Finally, to what extent and in what ways are the faculties at Catholic schools changing?

To answer these questions, I consulted the 1960, 1980, and 2001 editions of the *Official Catholic Directory*, which include data on the number of Catholic schools, students, and teachers in each year. To summarize the trends in each category, I have computed the percent change that has occurred between 1960 and 2001. All data are for the U.S., where the Catholic population has grown from 41 million in 1960 to 61 million in 2001 (excluding outlying areas such as Puerto Rico).

TABLE 4.4 Trends Among Catholic Schools, Students, and Teachers, 1960–2001

	1960	1980	2001	% Change
Total Institutions	*13,595*	*10,259*	*8,576*	*-37*
Seminaries	525	344	196	-63
Colleges/univ.	265	239	230	-13
Diocesan/parochial high schools	1,567	894	734	-53
Private high schools	866	633	513	-41
Diocesan/parochial elemen. schools	9,897	7,847	6,600	-33
Private elementary schools	475	302	303	-36
Total Students	*5,472,999*	*3,682,061*	*3,355,545*	*-39*
Seminarians	39,896	13,226	4,811	-88
College/university students	302,908	505,076	683,716	+126
Diocesan/parochial H.S. students	520,128	505,955	375,125	-28
Private high school students	324,171	340,604	281,539	-13
Diocesan/parochial elementary school students	4,195,781	2,251,294	1,913,554	-54
Private elementary school students	90,115	65,906	96,800	+7
Total Teachers	*160,447*	*167,713*	*162,471*	*+ 1*
Priests	10,890	5,444	1,849	-83
Scholastics	802	200	33	-96
Brothers	4,778	3,271	1,044	-78
Sisters	98,471	41,135	7,972	-92
Lay	45,506	117,663	151,573	+233

Overall, there has been a 37 percent decline in the number of Catholic educational institutions. The most precipitous decline has been in the number of seminaries, which fell 63 percent. There also have been steep declines in the number of diocesan and parochial high schools (53 percent) and private high schools (41 percent). Catholic elementary schools have declined by about one-third. The number of Catholic colleges and universities has fallen 13 percent.

There also has been a 39 percent decline in Catholic school enrollments. The sharpest declines have been in the number of seminarians (down 88 percent) and the number of students in diocesan and parochial elementary schools (54 percent). Enrollment also is down in diocesan and parochial high schools (28 percent). The number of students in private high schools increased between 1960 and 1980, but has declined to the point where it is now 13 percent less than it was in 1960. On the positive side, despite the decline in the number of Catholic colleges and universities, enrollments at these institutions have jumped 126 percent. Also, after declining between 1960 and 1980, the number of students enrolled in private elementary schools has increased to the point where it is 7 percent larger than in 1960.

The total number of faculty in Catholic institutions increased between 1960 and 1980, but has declined to the point where it is now only 1 percent larger than it was in 1960. Even though the total number of faculty has not changed much since 1960, there have been huge changes in the types of people teaching in Catholic schools. There has been a 96 percent decline in the number of scholastics, a 92 percent drop in the number of sisters, an 83 percent decline in the number of priests, and a 78 percent drop in the number of brothers. Meanwhile, there has been a 233 percent increase in the number of lay teachers. In 1960, only 28 percent of teachers are laypeople; now 93 percent are laymen and women.

The 2004 *Official Catholic Directory* reports 196 seminaries (no change); 226 colleges and universities (4 fewer); 722 diocesan/parochial high schools (12 fewer); 513 private high schools (no change); 6,379 diocesan/parochial elementary schools (221 fewer); 299 private elementary schools (4 fewer); 4,241 seminarians (570 fewer); 724,883 college and university students (59,167 more); 360,865 diocesan/parochial high school students (14,260 fewer); 287,472 private high-school students (5,933 fewer); 1,767,368 diocesan/parochial elementary-school students (146,186 fewer); 71,554 private elementary-school students (25,246 fewer); 1,705 priests teaching (144 fewer); 51 scholastics teaching (18 more); 1,159 brothers teaching (115 more); 7,579 sisters teaching (393 fewer); and 164,826 laypeople teaching (13,253 more).

In short, there have been dramatic changes in Catholic schools, students, and teachers. There are fewer Catholic schools, fewer students in these schools (especially in seminaries and in diocesan and parochial schools), and fewer teachers who are priests, brothers, sisters, and scholastics. But, the number of students in Catholic colleges and universities has increased, as has the number of students in private elementary schools, and the increase in lay teachers has made up for the loss of faculty who are priests, brothers, sisters, or scholastics.

Seven Sure-Fire Ways to Increase Financial Contributions

In the 1960s, Protestants and Catholics gave about 2 percent of their incomes to their respective churches. Since then, Protestant contributions have remained relatively stable, while Catholics' financial contributions have declined. Catholics now give only about half as much (about 1 percent) as Protestants do (2 percent). Meanwhile, due to factors such as the increased number of laypeople employed by dioceses and parishes, and the needs of a growing Catholic population, Church expenses continue to increase. As a result, many dioceses and parishes face operating deficits.

Villanova University economist Charles Zech addresses these financial issues in an important and highly readable book, *Why Catholics Don't Give, And What Can Be Done About It.*[7] The book is based on a national study Zech and several colleagues did on giving in five religious groups: the Catholic Church, the Presbyterian Church, the Lutheran Church, the Southern Baptist Convention, and the Assemblies of God. Zech compares Catholic giving patterns with those of mainline and evangelical Protestants; separates the facts from the myths about Catholic giving; and, based on his findings, offers seven foolproof ways to increase financial contributions to the Church. Here is a brief synopsis of Zech's main findings and recommendations, in their order of importance.

1. Catholics who feel a need to return "a portion of the bounty that God has given [them]" contribute more of their time, talent, and treasure to their parishes than other Catholics do. Zech concludes that the Church needs to "instill a sense of stewardship among its members." One important goal is to increase Catholics' commitment to planning their religious giving on an annual basis. Zech says that "pledging" is especially important among the wealthiest and most-highly committed Catholics,

whose levels of giving tend to lag behind those of wealthy and committed Protestants.

2. Studies show that Catholics generally, and young adult Catholics in particular, want more say in the operation of their parishes. Moreover, parishioners who feel they share in parish decision-making tend to be most generous. Zech concludes that increasing members' involvement in all aspects of parish life increases giving.

3. Members of middle-sized parishes with 1,000 to 2,500 members donate more money than members of small parishes with fewer than 1,000 members and large parishes with over 2,500 members. According to Zech, middle-sized parishes "are large enough to support an array of programs that Catholics value…but small enough so that an effective pastor can inspire a sense of ownership and community among parishioners." While acknowledging that there may be other reasons to maintain small parishes, Zech concludes that "we can think of no justification, either pastoral or financial, for allowing parishes to rise above 2,500 members."

4. Zech shows that "parents who send their children to parochial schools contribute more than do other parents of school-aged children." Moreover, other "members of parishes that sponsor their own parochial school [also] contribute more" than Catholics belonging to parishes that do not have schools of their own. Zech says that Catholic schools are a valuable asset to those parishes that already have schools, but warns that starting new schools does not automatically increase contributions. He says that parishes without schools ought to "find some other activity that [they] can rally around in order to generate the same sort of benefits as a school."

5. Zech shows that three Church teachings are closely tied to giving. Parishioners who value the Church's ecumenical attitude toward other faiths, emphasize Catholic traditions and sacraments, and agree with the Church's goal of reducing social injustice are more generous benefactors than other Catholics. The Church's emphases on ecumenism, traditions and sacraments, and social justice are not only important in their own right; they also result in increased financial contributions.

6. According to Zech, Catholics who believe that the Church has serious financial needs contribute more than Catholics who believe the Church is wealthy and doesn't need their support. Thus, Church leaders need to explain the Church's needs and how resources will provide important services to members and others in the community.

7. Finally, Catholics who believe their parishes are meeting their spiritual

and social needs tend to give the most. Parishes that meet their members' needs (including the needs of young adults, who will be the backbone of the Church in the years ahead) receive the largest contributions.

Zech's book is "must reading" for Catholics wanting to build strong parishes and dioceses.

Questions for Reflection

1. Which of Bolman and Deal's four approaches to organizations do you use most often? Which one are you least likely to use?
2. With the data related to the Church's "golden years" in mind, in what ways are you optimistic and/or pessimistic about the Church's future?
3. Are your assessments of your parish similar to or different from those of American Catholics in general? In what areas is your parish unique? In what ways is it pretty typical?
4. If you could do one thing that would increase your parish's ability to affect the daily lives of parishioners (such as in their families and work-places), what would you do?
5. What are the benefits of, and challenges faced by, racially and ethnically integrated parishes?
6. If you could do one thing that would increase your parish's ability to promote social justice and equality in your community, what would you do?
7. How do you interpret the changes that have taken place in Catholic schools? In what ways are the changes indications of decline in the Church? In what ways are they indications of the Church's ability to adapt to new circumstances?
8. What additional step(s) could your parish take toward having enough money to do all the things you would like it to do?

Chapter 5

Challenges with Authority, Sexual Abuse, and Other Problems

The Church faces several challenges having to do with authority, especially the authority of bishops. Research shows that a majority of Catholics do not know who their bishop is, and less than half of parishioners read their diocesan newspaper. Due to a number of conditions, including longstanding conflicts between liberals and conservatives and the recent sexual abuse scandal, there has been a marked decline in recognition of episcopal authority. There also are differences over the extent to which authority should be based on religious tradition and/or legal-rational considerations. Studies document the laity's continuing support for their parishes, but also their insistence on financial accountability, especially at the diocesan and national levels of Church life. The conclusion of this chapter indicates the relative importance laypeople attach to a dozen problems facing the Church today.

Study Shows Which Catholics Know Their Bishop

In a survey sponsored by the University of Notre Dame, Dean Hoge and I asked a random sample of 1,119 U.S. Catholics if they could name their bishop.[1] Those who said "yes" were then asked to give the bishop's name. While we cannot be absolutely sure that our respondents got their bishop's name correct in every case, 41 percent of U.S. Catholics were able to provide the name of someone they thought was their bishop.

What makes it possible for some Catholics to name their bishops, while others cannot? An individual's spirituality certainly has some influence. For example, 45 percent of Catholics who say they frequently have experienced God's presence in a special way know their bishop, compared to only 17 percent of Catholics who have never had such an experience. Forty-six percent of Catholics who pray privately on a regular basis, but only 18 percent of those who never pray, know the name of their bishop. Half of the people who say being Catholic is very important to them and 52 percent of those who say the Church is very important to them know their bishop's name.

But spirituality is only part of the story. A much bigger part has to do with Catholics' stake in the Church. Several questions in the survey indicate the extent to which people invest their time, talent, and money in the Church. These questions deal with issues such as the amount of Catholic schooling and Catholic instruction respondents have had, the extent of their involvement in a parish, and their participation in other aspects of Church life.

The more Catholics are invested in the Church, the more likely they are to know their bishop's name. Catholics who have received a great deal of Catholic instruction outside of Catholic schools are more likely than Catholics with no such instruction to know who the bishop is (50 percent versus 37 percent). Those who have had ten or more years of Catholic schooling are much more aware of their bishop than laypeople who have not attended Catholic schools (58 percent versus 38 percent).

Registered parishioners (53 percent) and parishioners who attend Mass weekly or more (57 percent) are regular financial contributors (59 percent), read the parish bulletin regularly (60 percent), attend parish programs (63 percent), and donate lots of time to the parish (66 percent) are also more likely to know the name of their bishop.

Laypeople who are invested in other ways also are more aware of their bishop's name. Forty-six percent of Catholics belonging to groups trying "to modernize the Church in some way" and 49 percent of those participating in groups trying "to restore the Church's traditional beliefs and practices" know who their bishop is. Sixty-four percent of people who read the diocesan newspaper and 68 percent of people who contributed $2,000 or more to the Church in 2002 know their bishop by name.

Two demographic groups that have a somewhat greater stake in the Church are pre–Vatican II Catholics (55 percent of whom know who their bishop is) and whites (45 percent know their bishop). Younger Catholics, Hispanics, and racial minorities are not as heavily invested in the Church and are less likely to know who their bishop's name. Men and women are equally aware of their bishop.

Thus, in addition to personal spirituality, having a stake in the Church significantly increases Catholics' knowledge of their bishop. About four in ten Catholics are heavily enough invested in the Church to know their bishop's name. But, six in ten are not. These people are found in all categories of Catholics, especially among young adults, Hispanics, and racial minorities.

The more the Church can do to increase the laity's stake in the Church, the more laypeople will know the name of their bishop.

How Many Parishioners and Which Ones Read Diocesan Newspapers?

Diocesan newspapers are one of the means by which bishops try to communicate with Catholic laypeople. Diocesan papers include news stories about worldwide developments in the Catholic Church and articles about recent and forthcoming events in their dioceses. They also include columns in which bishops share their views on key issues and other writers interpret events and changes in the Church. Letters-to-the-editor also give laypeople a chance to share their views with bishops and other readers.

How successful are diocesan papers in reaching Catholic parishioners? How many Catholic parishioners read their diocesan papers? What are the social and religious characteristics of those who do? How are they different from parishioners who do not read diocesan newspapers?

As part of a larger study of U.S. Catholics, sociologist Dean Hoge and I asked registered parishioners if they "read their diocesan newspaper on a regular basis." Thirty-nine percent said "yes." This figure is a national average; it is higher in some dioceses and lower in others.

Three attributes set regular readers apart from parishioners who do not read their diocesan paper. First, the more parishioners participate in a variety of spiritual practices and feel that God is part of their daily lives, the more they are likely to be regular readers. Here are just two examples. Catholics who pray at least weekly are three times more likely to be regular readers (42 percent) than those who pray once a month or less (only 14 percent). Parishioners who say they have experienced God's presence in special ways "many times" are four times more likely to read diocesan papers (47 percent) than parishioners who say they have never had this experience (12 percent). Similar patterns were found when we examined the frequency with which people pray the rosary, read the Bible, and read books on spirituality.

Another set of attributes has to do with Catholics' stake in the Church. Consider these four examples. First, parishioners who say "being Catholic is a very important part of who I am" are nearly twice as likely (42 percent) as those who disagree with that statement (24 percent) to read diocesan papers. Second, those who say the "Catholic Church is very important to me personally" are more than twice as likely to be regular readers (41 percent versus 17 percent). Third, half of Catholics who have had "a great deal" of Catholic instruction (apart from Catholic schools) read diocesan papers. Among those who have had "a great deal" of Catholic instruction, the figure is 44 percent. It slips to 39 percent among Catholics who have had only "some" instruction and 30 percent for those who have had "none." Finally, 45 percent of people who go to Mass weekly or more read the paper, compared to only 21 percent of Catholics who attend once a month or less.

Finally, of all the demographic factors we examined (including race, gender, education, and income), the one that produces the biggest differences is generation. Fifty-seven percent of pre-Vatican II parishioners (who were born in or before 1940) read diocesan papers, compared to 38 percent of Vatican II parishioners (born between 1941 and 1960), and only 30 percent of post-Vatican II and millennial parishioners (born between 1961 and 1985).

Thus, diocesan newspapers reach about four out of every ten parishioners, especially those who tend to be spiritual, are heavily invested in the Church, and are somewhat older. They face greater challenges in reaching parishioners who are less spiritual, do not have much of a stake in the Church, and are younger.

Are Church Leaders Out of Touch With the Laity?

How do Catholic laypeople perceive their relationship with Church leaders? There are many ways to examine that question, some of which I have considered in previous publications, others of which I will explore in the future. This study looks at the responses that a 1999 national sample of American Catholics gave when asked how strongly they agree or disagree with the following statement: "Catholic Church leaders are out of touch with the laity."[2]

Overall, it appears that Catholics have quite different views on this subject. Fifty-two percent of laypeople believe that Church leaders are out of touch with the laity (17 percent strongly agree with the statement and 35 percent agree somewhat). Forty-one percent disagree (with 24 percent disagreeing somewhat and 17 percent strongly disagreeing). Seven percent are unsure.

If Catholics have such diverse views on the subject, which laypeople believe Church leaders are tuned into the thoughts and actions of the laity, and which ones think otherwise? For example, who is more likely to think Church leaders are out of touch with the laity: the most educated/prosperous Catholics, or laypeople with less education and lower-family incomes? Who has more confidence in Church leaders: Catholics who are most highly attached to the Church, or those who are least involved?

I examined a dozen possible influences. Six of them revealed sizable differences. Catholics who have furthered their education beyond high school are more likely than Catholics who have not to believe that Church leaders are out of touch (58 percent versus 45 percent). Among Catholics with at least some Catholic schooling, those with thirteen or more years of Catholic education also are more likely than Catholics with one to twelve years of parochial schooling to think Church leaders are out of touch (66 percent versus 53 percent). Catholics who say the Church is of relatively little importance to them personally are most likely to have a negative view of Church leaders (67 percent versus 44 percent for those who say the Church is one of the most important parts of their lives). So are Catholics who attend Mass least often (57 percent versus 42 percent for weekly Mass attendees) and those who say they can conceive of circumstances under which they might leave the Church (67 percent versus 43 percent for those who say they cannot imagine leaving the Church). Middle-income Catholics are more likely to agree (59 percent) than either high-income Catholics (49 percent) or low-income Catholics (48 percent).

Thus, the Catholics who are most likely to say that Church leaders are out of touch with laypeople are the most highly educated (including those who have the most years of Catholic schooling), are least attached to the Church, and have incomes between $30,000 and $75,000 a year. Catholics with the most confidence in Church leaders are less educated (including fewer years of Catholic schooling), indicate in numerous ways that the Church is very important to them, and have either high incomes (over $75,000) or low incomes (under $30,000).

What do these findings imply for Church leaders? First, Church leaders might want to consult with highly educated middle-class parishioners to see what could be done to increase their confidence in Church leaders. Second, I suspect that there is a reciprocal relationship between attachment to the Church and people's views of Church leaders. Catholics who are least attached to the Church are most likely to conclude that Church leaders are out of touch with the laity, and those who believe that leaders are out of touch are most likely to drift away from the Church. Thus, to the extent that leaders cultivate the laity's involvement in the Church, they are likely to increase laypeople's confidence in Church leaders. Likewise, to the extent that they stay in close contact with laypeople, leaders are likely to increase the laity's attachment to the Church.

Is the Church's Teaching Authority Important to Catholics?

In a day when Catholics seem to disagree with Rome on many issues of faith and morals, one could easily get the impression that Catholics no longer value the teaching authority of the Church. But that would be an overstatement.

In a 1999 national survey, colleagues and I asked American Catholics how much importance they attach to "the teaching authority claimed by the Vatican."[3] Forty-two percent of Catholics said it is "very important;" 43 percent said it is "somewhat important;" only 16 percent said it is "unimportant" or that they "don't know." In other words, the vast majority of Catholics attach at least some importance to the Church's teaching authority. Only a minority of Catholics consider it unimportant.

It also is clear that some Catholics cherish the Church's teaching authority more than others do. Which Catholics are most likely to see it as "very important"? Which are least likely to do so?

TABLE 5.1 Teaching Authority Is "Very Important" (percent)

All Catholics	**42**
Generation	
Pre-Vatican II	64
Vatican II	45
Post-Vatican II	30
Education	
High school or less	49
Some college	41
College or more	28
Income	
Less than $30,000	50
$30,000–$49,999	41
$50,000+	32
Importance of Church	
Among most important parts of life	64
Quite important	27
Not important	9
Mass attendance	
Weekly or more	64
Monthly	37
Seldom or never	20

Ethnicity, religion at birth, and gender are of little or no consequence on this issue. There are no statistically significant differences between Hispanics and non-Hispanics, converts and cradle Catholics, or men and women.

However, three other factors do produce important differences. First, there are important generational differences in the way Catholics think about the Church's teaching authority. Older Catholics are much more likely than middle-aged and younger Catholics to say the Church's teaching authority is important. Sixty-four percent of people in the pre-Vatican II generation say it is very important, compared to 45 percent of people in the Vatican II generation, and only 30 percent of people in the post-Vatican II generation.

Second, there also are class differences in the way Catholics view the Vatican's teaching authority. Forty-nine percent of Catholics with a high-school education or less, and 50 percent with an income of less than $30,000, say that the Church's teaching authority is very important. As education and income increase, the importance of the Church's teaching authority declines. Only 28 percent of Catholics with a college education or more and only 32 percent of Catholics with an income of $50,000 or more say it is that important.

Third, the more committed Catholics are to the Church, the more they value the teaching authority of the Vatican. Sixty-four percent of Catholics who say the Church is among the most important parts of their life and the same percent of people who attend Mass at least weekly report that the Church's teaching authority is very important. Only one in ten Catholics who say the Church is unimportant and only two in ten who seldom or never attend Mass say the Church's teaching authority is that important.

In short, older, less prosperous, and more committed Catholics are most likely to attach importance to the Vatican's teaching authority. Young, more prosperous, and less committed Catholics are far less likely to do so. Although there is a pastoral challenge to explain the Church's teaching authority to all Catholics, that challenge is greatest among young adults, Catholics with the most resources, and those who identify as Catholic but are only loosely connected to the Church.

Decline in Recognition of Episcopal Authority

In the late 1800s and the first half of the twentieth century, the pope and bishops accumulated considerable authority over lower ranking clergy and laypeople. They employed an elaborate system of rewards and punishments to produce compliance with Church teachings and codes of conduct.

For clergy, rewards included assignments to bigger and better parishes and promotions to monsignor. Punishments included being overlooked when choice assignments were made or being assigned to lesser parishes. For laypeople, rewards included elevation to leadership roles in a vast array of Catholic organizations and occasional expressions of appreciation by priests for one's contributions to the Church. In addition to the possibility of excommunication, punishments included guilt, fear of hell, and penance for one's sins.

The pope and bishops were able to exercise this authority because lower ranking clergy and laypeople perceived the hierarchy's authority as legitimate. As a result, even when the rewards and punishments might have seemed severe and manipulative, they produced high levels of conformity in belief and practice.

In the last thirty to forty years, there has been a marked decline in recognition of episcopal authority. This decline has been evident in the growing tendency for clergy and laypeople to question the abilities, motivations, and decisions of the hierarchy. For example, in his 1977 book, *The American Catholic: A Social Portrait*, Andrew Greeley accused American bishops of being "bumbling, incoherent nonentities" that range from "dull to psychopathic."[4] It also has appeared in the laity's increased willingness to challenge their bishops on issues such as the closing of parishes and parochial schools. It has been found in numerous national surveys, such as our 1999 study, that a declining percentage of Catholics (including only 30 percent of young adults) believe the hierarchy's teaching authority is an important part of their faith.[5] More and more Catholics believe they alone have responsibility for making decisions on faith and morals and, according to most studies, more and more people are doing just that.

The decline in recognition of episcopal authority has many roots. With the decline of the so-called Catholic ghetto in the 1950s and 1960s, Catholics were increasingly exposed to American culture's suspicion of social institutions, especially ones that are hierarchically organized. Also, Vatican II urged Catholics to take responsibility for their own faith, thus shifting the locus of authority from the hierarchy to one's personal conscience. Other influences have included changes in rules many people thought were unchangeable, such as dropping the no-meat-on-Friday regulation, and decisions not to change rules they felt should be changed, such as Pope Paul VI's decision to uphold the ban on artificial birth control.

Another contributing factor has been the rising level of education among the laity and, as I have documented in previous columns, the increased tendency for laypeople to think for themselves. Still another factor has been the tendency for both liberal and conservative Catholic organizations to call episcopal authority into question as they promote their own agendas. Books, such as Garry Wills' *Papal Sins*,[6] also have increased the laity's awareness of historical cases of corruption and poor judgment among episcopal authorities.

Thus, as Peter Steinfels rightly observes, the recent scandal relating to sexual misconduct by priests is not the root cause of the decline in recognition of episcopal authority.[7] That decline was well under way long before this scandal. However, the scandal, and the way the hierarchy has handled it, is hastening the decline, especially among young Catholics. According to a study published in 1996, 35 percent of pre-Vatican II Catholics, 51 percent of Vatican II Catholics, and 58 percent of post-Vatican II Catholics said that reports of pedophilia among Catholic priests had weakened their commitment to the Church.[8]

The Sexual Abuse Scandal, Bishops, and the Media, as Seen by the Laity

When 1,119 American Catholics were interviewed in fall 2003, 91 percent said they had heard of the recent sexual abuse scandal in the Church.[9] Of those who had heard of the scandal, 78 percent said they are "ashamed and embarrassed for my Church." Seventy-two percent said, "The failure of bishops to stop the abuse is a bigger problem than the abuse itself." Two-thirds (66 percent) believed "the cases that have been reported to date are only the tip of the iceberg." Clearly, laypeople feel ashamed, hold clergy accountable, and fear that the problem might be bigger than it seems.

When laypeople were asked about the bishops' handling of the scandal, 62 percent said the bishops "are covering up the facts." Only 20 percent said the bishops "are being open and honest." The rest are not sure or believe the situation involves some mixture of truth and coverup. The bishops clearly have a credibility problem on this issue.

Catholics also perceive the media as playing at least some role in the scandal. Sixty-nine percent of laypeople indicated that "the media has prolonged the scandal by reporting the same stories over and over again." Fifty-six percent said "the media reports have been too anti-Catholic." Catholics are more critical of the media for rehashing stories than for being biased against the Catholic Church, although both issues are of concern to a majority.

Clearly, Catholics are disturbed by the scandal, the way the bishops have handled it, and the way the media has covered it. But, there also are differences in the way laypeople interpret the scandal. Some are more ashamed than others. Some are more inclined to blame the bishops, while others are more inclined to blame the media.

Hypothesizing that Catholics' attachment to the Church might affect their interpretations of the scandal, sociologist Dean Hoge and I compared the responses of registered parishioners with those of nonparishioners. Feelings of shame and embarrassment are widely shared by both groups. Although both groups also have serious doubts about the bishops' honesty, parishioners express more confidence in the bishops than nonparishioners do. Registered parishioners also are more likely than nonparishioners to believe the media has contributed to the problem by distorting the facts.

We also compared the responses of four generations: pre-Vatican II Catholics (who were 63 years of age or older when the study was done), Vatican II Catholics (who were 43 to 62 years old), post-Vatican II Catholics (who were 26 to 42), and millennial Catholics (who were 18 to 25). Pre-Vatican II Catholics are a bit more likely than younger Catholics to feel ashamed, but are not as likely to question the bishops' honesty, and are more likely to believe the media has prolonged the scandal and has been anti-Catholic. Younger Catholics are more likely to say the reported cases of sexual abuse are just the tip of the iceberg.

In short, most Catholics—whether they are registered parishioners or not—are ashamed and embarrassed by the scandal. Parishioners are not as quick to blame the bishops and are more likely to blame the media. The pre-Vatican II generation is more likely to feel ashamed and embarrassed, but they are not as likely to accuse bishops of being dishonest and is more likely to believe the media has been biased in its coverage of the scandal. Although younger Catholics are not as ashamed, they are more likely to blame the bishops and less likely to blame the media.

Interpreting the Data on the Sexual Abuse Scandal

In the early months of 2004, three separate reports were published on the sexual abuse scandal in the Catholic Church. In January, the Gavin Report documented the extent of diocesan compliance with the *Charter for the Protection of Children and Young People* initiated by the Conference of bishops in Dallas back in 2002.[10] In February, the John Jay College of Criminal

Justice reported data on the number of priests and victims involved in incidents of abuse, and the National Review Board released its analysis of the scandal.[11]

As I try to interpret these reports and their significance for the Church, I ask how much they reflect the four approaches social scientists use when they study any kind of organization, including churches: (1) structural approach, (2) human-resource approach, (3) symbolic approach, and (4) the political approach.[12]

With regard to the structural approach, to what extent do the reports address the rules and regulations governing the behavior of the people who occupy leadership positions in the Church? The Gavin Report shows that the vast majority of dioceses are making good-faith efforts to comply with the Charter, although some dioceses are further along in this process than others. The National Review Board's report says there has been a lack of accountability in the Church, with existing governance structures (such as diocesan councils) being ignored or ineffective and laypeople not being sufficiently involved in all levels of church life. It offers several recommendations for structural change in these areas. It also argues that policies related to the screening of seminary candidates and the formation of clergy have not worked well in the past, but have improved in recent years.

The human-resource approach assumes that an organization is only as good as the people in it. The National Review Board asserts that the vast majority of priests and bishops have been mature and faithful leaders. However, it says, many emotionally immature men have been admitted to the seminary and ordained. Based on the John Jay study, it shows that—between 1950 and 2002—4,392 priests were accused of at least one credible incident of immoral sexual conduct with 10,667 young people. In no uncertain terms, the Board says the priests' behavior was both immoral and criminal and that these priests quite rightly have been removed from active ministry. The Board just as strongly chastises those bishops who, often with a "haughty attitude," abdicated their episcopal responsibilities. Although it does not call for their dismissal, it does call for significant changes in their behavior.

The symbolic approach calls attention to an organization's culture. The National Review Board concludes that one important source of the misconduct by priests and bishops is the extent of clericalism in the Church. Clericalism encourages bishops and priests to consider themselves a separate and superior class that is not accountable to others in the Church. The Board calls for an end to this culture, and the secrecy it breeds, beginning with greater trust of the laity and increased lay involvement in decision making at the parish, diocesan, and national levels. Noting the culture of moral relativism and the gay subculture that arose in some seminaries in the 1970s and 1980s, the Board also calls for a culture of chastity among seminarians and priests, whether they are heterosexual or homosexual in orientation.

The political approach highlights the conflicts between factions that are involved in a power struggle for control of an organization. The National Review Board's report speaks to this issue when it refers to the tendency for liberal Catholics to blame the scandal on celibacy (and, thus, to promote a married priesthood) and for conservative Catholics to blame it on homosexual priests (and, thus, to exclude gay men from ministry). The Board challenges both sides and calls for more dispassionate considerations of homosexuality and the role of celibacy in the Church in general and in this scandal in particular.

These studies certainly leave some questions unanswered and invite further study of the scandal in the Church. However, they address all four dimensions of church life, point to problems in each area, and specify improvements that should be made in each one. Together, they are the most comprehensive, objective, and credible studies of sexual abuse in any organization I know.

Types of Authority in Today's Church

Years ago, sociologist Max Weber developed a theory about the nature of authority in organizations. His theory included a distinction between "traditional" authority and "legal-rational" authority. I find Weber's insights helpful as I try to understand recent events in the Church.

In Weber's words, traditional authority is based "on a belief in the sanctity of immemorial traditions and the legitimacy of the status of those exercising authority under them."[13] In groups emphasizing traditional authority, emphasis is put on the worldview and customs that have evolved over time. The group's traditions reflect deep-seated cultural values and codes of conduct that might not be written down but are understood and shared by members of the group.

In such groups, leaders are expected to exemplify and uphold the group's traditional ways of doing things. To the extent that leaders cherish and personify the group's traditions, members will honor them and respect their judgments. Confident that their leaders are thinking and acting in accord with the group's traditions, members will tend to do what their leaders ask of them.

In some tradition-oriented groups, leaders come from a single family and see themselves as passing on family traditions. In cases where leaders are not actually family members, they tend to think of themselves as family. There is an emphasis on fraternal relationships. In such groups, deviance is defined as a departure from tradition. The normal place to deal with deviance is in private, and the normal way to deal with it is through informal means of social control.

With the group's emphasis on tradition, there is a tendency to resist change. If change must take place, leaders look to the past for precedents, because they must interpret change as being consistent with tradition.

Legal-rational authority, on the other hand, rests "on a belief in the 'legality' of patterns of normative rules and the right of those elevated to authority under such rules to issue commands." This definition stresses the legality of the constitution, bylaws, and formal procedures that govern the group's actions.

Leaders are selected according to clearly defined organizational rules and procedures. The emphasis is on individual talents, prior achievements, and the qualifications needed to do work that is described in job descriptions. Once chosen, leaders interact mostly on the basis of tasks they must accomplish. Their authority is rooted in organizational rules, which they are to abide by and enforce. Deviations from the rules are addressed according to public procedures stressing accountability.

In groups where legal-rational authority prevails, there is an emphasis on the present and an openness to change. This is reflected in a tendency to review and update the rules. As older regulations are found wanting, new ones are introduced.

These two types of authority are not mutually exclusive. There are elements of both in almost any organization. Thus, one issue most groups face has to do with the weight they attach to each type. In the wake of the sexual abuse scandal, bishops and laity are struggling with this very issue. By and large (although not in every individual case), bishops seem to prefer a traditional model of authority. One indication is their desire to address issues of deviance informally among "brother bishops." On the other hand, laypeople participating on the National Review Board and in groups such as Voice of the Faithful and the Leadership Roundtable in Philadelphia stress legal-rational authority (note their emphasis on the need for transparency and public accountability in the Church). The future of the Church depends on how the relationship between traditional and legal-rational authority is resolved.

Studies of Giving Contain Good News and Bad News

Since the sexual abuse scandal began to rock the Catholic Church in January 2002, people have wondered what its impact would be on Catholics' financial contributions to the Church. How many Catholics would give less money? How many would continue to give at earlier levels? How many would increase their contributions? Where would the financial impact of the scandal be felt the most: at the parish level, the diocesan level, or the national level?

Two recent studies provide some answers. One study was conducted by FADICA (Foundations and Donors Interested in Catholic Activities) in conjunction with Villanova University economist Charles Zech and the Gallup Organization.[14] In October 2003, FADICA re-contacted 309 of the 656 weekly Mass attendees who had participated in its 2002 survey of U.S. Catholics. FADICA's goal in its 2003 survey was to see if Catholics' attitudes about Church finances and their own contributions had changed. In the other study, Church consultant Joseph Claude Harris analyzed figures published by the International Catholic Stewardship Council relating to Offertory collections and annual appeals in 2000, 2001, and 2002.[15]

FADICA's data point to the four conclusions. First, religiously active Catholics continue to favor financial accountability. "In 2002, 80 percent of the sample called for the bishops to give a full accounting of the financial costs of the settlements. In 2003, that figure had risen modestly to 84 percent."

Second, "The 2003 survey showed virtually no difference in the impact of the scandal on parishioners' willingness to contribute to their parish." In both years, 64 percent of the respondents said the scandal had not affected their giving, about 10 percent said they had reduced their contributions because of the scandal, and 3 to 5 percent said they had increased their giving.

Third, although a majority of Catholics who attend Mass weekly continue to support diocesan collections, there have been significant changes in Catholics' attitudes about these collections. In 2003, the percentage of respondents saying they had not changed their contributions "because they supported their bishops" fell (from 30 to 24 percent), and the percentage saying they had not changed their contributions "because they did not want to punish diocesan charities" increased (from 21 to 35 percent).

Fourth, while a majority of these Catholics also continue to support national collections, the number of saying they do not expect to support such collections rose from 19 percent in 2002 to 27 percent in 2003.

Harris drew two conclusions from his data. First, among the dioceses that participated in the study (63 percent of all dioceses), offertory collections—which account for nearly three-quarters of total parish revenues—increased by 4.9 percent (from $5.6 billion in 2001 to $5.8 billion in 2002). Had the Archdiocese of Boston—the epicenter of the sexual abuse scandal—participated in the study, Harris estimates the national increase would have been 4.2 percent.

Second, contributions to diocesan appeals "dropped from $650 million for 2001 to $635 million for 2002, a decline of 2.3 percent. About half of the total $14 million drop in pledges occurred in the Archdiocese of Boston where pledges plummeted from $16 million in 2001 to $8.8 million for 2002. The remaining shrinkage of pledges was evenly distributed around the country."

Taken together, these studies show that laypeople want the Church to be accountable for its finances, continue to support local parishes through offertory collections, are giving less money more conditionally to diocesan appeals, and are increasingly unwilling to contribute to national collections.

The Laity's Perceptions of Problems in the Church

Even optimistic Catholics admit the Church faces at least some challenges in the years ahead. But, which ones are most serious: the growing shortage of priests and sisters, the quality of religious education, homosexuality among priests, the sexual abuse scandal, or something else?

In fall 2003, Dean Hoge and I (along with several colleagues at the University of Notre Dame) created a list of twelve possible problems. We, then, asked a random sample of 1,119 American Catholics to rate each issue as "a serious problem," "somewhat of a problem," or "not a problem." Here's what we found.[16]

TABLE 5.2 Percent Saying Each Item Is a "Serious" Problem in the Church

That some priests have sexually abused young people.
85

That some bishops have not done enough to stop priests from sexually abusing young people.
77

The shortage of priests and sisters.
62

That young adults are not as involved in the Church as much as they should be.
53

That parents don't teach their children the faith the way they should.
49

That there are too many men with a homosexual orientation in the priesthood.
42

That the Church's teachings on sexual morality are out of touch with reality today.
40

That women are not involved enough In Church decision making.
38

That laypeople are not consulted enough in forming the Church's moral and social teachings.
31

That laypeople no longer live up to the obligations involved in practicing the Catholic faith.
30

That there is poor religious education in parishes and Catholic schools.
27

That bishops and priests no longer hold Catholics accountable to Church teachings.
25

A majority of Catholics point to four problems. The top two have to do with the sexual abuse scandal: "That some priests have sexually abused young people" (85 percent) and "that some bishops have not done enough to stop priests from sexually abusing young people" (77 percent). Next, 62 percent of Catholics say that the "shortage of priests and sisters" is a serious problem. Fourth, 53 percent say it is a serious problem that "young adults are not involved in the Church as much as they should be."

Then there are four issues that one-third to one-half of Catholics believe are serious problems. These include concerns that "parents don't teach their children the faith the way they should" (49 percent), "there are too many men with a homosexual orientation in the priesthood" (42 percent), "the Church's teachings on sexual morality are out of touch with reality today" (40 percent), and "women are not involved enough in Church decision making" (38 percent).

At the bottom of the list are four issues that less than one-third of Catholics consider serious. These issues are that "laypeople are not consulted enough in forming the Church's moral and social teachings" (31 percent), "laypeople no longer live up to the obligations involved in practicing the Catholic faith" (30 percent), "there is poor religious education in parishes and Catholic schools" (27 percent), and "bishops and priests no longer hold Catholics accountable to Church teachings" (25 percent).

Thus, laypeople clearly think some problems are more serious than others. The sexual abuse scandal, the shortage of priests and sisters, and the limited participation of young adults are at the top of their list. Church leaders who commit to solving these four problems can expect support from the vast majority of Catholics. While other problems are major concerns to some laypeople, there is not as broad a base of support for addressing these issues.

Questions for Reflection

1. Do you know the name of your bishop? If so, how did you come to know his name? If not, how do you explain that fact?
2. How often, if ever, do you read your diocese's newspaper? How much and which parts of it do you read?
3. Do you personally believe Church leaders are out of touch with laypeople? Which ones are most and least out of touch? How do you explain the difference? What can be done to close the gap between leaders and others in the Church?

4. Which of the explanations offered in these sections (for example, teaching children to think for themselves, the conflict between liberals and conservatives, the sexual abuse scandal) do you think are most helpful in explaining the decline in the recognition of episcopal authority? Why?
5. What has been your response to the recent sexual abuse scandal? Has it affected your perception of bishops, their authority, and the accountability? Has it altered your participation in and/or support of the Church? If so, in what way?
6. Beside the sexual abuse scandal, what other problem(s) do you consider most serious, and why?

Chapter 6

Leadership: Priests, Deacons, and Lay Ministers

This chapter deals with changes in Church leadership. First, it reminds us that, relative to other parts of the global church, the Church in America has more than its fair share of priests. U.S. priests, who work about fifty-eight hours a week, are quite different from one another in their understanding of the priesthood—with some preferring a cultic model and others favoring a servant-leader approach. They also are quite different from laypeople in terms of age, with the effect that older Catholics have more access than young Catholics do to priests of their own age. Moreover, the number of priests is declining sharply, as a result of fewer men being ordained and attrition among newly ordained priests who are dissatisfied with their workload and lifestyle. As ways of coping with the growing shortage of priests, laypeople seem willing to accept lay leaders and some reduction in the number of Masses if necessary, but they want priests to visit the sick and provide the sacraments. There are growing numbers of permanent deacons (all of whom are men) and lay ministers (most of whom are women). These new leaders bring considerable experience and dedication to their work. However, they face important challenges resulting from ambiguities and conflicts in these new leadership roles and from the differences between themselves and the laity they serve. Almost all lay ministers participate in a core set of spiritual practices, but they also have distinctive styles of spiritual practice.

American Catholicism and Global Catholicism

In 2000, the U.S. population totaled about 280 million people, 61 million of whom were Catholic. There were about 45,000 priests, or about 1,355 Catholics for every priest.

But, what do these statistics mean in the context of the world population and global Catholicism? What percent of the world's population lives in the United States? Comparatively, does the U.S. have a large or small percentage

99

of Catholics? What percent of all Catholic priests are located in the U.S.? How does the ratio of laypeople to priests in this country compare with laity-to-priest ratios in other places?

To answer these questions, I consulted Bryan Froehle and Mary Gautier's book *Global Catholicism*.[1] It provides worldwide data on Catholicism, as well as data for five continents: Africa, America (including North America, Mesoamerica, South America, and the Caribbean), Asia, Europe, and Oceania (23 countries and territories in the Australia-New Zealand area of the southwest Pacific). The book is a great resource for anyone wanting to know about the Church worldwide.

At the outset of the twenty-first century, there were 6 billion people in the world. The largest share of the world's population (61 percent) was located in Asia, which had about 3.7 billion people. The American continent ranked a distant second with 14 percent of the world's population (826 million people, about one-third of whom lived in the United States). Africa was a close third, with 13 percent of the world's population (789 million people). Europe was fourth, with 12 percent (702 million people). In fifth place was Oceania, which had only 1 percent (30 million people). The U.S. population of 280 million was about 5 percent of the total world population—more than Oceania, but less than Europe.

The world's Catholic population was just over 1 billion people (about 17 percent of the world's total population). The most Catholic continent, percentagewise, was America, which was 63 percent Catholic (a total of 519 million Catholics in North and South America, Mesoamerica, and the Caribbean). Europe was second, with 40 percent of its population being Catholic (280 million people). Oceania ranked third percentagewise (27 percent Catholic), although it was last in the total number of Catholics (only 8 million). The United States was most similar to Oceania percentagewise, but had a much larger number of Catholics. Africa was fourth, with a population that was 16 percent Catholic (130 million people). Asia was the least Catholic continent (only 3 percent), although its Catholic population totaled 107 million people.

In 2000, there were 405,178 priests worldwide. Fifty-one percent of all priests (208,659) lived in Europe. Thirty percent (120,841) were in North and South America, Mesoamerica, and the Caribbean (with 11 percent of the world's priests being in the United States). Next came Asia at 11 percent (43,566 priests) and Africa at 7 percent (27,165 priests). Oceania was last, with only 1 percent (4,947 priests).

On a global basis, there were 2,579 Catholics for every Catholic priest.

As far as Catholic laypeople are concerned, the most favorable ratio was in Europe, which had 1,343 Catholics for each priest (about the same ratio as in the United States). Oceania ranked second, with 1,658 Catholics per priest. Coming in third was Asia, which had 2,463 laypeople per priest. America ranked fourth, with 4,298 Catholics per priest. In last place was Africa, which had 4,786 Catholics per priest.

In short, the United States had about 5 percent of the world's population, about 6 percent of all Catholic laypeople, about 11 percent of all Catholic priests, and among the most favorable Catholics-to-priests ratios anywhere in the world.

A Week in the Life of a Parish Priest

Have you ever wondered how many hours a priest works each week? Have you ever wondered how much time he spends on activities such as preparing homilies, counseling parishioners, and taking care of administrative matters? Have you ever wondered how a priest's weekly activities compare with those of a Protestant minister?

Some answers are found in a study of Catholic priests and Protestant ministers in Milwaukee County, Wisconsin, by sociologists Sandi Brunette-Hill and Roger Finke.[2]

Priests work about fifty-eight hours a week. Their total hours are comparable to clergy in "conservative mainline" denominations, such as the Lutheran Church-Missouri Synod and the Southern Baptist Convention. Priests work longer hours than clergy in "traditional mainline" groups, such as the Episcopal and Presbyterian churches (53 hours a week) and "sectarian" groups such as the Assemblies of God and the General Association of Regular Baptists (51 hours a week).

Priests spend the most time on "priestly" activities (24 hours), followed by "administration" (18 and a half hours), "pastoral" work (11 hours), and "teaching" (5 hours). Here is how priests spend their time in each of these categories.

In the priestly category, Catholic clergy spend about seven and a half hours on special services and ritual activities, such as weekend Masses. They allocate another seven hours to prayer. They spend five hours preparing homilies, four hours reading Scripture, and an hour and a half working on spiritual conversions. Overall, priests devote more time to these activities than clergy in any other religious group. They spend considerably more time than Protestant ministers do on ritual activities, mainly because Catholics conduct more worship services each weekend. Priests also give more time to prayer. They spend only half as much time preparing homilies as Protestant ministers and less time than Protestant clergy do with the choir. They devote more time to conversion activities and Scripture reading than clergy in mainline denominations but less than clergy in sectarian groups.

When it comes to administrative matters, priests spend nearly eight hours a week on paper work, four hours on planning, four hours on local meetings, two hours on civic organizations, and an hour and a half on diocesan and ecumenical work outside the parish. Priests and clergy in traditional mainline denominations spend five to six hours more than clergy in conservative mainline and sectarian groups do on administration. Priests give more time to paperwork than clergy in any other group. In most other administrative areas, they are comparable to traditional mainline and conservative mainline clergy and busier than clergy in sectarian Protestant groups.

Regarding pastoral work, priests spend about five hours on counseling, three visiting the sick, two visiting parishioners, and two on other personal contacts. They give about as much time as other clergy do to counseling. They also are similar to most other clergy in the hours they give to visiting the sick and visiting members, except for clergy in conservative mainline groups, who spend two to three hours more per week on visiting the sick.

In the area of teaching, priests spend about two and a one half hours a week teaching children, an hour and three quarters teaching adults, and three quarters of an hour teaching youth. Priests and clergy in traditional mainline and sectarian groups spend considerably less time on teaching than clergy in conservative mainline groups.

In short, priests work long hours on a wide range of functions. Their efforts—which laypeople value, but often take for granted—are indispensable to the Catholic way of life.

Generational Differences Among Priests

In *Evolving Visions of the Priesthood*, Dean Hoge and Jacqueline Wenger of Catholic University have published an important study of priests and their views of the priesthood.[3] The book is based on a study of diocesan and religious-order priests in 2001, but it also makes excellent use of studies done in the 1970s, 1980s, and 1990s, thus allowing the authors to document trends over the last thirty years.

Hoge and Wenger assert that today's priests have much in common. For example, virtually all priests agree on "their love of God's people, desire to serve God's people, love for the Catholic Church, desire for personal fulfillment, and acceptance of celibate homosexual priests."

However, there also are differences, many of which have to do with priests' views of the priesthood. Drawing on the work of Father James Bacik and historian Robert Schwartz, Hoge and Wenger explore two models of priesthood.

The "cultic" model stresses the importance of the priest as the main provider of worship and sacraments. In the cultic model, the priest is a man set apart from laity by virtue of the sacrament of holy orders. In other words, as a result of the sacrament of holy orders, the priest is ontologically different from the laity. He occupies a higher status and has more influence in the Church than the laity. He is seen as mediating the laity's relationship with God. He also has a distinctive lifestyle, as indicated by the discipline of celibacy, distinctive clerical attire, and separate living quarters in a rectory.

The "servant-leader" model stresses the importance of baptism as the sacrament that calls all Christians (laypeople as well as priests) to ministry. In other words, a priest is not set apart in any ontological sense. Rather, his distinctiveness emanates from his role as a pastoral leader. As a parish or diocesan leader, he collaborates with the laity, especially the lay ministers who also serve on parish and diocesan staffs. His lifestyle is not much different from that of laity. For example, he often wears civilian clothes, frequently has his own apartment, and thinks celibacy should be optional.

Hoge and Wenger find that older priests, who went to the seminary in the pre-Vatican II years of the 1940s and 1950s and are now over sixty-five years of age, embrace the cultic model. Priests fifty-six to sixty-five years of age, who were in seminary in the 1960s and early 1970s, put more emphasis on the servant-leader model. Younger priests, who went through seminary in the 1980s and 1990s, tend toward the cultic model more than the servant-leader model. The researchers also compared the attitudes of today's priests and priests in earlier surveys. They consistently find that today's younger priests support the cultic model more than young priests did in 1970.

According to Hoge and Wenger, their findings point to two shifts among priests in the last thirty years. "The first occurred at the time of Vatican II—from the older [cultic] model of priest as administrator of the sacraments and teacher of the faith, to a model of priest as spiritual and social leader of the community" (p. 59). The second shift began in the early 1980s and continues to this day. In Hoge's and Wenger's words, "The direction of the second transition is open to interpretation. Many older priests see it as a return to the cultic model of the priesthood dominant in the 1940s and 1950s, whereas many of the newly ordained see it as an innovative blending of pre-Vatican II and post-Vatican II elements into a new vision of the priest-hood" (p. 113).

Whichever interpretation one prefers, it is clear that there are important generational differences among today's priests. While priests who were formed in the Vatican II years of the 1960s and early 1970s embrace a servant-leader model of the priesthood, priests in pre-Vatican II and post-Vatican generations are more inclined to think of the priest in terms that are more compatible with the cultic model.

Comparing the Ages of Priests and Laypeople

In *Catholicism USA*, Bryan Froehle and Mary Gautier report that the average age of active diocesan priests is fifty-nine years. Fifty-nine percent are fifty-five years of age or older, 36 percent are between thirty-five and fifty-four, and only 5 percent are thirty-four or less.[4] In a recent study of American Catholics, colleagues and I found that the average age of laypeople is forty-eight years. Twenty-six percent are fifty-five years of age or older, 39 percent are thirty-five to fifty-four, and 35 percent are thirty-four or less.

Putting these two studies together, we see a striking difference between the ages of priests and laypeople. Although there are similar percentages of middle-aged priests and laypeople, there are dramatic differences at the older and younger ends of the scale. The percentage of older priests is more than twice as large as the percentage of older laypeople. On the other hand, the percentage of younger laypeople is seven times larger than the percentage of younger priests.

TABLE 6.1 The Ages of Priests and Laypeople

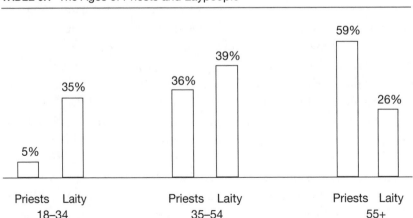

Why is this age difference important? Because other research shows that people are more likely to identify and interact with people who are similar in age than they are to gravitate toward people who are significantly older or younger. Older people are more likely to associate with older people than they are to hang around with younger people. Younger people are more likely to seek out one another than they are to befriend older people. When it comes to age, "birds of a feather flock together."

Therefore, when older laypeople seek interaction with a priest, they are inclined to prefer older priests, and they have many priests to choose from. Middle-aged laypeople also prefer interaction with priests of their own age, but when they seek such interaction, they do not have quite as many priests of their own age to choose from. Young Catholics are even less fortunate. It is only natural for them to want to associate with priests of their own age, but they have very few opportunities to do so. When they want to talk with a priest of their own age, they have a hard time finding one.

It is reasonable to assume that this situation contributes to older Catholics' identification with and involvement in the Church. It is also a good bet that it has something to do with the fact that young people are least inclined to identify with and participate in the Church.

If so, what can be done to increase young laypeople's attachment to the parishes and dioceses? One possibility is to increase the presence and visibility of eighteen- to thirty-four-year-old lay ministers in programs and activities oriented to young adults. The more young adults see same-age people in leadership roles, the more they will feel the Church includes people with whom they can relate.

Historical View of the Priest Shortage

By now, you have probably heard that there is a "priest shortage." The Church does not have as many priests as it used to have. Meanwhile, the number of American Catholics continues to grow. The combination of these trends is fostering a great deal of concern among clergy and laity.

Let's put today's priest shortage in historical perspective. One way to do that is to look at the total number of priests and the total number of laypeople throughout the twentieth century. When we do that, we see that there has been a U-shaped ratio of priests-to-people over the last hundred years. There was a priest shortage at the beginning of the twentieth century, when the growing number of immigrants outstripped the supply of priests. That priest shortage diminished through the 1940s as the Catholic population stabilized and the supply of priests increased. However, the priest shortage has become increasingly serious ever since, as the supply of priests has not kept pace with the increasing size of the Catholic population.

TABLE 6.2 Priest to Laity Ratio Since 1900

Year	# Priests	# Laity	Ratio
1900	11,987	12M	1:1,001
1910	16,550	16M	1:967
1920	21,019	20M	1:952
1930	27,864	20M	1:718
1940	35,839	22M	1:614
1950	43,889	29M	1:661
1960	54,682	42M	1:768
1970	58,161	48M	1:825
1980	58,398	50M	1:856
1990*	53,088	59M	1:1,111
1999*	46,603	62M	1:1,330

* Figures include Puerto Rico, Virgin Islands, and Guam

In 1900, 11,987 priests served a Catholic population of 12 million laypeople (a ratio of one priest for every 1,001 laypeople). In 1910, 16,550 priests served 16 million lay Catholics (a ratio of one priest for every 967 laypeople). The ratio of priests to laypeople improved as the number of priests grew steadily, while the number of laypeople leveled off (due mainly to the slow down in immigration after 1924). The priest-to-people ratio peaked in 1940, when there was one priest for every 614 laypeople. Since then, the number of priests has not kept up with the growing number of Catholics. By 1960, there was one priest for every 768 Catholics. By 1970, the ratio was 1:825. By 1980, it was up to 1:856. By 1990, it had risen to 1:1,111. By 1999, it was 1:1,330, and in 2004 there were 43,422 priests, for a ratio of 1:1,562.

These data point to three conclusions. First, this is not the first time we have had a priest shortage. We had one at the beginning of the twentieth century. Second, the current shortage is more serious than the one we experienced a hundred years ago. There was one priest for every 1,001 laypeople in 1900; in 2004 there was only one priest for more than 1,562 laypeople. Third, given the continuing decline in the number of priests and the continuing increase in the number of laypeople, the current priest shortage will become even more serious in the years ahead.

A Rational Choice Explanation for the Decline in Vocations

In December 2000, sociologists Rodney Stark and Roger Finke offered a provocative explanation for the recent declines in the numbers of priests, brothers, sisters, and seminarians.[5]

Their explanation is based on "rational choice" theory of human behavior. This theory assumes that, when people are faced with important decisions in life, they weigh the costs and benefits of various options. It also assumes that people tend to choose the options where the benefits outweigh the costs, and avoid the ones where the costs outweigh the benefits. (It is the weighing of costs and benefits that gives this thesis its name: "rational choice.") Applying this theory to the issue of vocations, Stark and Finke believe that Catholic men and women tend to weigh the costs and benefits of entering the priesthood and religious life. When they believe the benefits outweigh the costs, they will consider priesthood and/or religious life an attractive choice; when they believe the costs outweigh the benefits, they will not.

According to Stark and Finke, before Vatican II the benefits of entering the priesthood and religious life outweighed the costs. The benefits associated with the priesthood and religious life included increased access to holiness and eternal salvation, the rewards of community life, and a life set apart from the secular world. Costs, such as "vows of celibacy, obedience, and in the case of those entering orders, poverty" were seen as being worth it.

Stark and Finke argue that Vatican II produced a dramatic change in this cost/benefit ratio. They contend that this shift was tied to three Vatican II documents. First, they say that "*Lumen Gentium* declared that all Christians were called 'to holiness' simply by having been baptized, and those who pursued a religious vocation could no longer aspire to a superior state of holiness. Previously the Church had taught that priests and the religious were in a superior state of holiness. Now, despite their vows, they were just like everyone else."

Second, in Stark and Finke's words, "*Gaudium et Spes*...revoked centuries of preference for withdrawal from the 'sinful world' and proclaimed that it now was inappropriate for the religious to pursue a cloistered life, but that they should become full participants in the secular world. Indeed, this document stressed the need to modernize the entire lifestyle of the orders."

Third, *Perfectae Caritatis* proclaimed that "the manner of life, of prayer and of work should be in harmony with present-day physical and psychological conditions of the members." According to Stark and Finke, "Soon, entire orders abandoned their convents for a new life as scattered apartment dwellers, often without roommates, and dressed like everyone else."

Stark and Finke believe this shift in the cost/benefit ratio accounts for the decline in vocations. They state that "the rapid decline in Catholic vocations was in response to a cost/benefit ratio that had suddenly gone from positive to negative." When the Church "withdrew many of the most compelling motivations for the religious life, while retaining the most costly aspects of vocations," vocations to the priesthood and religious life began to decline.

Stark and Finke's theory is not the only possible explanation for the decline in vocations to the priesthood and religious life, and it does not take into account all of the factors that might contribute to the so-called "vocation crisis." However, their explanation is grounded in a very legitimate theory of human behavior and, unlike many other theories that stress external (societal) influences over which Church leaders have little or no control, their thesis deals with internal (Church) conditions over which leaders do have some control. Their argument suggests that the Church could solve the vocation crisis by lowering the costs and/or increasing the rewards associated with the priesthood and religious life. It's worth considering where that implication might lead us.

Newly Ordained Priests:
Who Stays and Who Leaves the Priesthood?

In his book, *The First Five Years of the Priesthood*, sociologist Dean Hoge compares diocesan priests and religious order priests who were ordained between 1995 and 1999 with men who resigned from the priesthood between 1992 and 1999.[6] Among other things, the book provides insights into these groups' experiences before ordination and during their first assignments as priests. It also indicates why some newly ordained priests leave the priesthood. Finally, Hoge compares men who left the priesthood recently with men who left the priesthood in the 1970s.

Currently active priests and those who have recently left the priesthood were a bit different before they were ordained. Among diocesan and religious order priests who remain in the priesthood after five years, 80 percent were born in the U.S., and six in ten had worked full time for over five years before entering the seminary at thirty-six to thirty-seven years of age. Among priests who have left the priesthood, 96 percent were born in the U.S., and six in ten had worked four years or less before entering the seminary. On average, these former priests were ordained when they were thirty-two years of age and left the priesthood when they were thirty-six.

While those who remained in the priesthood and those who left had many similar views of their seminary experiences, those who left the priesthood were less likely to say their seminaries had done a good job in four areas: understanding themselves as sexual persons, handling problems of loneliness, developing personal support networks, and understanding changes in the priesthood. The men who had left the priesthood also had less positive experiences in their first assignments. They were much more likely to say the pastor in their first parish was not supportive. They also cited too little privacy and having too public a life. When Hoge compared active priests' satisfaction with their current assignments and the satisfaction of men who left the priesthood with respect to their last assignment, he found high levels of personal and professional satisfaction among recently ordained diocesan and religious order priests who remain in the priesthood. Those who left the priesthood indicated much less satisfaction with "living a celibate life," their "living situation," their "current work in ministry," and their "relationship with the bishop or superior."

One might ask whether those who left the priesthood were unsure of their calling to the priesthood well before they were ordained. That does not appear to be the case. Two-thirds say they had not thought about leaving the priesthood until after ordination. When asked why they left the priesthood, their most frequent response was a desire to marry. In Hoge's words, "Some were in love, others were not but had difficulties with celibacy." Other factors included dissatisfaction with Church leadership and loneliness.

Interviews with men who left the priesthood in the 1990s suggested that the men fell into four categories. Twenty to 30 percent are heterosexual men who felt lonely or unappreciated and fell in love with a woman. Another 20 to 30 percent have much in common with the first type, except these men felt they could not continue to lead a celibate life, even though they were not in love with any particular woman. Thirty to 40 percent are heterosexual or homosexual men who felt lonely and were disillusioned with their fellow priests or the Church hierarchy. Five to 15 percent are homosexual men who were lonely, felt unappreciated, and wanted an open relationship with a man.

When Hoge compared the reasons why men left the priesthood in the 1970s and why some are leaving today, he reached the following conclusion: "In 1970, the main two reasons for resignation were the desire to marry and a rejection of authoritative institutional Church structures. In 2000 the desire to marry was clearly in first place, with institutional criticism far behind. The priests in our 2000 research were not, for the most part, institutional rebels."

The Laity's Views on Coping With the Priest Shortage

It is a well-known fact that the Catholic Church in America is experiencing a priest shortage. The Catholic population continues to grow, while the number of priests continues to decline. According to 2004 figures for the U.S., Puerto Rico, the Virgin Islands, and Guam, there are about 68 million American Catholics but only 43,422 priests.

One way to address this problem is to attract more men into the priesthood. Although this option is being pursued quite vigorously, the results to date suggest that these efforts are having only a limited impact. Another possibility is to increase the number of permanent deacons, who are able to perform a number of functions that traditionally have been performed by priests. There are already over 12,000 permanent deacons, but this solution is limited by the fact that permanent deacons cannot hear confessions, anoint the sick, or consecrate the Eucharist. A third possibility is to allow women and married men to be priests. Pope John Paul II made it clear that this is not a viable option.

At least in the short term, American Catholics are faced with two main options. One is to redefine the roles of priests and laypeople, so that laypeople take on some of the responsibilities that used to be performed only by priests. The other is to reduce the frequency of Masses and other sacramental services. Both of these options are under consideration, or are already in process, in many dioceses and parishes.

What do American Catholics think of these options? To what extent do they approve of giving laypeople responsibilities that used to be assigned to priests? What do they say about reductions in services? Some answers are found in a 1999 national survey that I did with colleagues William V. D'Antonio, Dean Hoge, and Katherine Meyer.[7] Here is what we found.

TABLE 6.3 Coping With the Priest Shortage

	Percent Who	
	Approve	*Disapprove*
Lay administrator, visiting priest	51	47
Reduce Masses to		
less than one a week	41	58
No priest to visit the sick	34	65
No priest for anointing of the sick	20	79

First of all, American Catholics wish there were no priest shortage. They value the Church's sacraments and, in the best of all worlds, wish there were enough priests to celebrate the sacraments as often as they have been celebrated in the past. Second, no single way of coping with the priest shortage receives the wholehearted support of all Catholics. Catholics have mixed feelings about each of the options we presented them.

Within this context, laypeople are more willing to pursue certain options more than others. Of the options we explored, the one that seems most acceptable is having a lay parish administrator and a visiting priest. Fifty-one percent of American Catholics are open to this possibility; 47 percent say this option is unacceptable.

The second most acceptable option is to reduce the number of Masses. We asked what Catholics think of having Mass less than once a week. Only 41 percent of Catholics endorse this option; 58 percent oppose it. Although reducing the frequency of Masses to less than once a week is not a popular option, it still might happen in some locations. So we posed the possibility that Sunday Mass could not be celebrated, then asked if a Communion service led by a layperson using consecrated hosts would be a satisfactory substitute. Only 12 percent of Catholics approve of a Communion service on a regular basis; 57 percent say it would be acceptable on an occasional basis; and 31 percent say it is unacceptable.

We also asked what Catholics think about the possibility of not having a priest to visit the sick. Only one-third say this is acceptable; two-thirds disapprove. The least attractive option is not having a priest for the sacrament of anointing of the sick. Only 20 percent of Catholics are open to this idea; 79 percent clearly dislike it.

Laypeople lament the fact that there is a priest shortage, but they are coming to terms with it. In the process, they are deciding that laypeople can perform some administrative functions that used to be reserved for priests. They might be willing to reduce the number of Masses and to have Communion services on an occasional basis, but they still want priests to visit and anoint the sick.

Do Other Churches Also Face a Clergy Shortage?

It is a well-established fact that there is a growing shortage of Catholic priests in the United States and territories such as Puerto Rico and the Virgin Islands. In 1981, there were 51.2 million Catholics and 58,534 priests (one priest for every 875 Catholics). By 1991, the number of Catholics had increased to 58.2 million, but the number of priests had fallen to 52,277 (one priest for every 1,113 Catholics). By 2001, the Catholic population had risen to 65.2 million, but there were only 45,713 priests (one priest for every 1,426 Catholics). In other words, although there were 14 million more Catholics (a 27 percent increase), there were 12,821 fewer priests (a 22 percent decline).

As Catholics try to understand the growing shortage of priests, they sometimes ask if the Catholic Church is the only religious group with a declining number of clergy, or if this decline also is occurring in other religious groups. To explore this question, I consulted the *Yearbook of American and Canadian Churches*, which publishes membership figures for major religious groups and information on the total number of clergy in each group.[8] The 2003 issue of the *Yearbook* reports data on these two topics for 2001, the 1993 edition contains data for 1991, and the 1983 edition has data for 1981.

In each edition, I selected seven mainline Protestant denominations: the Episcopal Church, the Presbyterian Church, the United Church of Christ, the United Methodist Church, the Evangelical Lutheran Church in America, the Christian Church/Disciples of Christ, and the American Baptist Churches in the USA. I also gathered information on three Christian groups that are considered more theologically conservative: the Assemblies of God, the Lutheran Church-Missouri Synod, and the Church of the Nazarene.

In terms of membership trends, the groups fall into two categories. Memberships in the Presbyterian Church, the Assemblies of God, and the Church of the Nazarene have increased since 1981. On the other hand, the American Baptist Churches, the Episcopal Church, the United Church of Christ, the United Methodist Church, the Evangelical Lutheran Church, the Christian

Church/Disciples of Christ, and the Lutheran Church-Missouri Synod had fewer members in 2001 than they had in 1981.

What about trends among the clergy? In every group, including those in which membership has declined, the total number of clergy has increased.

TABLE 6.4 Total Clergy by Religious Group

Religious Group	Total Clergy			
	1981	*1991*	*2001*	*%Change*
Membership has increased				
Assemblies	23,898	30,746	32,374	+35
Catholic	58,534	52,277	45,713	-22
Nazarene	7,945	9,363	9,898	+25
Presbyterian	20,471	20,357	21,150	+3
Membership has declined				
Am. Baptist	6,951	8,421	8,856	+27
Disciples	6,608	6,912	6,936	+5
Episcopal	12,908	14,878	16,712	+29
Lutheran-ELCA	15,934	17,426	17,693	+11
Lutheran-MS	7,376	8,389	8,497	+15
Methodist	36,676	38,502	44,539	+21
UCC	10,008	10,171	10,347	+3

Source: *Yearbook of American and Canadian Churches*, 2003, 1993, and 1983.

In the Christian Church/Disciples of Christ, United Church of Christ, and Presbyterian Church the increases have been rather modest (3 to 5 percent). In the Evangelical Lutheran, Lutheran-Missouri Synod, and United Methodist churches, they have been larger (11, 15, and 21 percent, respectively). In four groups, the increases have been larger yet. These denominations include the Church of the Nazarene (25 percent), American Baptist Churches (27 percent), Episcopal Church (29 percent), and the Assemblies of God (35 percent).

While this exploration certainly does not address all of the complicated issues involved in a comprehensive analysis of the priest shortage, it indicates that the Catholic Church is the only one of these eleven religious groups that has a declining number of clergy. This fact suggests that the sources of the priest shortage are more likely to be found in the Church itself than in societal conditions adversely affecting churches in general. If so, it will be up to clergy and lay leaders representing many different intellectual disciplines, theological perspectives, and walks of life to identify what the root causes might be and what, if anything, might be done to increase the number of priestly vocations.[9]

The Permanent Diaconate:
The Promise and the Problems

At Vatican II (1962–65), Church leaders reintroduced the permanent diaconate. Deacons would come from the ranks of the laity and could be married, but they would be ordained clergy who could perform all the duties of priests except for the sacrament of reconciliation, the anointing of the sick, and the consecration of the Eucharist.

Frank DeRego and I examined the history and implementation of the permanent diaconate (relying heavily on data from a 1981 study by American bishops, a 1987 study by sociologist Dean Hoge, and a 1996 study by the National Conference of Catholic Bishops).[10]

At Vatican II, bishops were concerned about the growing shortage of priests, especially in Third World countries. Reintroducing the early-Christian order of a permanent diaconate was seen as one way of dealing with this problem. But the bishops were divided over the concept of a permanent diaconate. Some bishops feared that it would overturn more than a millennium of tradition establishing the connection between celibacy and ordained ministry. If the Church allowed married men to be deacons, that might be a step in the direction of a married priesthood. Other bishops saw the permanent diaconate as a "leaven in the loaf." Since the permanent deacon lived in the workaday world and in many cases would be married, his ministry would directly relate to the lives of the people he served. In the end, the permanent diaconate was approved, with the proviso that celibacy would remain in force for the priesthood.

Since being reintroduced, the diaconate has grown, but in an unexpected fashion. By 1997, there were 21,900 deacons in 121 countries. Although bishops expected the diaconate to expand most rapidly in relatively poor countries where the priest shortage is most acute, 81 percent of all deacons are in affluent countries, where the priest shortage is less severe. Half of all deacons are in the United States alone. The number of American deacons increased from only 1,900 in 1977 to 11,788 in 1997. As of 2003, there were 14,308 deacons in the United States.

The response to the permanent diaconate has been mixed. On the positive side, the 1981 study indicated that 88 percent of deacons "would seek ordination if they had to do it over again." Data from deacons' wives, supervisors, and bishops indicated overall satisfaction with the diaconate program. The 1996 study called the diaconate "hugely successful," saying there is "widespread and enthusiastic acceptance of the ministries performed by deacons." Deacons' wives "describe themselves as supportive of their husbands' ministry and their family as greatly enriched by his ordination."

Nevertheless, deacons often face conflicting expectations from bishops, priests, laypeople, and members of their families. Priests often feel that deacons, most of whom work part time, should give more time to the Church. Meanwhile, deacons' wives feel that their husbands' ministerial work often takes time away from their family lives. Some Catholic laypeople believe the restoration of the permanent diaconate clericalizes the Church and detracts from lay roles and responsibilities. Religious sisters and laywomen who serve as administrators of priestless parishes report that ordination gives deacons status advantages.

There also is evidence of role ambiguity. The 1981 study indicated that more than half of deacons had no job descriptions or formal work agreements with parishes. The 1996 study shows that lay leaders are inclined to see deacons as "underqualified priests or overqualified laity." A majority of lay leaders do not think ordination is necessary for the work deacons do. Fewer than one-third of parish council members say they have a "very good" understanding of the diaconate; even fewer are convinced that laypeople really understand the role of deacons. Deacons believe that most priests, lay ministers, and parishioners do not fully understand deacons' role in the Church.

If the permanent diaconate is to be an effective form of ministry in the years ahead, these conflicts and ambiguities will have to be addressed.

Lay Ministers Have Lots of Experience, Dedication, and Faith

Research indicates a rapid increase in the number of laypeople assuming leadership roles in the Church. In 1992, Rev. Philip Murnion reported that 21,569 people were working at least twenty hours per week in parish ministries.[11] By 1999, Murnion and David DeLambo reported that the number of lay ministers had risen to 29,146 (a 35 percent increase).[12]

Who are these lay ministers? What types of laypeople are stepping into leadership roles in the Church? Several colleagues and I explored these questions in a study of lay ministers in the archdioceses of Indianapolis and Louisville, the dioceses of Lafayette and Evansville in Indiana, and the diocese of Owensboro, Kentucky. The social profile of lay ministers in these five dioceses is very similar to profiles Murnion and other researchers have reported. For example, the typical lay minister in these dioceses and elsewhere is a fifty-year-old, college-educated, married, white woman.

According to our findings, lay ministers bring lots of experience, dedication, and faith to their work in the Church. The vast majority of lay ministers have very Catholic and very religious backgrounds. Eighty-three percent grew up Catholic, 77 percent attended Mass regularly as children, and nearly half were actively involved in Church activities during their youth. Eighty-five percent attended Catholic grade schools, three-quarters went to Catholic high schools, and 59 percent were students at Catholic colleges and universities.

They also have active lifestyles that include many family, community, and personal commitments. Seventy-eight percent are married. Fifty-one percent have school-age children. Sixty percent spend twenty or more hours a week on family responsibilities. Forty-three percent are the primary-wage earner in their families. Thirty-five percent spend twenty or more hours a week working at another job. Twenty-seven percent devote five or more hours a week to community activities. Twelve percent spend five or more hours pursuing their own educations.

Lay ministers have many years of experience in Church work and are deeply committed to a variety of ministries. Thirty-two percent have worked in the Church for over twenty-one years, and another 30 percent have eleven to twenty years of experience. Half are full-time paid staff people, 21 percent work part time, and 29 percent are volunteers. Fifty-three percent spend thirty or more hours a week on their ministries, and an additional 14 percent work between eleven and twenty-nine hours a week. A majority of lay ministers are involved in religious education, music ministries, school administration, and youth ministry. Others are pastoral associates, leaders in RCIA, diocesan office staff people, business managers, and family-life coordinators.

People in these positions also are quite spiritual. Ninety-four percent say their current ministry strengthens their spirituality. Seventy-nine percent say the parish where they work nurtures their spiritual life. Seventy percent see their work in the Church as a calling (not simply as a job or a career). Twenty-two percent spend more than ten hours a week in worship and prayer. Another 45 percent devote five to nine hours a week to such activities. On average, lay ministers set aside about eight hours a week for spiritual practices.

Certainly, clergy and lay leaders face many challenges as lay ministry emerges in the Church. Given the fact that Hispanics, African Americans, Asians, and Native Americans are underrepresented relative to the numbers in the Church as a whole, one challenge is to attract young people of both sexes and all racial and ethnic backgrounds to lay ministry. At the same time, however, leaders ought to be impressed with the qualifications and Catholicity of the people who are moving into positions of leadership in our parishes and dioceses. They are well grounded in their communities, highly committed to their work in the Church, and deeply involved in their faith.

Challenges Facing Lay Ministers in Their Work With the Laity

A growing number of laypeople are assuming leadership roles in the Church. These "lay ministers" include liturgists, diocesan directors of religious education, youth ministers, music ministers, business managers, family-life co-ordinators, and catechists.

As members of a new category of Church leaders, these lay ministers face many challenges. Some challenges have to do with their relationships with bishops, priests, and one another. Others have to do with their relationships with the laity.

Lay ministers and the laypeople they serve have much in common. For example, the vast majority of people in both groups have been born and raised in the Catholic Church. Most accept the core teachings of the Church, such as belief in Incarnation (Jesus was fully human and fully divine), Resurrection (Jesus died and rose for our sins), and Real Presence (at Mass, the bread and wine actually become the Body and Blood of Christ). Most also believe God has been, and continues to be, present in their lives. These similarities increase the chances of good communication and the likelihood of cooperation between lay ministers and the laypeople with whom they serve.

Recent studies show, however, that the two groups also are different. Over 90 percent of lay ministers are white, compared to only about 70 percent of laypeople in general. Three out of four lay ministers, but only about half of all laypeople, are women. Three-quarters of lay ministers are married, compared to just over half of other laypeople. Half of lay ministers, but only one-third of other laypeople, have preschool-age or school-age children living at home.

Lay ministers are almost twice more likely to have attended a Catholic grade school (85 percent), three times more likely to have attended a Catholic high school (75 percent), and are six times more likely to have attended a Catholic college or university (60 percent). They are twice as likely to have completed college or gone to graduate or professional school, and they are more likely to have white-collar jobs.

Lay ministers and the laity also belong to different generations. Although nearly half of all adult Catholics belong to the post-Vatican II generation (that is, were born between 1961 and 1982), only about one-fifth of lay ministers are members of this generation. Lay ministers are far more likely to be members of the Vatican II generation. While two out of three lay ministers were born between 1941 and 1960, only about one-third of other laypeople are in that generation. About 15 percent of lay ministers and 20 percent of laypeople belong to the pre-Vatican II generation (that is, were born in or before 1940).

Laypeople and lay ministers also are quite different spiritually. Lay ministers are somewhat more likely to report that God has forgiven their sins, cared for them when they have needed help, answered their prayers, and been present to them in some special way. These differences, no doubt, are related to differences in the groups' spiritual practices. Virtually all lay ministers are registered parishioners who attend Mass and receive holy Communion at least once a week. By comparison, only two-thirds of laypeople are registered parishioners and only about one-third are weekly churchgoers. Compared to laypeople in general, lay ministers are more likely to go to confession, pray the rosary, read the Bible, and participate in a prayer group or Bible study group.

If these demographic and spiritual differences are not understood and addressed, they could become serious problems, fostering poor communication and even conflict. On the other hand, if they are taken into account, they need not stand in the way of new and fruitful relationships between lay ministers and laypeople.

The Spiritual Practices of Lay Ministers

Lay ministers are laypeople who work in parishes and dioceses carrying out a variety of ministries, such as religious education, youth programs, and social outreach. In a recent study, colleagues and I learned two things about the spiritual practices of lay ministers: there are certain practices that nearly all lay ministers engage in, and there are others that appeal to some lay ministers more than others.

Several religious practices are common to almost all lay ministers. Over 90 percent attend Mass at least once a week, receive holy Communion weekly, read the parish bulletin every week, and talk to God daily. Eighty to 89 percent start and end the day with prayer at least once a week, pray alone at least once a week, and pray before meals daily. And 63 percent say prayers such as the Our Father and the Hail Mary at least daily.[13]

Five styles or approaches to lay spirituality emerged from the study:

Traditional. This style includes spiritual practices that have been encouraged by the Church for many years. Sixty-six percent of lay ecclesial ministers attend Eucharistic Adoration at least once a year. Fifty-five percent practice Marian devotions at least once a year. Thirty-five percent confess sins to a priest several times a year. Thirty-five percent participate in other devotions, such as novenas and benedictions, several times a year. Twenty-nine percent pray the rosary at least once a week. Only nine percent practice the Liturgy of the Hours daily.

Service/Justice. This approach involves concern for others. Service includes assistance to needy individuals. Justice involves social reforms aimed at fostering fairness in society. Sixty percent of lay ministers are often involved in helping the poor. Fifty-two percent often participate in activities aimed at reducing racism or sexism. Fifty percent care for the elderly, and 35 percent care for the sick and dying. Thirty-one percent are involved in protecting the unborn. Twenty-five percent participate in ecology programs. Twenty-four percent are involved in caring for the homeless. Only nine percent are involved in activities aimed at ending the death penalty.

Cognitive. These practices stress the use and development of cognitive skills through reading and study. Seventy-one percent of lay ecclesial ministers read the diocesan newspaper at least once a week. Forty-eight percent are involved in a theology class at least once a year. Thirty-eight percent read books on spirituality at least once a month. Thirty-seven percent read books on theology and ministry at least once a month. Twenty-five percent read some other kind of religious magazine at least once a week.

Interactive. The fourth cluster includes Scripture-oriented activities that usually involve interactions with other people. Seventy percent of lay ecclesial ministers attend a retreat at least once a year. Forty-one percent study the Bible at least once a week. Thirty-six percent see a spiritual director at least once a year. Twenty-seven percent are in a prayer group at least once a month. Twenty-four percent attend a charismatic service at least once a year. Only 17 percent are in a Bible study group, and only 14 percent are involved in the prayerful reading of the Bible (*Lectio Divina*) every day.

Expressive. The last cluster includes practices stressing personal reflection and expressions of one's inner feelings. Fifty-three percent of lay ecclesial ministers are involved in centering prayer some time during the year. Forty percent keep a journal. Thirty-eight percent are involved in creative pursuits such as dance. Twenty-three percent meditate daily. Ten percent are involved in Yoga or Tai Chi.

Thus, almost all lay ministers engage in a core set of sacramental and devotional practices but, in addition, they have several different ways of being spiritual.

Questions for Reflection

1. Do you know how the pastor of your parish allocates his time during an average week? Is he spending time on activities that are healthy and wise for him personally and effective in meeting the needs of his parishioners?
2. Are the generational differences among priests and the age differences between priests and laypeople evident in your area? What, if anything, can be done to bridge these differences?
3. How is the growing shortage of priests impacting the church in your area? How are Church leaders and laypeople responding? For example,

how willing are laypeople in your area to support a lay pastoral administrator, have fewer Masses, or close parishes?

4. What could your diocese or parish do to improve the working conditions of priests so that more men would remain in the priesthood?

5. Who are the permanent deacons in your parish, how well do parishioners understand their work in the Church, and how have parishioners responded to them?

6. Who are the lay ministers in your parish? What have been their greatest contributions, what conditions are limiting their effectiveness, and what can be done to remove these obstacles?

7. To what extent do you engage in any of the spiritual practices found among lay ministers? Which styles, if any, do you favor?

Part III

The Beliefs and Practices of American Catholics

Chapter 7

Why Catholics Think and Act the Way They Do

Learning theory—with its emphasis on imitation, affirmation, and punishment—helps to explain why Catholics think and act the way they do. Role theory also helps to explain why people's behavior sometimes changes or seems to be inconsistent. People are motivated by values and interests, both of which need to be considered if one is to understand why people choose some courses of action over others. As many Church leaders assume, attitudes (and attitude change) frequently precede behavior (and behavioral change). However, it also is true that behavior (and behavioral change) often precede attitudes (and attitude change). This chapter invites readers to think about the way these ideas might apply to their own lives, and how they might account for beliefs and practices of others in their parishes and dioceses.

Learning Theory Explains Some Differences Among Laity

There is a great deal of variation in Catholics' beliefs and practices. For example, about two-thirds of Catholics are registered parishioners; one-third are not. Also, 30 to 40 percent of Catholics attend Mass on a weekly basis; the other 60 to 70 percent go less often. About 80 percent believe God is present in the sacraments; the rest are not sure or do not accept that idea. About one-fourth of Catholics agree with most all of the Church's teachings on sexual and reproductive issues; another one-fourth agree with some but not all of these Church teachings; about half disagree with the Church on most of these moral issues.

How do we account for these variations? Why do Catholics have such different religious beliefs and practice their faith in such different ways? One answer is found in what social theorists call learning theory. Here is a brief summary.

In any given society, social groups share at least some cultural values and norms (such as Americans' shared belief in democracy). However, groups also have subcultures or lifestyles of their own. These subcultures include religious ideas and codes of conduct that are usually linked to other matters, such as views about family, work, and politics. Ideas and actions that are normative in some groups are often inappropriate in others. What is considered acceptable conduct in some groups is unacceptable in others.

Individuals are born into these different groups. For example, some are born to parents with European roots, while others have parents who come from Hispanic, African American, Asian, or Native American backgrounds. Some are born into highly educated and prosperous white-collar families, others into blue-collar families that have fewer social and economic resources. Some are born during periods of religious traditionalism, while others are raised during periods of religious innovation and change.

Individuals learn the cultural and religious traits of the groups and times into which they are born. They learn in three ways. One way is by imitating the people around them, as when young girls copy their mothers' mannerisms and young boys emulate their fathers' behavior. Affirmation is another means by which people learn. Rewards take many forms, such as verbal expressions of approval from loving parents, colorful stars on grade-school students' papers, and pats on the back from coaches or mentors who are trying to encourage specific attitudes and behavior patterns. Punishment is a third mechanism for learning. Parents and other authorities use "time outs," curfews, and other sanctions to discourage unacceptable ideas and behaviors. In short, through imitation, affirmation, and punishment, people come to reflect the groups and times in which they grew up.

This is evident in Catholics' religious beliefs and practices. Given the cultural differences between racial and ethnic groups, it is not surprising to find that Catholics with Asian backgrounds are more likely to comply with official Church teachings than Anglos and Hispanics, who, in turn, are more traditional than Catholics with African American backgrounds. Considering the different lifestyles of the rich and poor, blue-collar Catholics develop more traditional beliefs and practices than affluent Catholics. It also is no wonder that pre-Vatican II Catholics (born in or before 1940) are more likely to agree with Church teachings than Vatican II Catholics (born between 1941 and 1960) and post-Vatican II Catholics (born since 1961).

Learning theory is not the only explanation, but it accounts for at least some of the variation in Catholics' beliefs and practices.

Understanding Changes and Inconsistencies in Human Behavior

In general, people look for continuity and consistency in one another's behavior. We like to think people will act in pretty much the same way whenever we observe them or interact with them.

As a result, we are often surprised when people act one way in one place but quite differently in another. We might be surprised to find that a pastor who is a bit of a tyrant at the parish in the morning is a softy when he visits his mother in the nursing home later in the afternoon. Or, we might know a lector who is very polite on the altar Sunday morning but curses when he plays golf with his buddies Sunday afternoon. A group of Catholic school principals recently told me of fourth-grade students who stand erect and behave themselves when they attend Mass at their parochial school but do not pay attention when they go to Mass with their parents on Sunday morning. We all have known young women who seldom attended church while they were single but became regular churchgoers when they got married and had children of their own.

Are these changes and inconsistencies signs of personality disorders? Not usually. Are these people hypocrites and phonies? In most cases, they are not. Then how are we to explain the changes and inconsistencies in their behavior? One way is to understand the nature of social positions and social roles. Social positions are the statuses people occupy, such as pastor, son, lector, golfer, student, child, single woman, and mother. Social roles are the behaviors that are expected of people who occupy these social positions.

People occupy many different social positions and tend to behave as they are expected to act in each one. The priest who is a bit authoritarian around the parish but does whatever his mother asks of him when he sees her at the nursing home does not have a personality disorder. He is simply changing positions (from being a pastor to being a son), and his behavior is changing accordingly (from acting like an authority figure to obeying his mother). The lector who is courteous at church but swears on the golf course is not schizophrenic. He is simply changing positions (from being a lector to being a golfer) and social roles (from being polite to expressing his emotions). Fourth-grade students who behave when they attend Mass at school during the week but do not pay attention when they go to Mass with their parents on Sunday morning are not being two-faced. They are simply changing social positions (from being students to being children) and social roles (from doing what their teachers expect them of them to acting as their parents expect them to act). Young women who seldom attend church while they are single but become regular churchgoers when they get married and have children of their own are not phonies. They are just changing social positions (from being single to being wives and mothers) and social roles (from doing whatever they want whenever they want to doing what is best for their families).

I find that the concepts of social positions and social roles are very useful when college students and I talk about what their lives will be like when they settle down and get married. When we discuss marriage, I ask them to describe how they will be expected to act as husbands or wives. Their responses usually include things such as maintaining a job, sharing household responsibilities and leisure time activities with their spouse, being lovers, and in some cases attending church with their spouse. When the conversation turns to becoming parents, students usually talk about spending time with the children; teaching them to walk, talk, and behave; and often making sure their children are raised in their Church. By the time we are finished, students understand some of the transitions they will make and some of the inconsistencies that will appear in their own behavior. They also understand the changes and inconsistencies that are likely to appear in their spouse's behavior.

Readers also might find the concepts of social positions and social roles to be helpful in explaining people's behavior in their parishes, parochial schools, families, and workplaces.

Values and Interests Affect the Way We Act

Whenever I am asked why people act the way they do, I stress the importance of two things: values and interests. Values are one's views of what is right and what is wrong, what is moral and what is not. Interests signify actions people are willing to take because they stand to gain socially, economically, or politically, and actions they are not willing to take because the costs outweigh the benefits.

TABLE 7.1 Values and Interests

		Interests	
		No	Yes
Values	Yes	Yes/No	Yes/Yes
	No	No/No	No/Yes

Sometimes people's values and interests are compatible. Something they think is right also might be in their best interest. Likewise, something they do not value also might be far too costly for them to consider.

At other times, people's values and interests are in conflict. Something they value might not be in their best interest. Conversely, their values might tell them not to do something, but it might be in their interest to do it anyway.

These combinations of values and interests explain why parishioners volunteer for some church activities but not others. When people think a parish project is important, and they can benefit from it, they are likely to volunteer. If they think it is important, but also think it will require too much time or money, they are more reluctant to get involved. When they think the project is not especially important, but can visualize some personal benefit from participating in it, they also will be reluctant to participate. Finally, if they are not convinced of the project's value and believe there is nothing in it for them, they usually shy away from it.

These circumstances have implications for Church leaders. Picture a pastor, parish council member, or the chair of a parish committee who wants to ask parishioners to participate in some activity, let us say a fund drive to build a new Catholic school. The leader needs to decide who to ask, and how to ask them.

Using the four cells in the accompanying box, the leader should make four lists (see table 7.1). There are some people who would not only think a school is important; they also would have something to gain from being involved. The project appeals to both their values and their interests. These are the people the leader should approach first, explaining how the project reflects their values and how they will benefit from being involved. They are likely to accept, and they will stick with the project through thick and thin.

There also are people who would think it is important to have a new school, but would have nothing to gain from it. When approaching these parishioners, the leader is faced with two challenges: explaining how the project is so valuable that the costs pale in significance, and convincing them that the personal benefits of participating might outweigh the costs. Unless these challenges are met, these parishioners are not likely to participate (and for very understandable reasons based largely on interests).

There also are some people who think there is no need for a new Catholic school, but who might benefit from participating in a project to build one. Here the leader faces a different set of challenges: explaining precisely how the parishioners would benefit personally from the project, and convincing them that there is enough value in the project to justify whatever costs might be incurred. If these challenges are not overcome, these parishioners will be reluctant to get involved (again for very understandable reasons, this time based mainly on values).

Finally, there are some people for whom the project is both unimportant and too costly. The project does not appeal to either their values or their interests. The leader probably should not waste much time trying to recruit these people for this project. Perhaps some other project will reflect their values and serve their interests, but not this one.

Attitudes and Behavior: A Two-Way Street

There is a well-established body of research showing that attitudes precede behavior. According to this research, people's values and beliefs affect their actions. Their perceptions affect the choices they make. Their ideas translate into actions.

Applying this principle to religion, we see that people's faith has consequences for the way they live their life. Their religious beliefs affect the way they act. Their religious worldviews carry over into their relationships with others.

By extension, this research suggests that, if Church leaders want to change the way people currently act, the first thing they have to do is change the way people think. If they want people to do things they have never done before, they need to change people's attitudes. If they would like people to volunteer for something new, they have got to convince them that the new course of action is worthwhile. If they want people to stand up for something they never stood up for before, they have got to educate them first.

This body of research underlies a great deal of ministry in the Church. It is the underpinning of much of what takes place in religious education and youth ministry. It also is found in ministry with young adults, and older adults as well. It is the framework within which a great deal of social ministry takes place. It is the bedrock of most weekend homilies and a great deal of pastoral counseling.

There is nothing wrong with this way of thinking. It works. Attitudes do affect people's actions.

However, there is another well-established body of research showing that people's actions also precede their values and beliefs. The choices people make affect their perceptions of reality. Their actions translate into ideas.

This approach also can be applied to religion. It suggests that religious practices affect people's religious beliefs. Their experiences in social ministry affect their views of the Church's social teachings. Their lifestyles impact their religious worldviews. Their involvement in parish life affects their views of the Church.

By extension, this research suggests that, if Church leaders want to change the way people think, the first thing they ought to do is change the way people act. If leaders want people to think things over, they ought to invite people to do something they have never done before. If they want to convince people that a new course of action is worthwhile, ask them to try it first. If leaders want people to understand why something is worth believing in, give them a chance to experiment with it.

According to professor David G. Myers of Hope College, the assumption that attitudes affect actions "lies behind most of our teaching, preaching, counseling, and child rearing."[1] He adds, however, that "the reverse is equally true: we are as likely to act ourselves into a way of thinking as to think ourselves into a line of actions....Individuals are as likely to believe in what they have stood up for as to stand up for what they believe."

Myers' observation challenges us to think about ministry in some new ways. Many Church programs—such as Bible study, social ministry, and small Christian communities—include the components of prayer, study, faith sharing, mutual support, and outreach. These components usually occur in just that sequence: prayer and study, followed by a faith sharing and mutual support, ending a commitment to action. This sequence is based on the familiar assumption that attitude precedes action.

Now, arrange the same components using the less familiar assumption that action precedes attitude. Suddenly, the sequence is reversed: action leads to mutual support and faith sharing, and ends in a commitment to further study and prayer.

I do not suggest that Church leaders abandon their traditional approach to ministry for a new one. Both approaches are legitimate ways for people to participate in the Church. After all, people have different ways of being faithful. Some prefer to study first; others want to roll up their sleeves and get right to work. Some like to start with prayer, then act; others prefer to get started, then end with prayer. Some prefer to think things over before acting; others prefer to dive right in, and explore the implications of their actions as they go along. The Church needs to provide a variety of ways for people to be faithful Catholics.

Questions for Reflection

1. How does learning theory explain your beliefs and practices and those of other Catholics you know? In what ways are your views extensions of what you have learned from your parents and peers?
2. How do the concepts of social positions and social roles help you to account for changes and/or inconsistencies in your own behavior?
3. Can you think of times when you and/or Church leaders have appealed to others on the basis of values, only to fail because you/they overlooked people's self-interests?
4. Can you think of a time when you have been especially motivated to participate in some course of action? Examine the extent to which your values and interests were at stake.
5. As a rule, are you more likely to assume that attitudes affect behavior or that behavior affects attitudes? When and how are these assumptions reflected in your behavior?
6. Can you recall a situation in which you became involved in some project or activity, only to find that your attitudes changed as a result of your involvement?

Chapter 8

Catholic Identity and Commitment to the Church

This chapter opens with an analysis of how Catholics are struggling with the truth-claims of Catholicism and other religious traditions. It then explores the relationships between and the consequences of Catholic identity and commitment to the Church. Although identity is often accompanied by commitment to the Church, the two do not always go hand and hand. Levels of Catholic identity exceed levels of commitment to the Church. As Catholics think about what it means to be Catholic, they distinguish between Church teachings they consider to be essential to the Catholic faith and ones they think are optional or peripheral. As the last three sections of this chapter show, identity and commitment have demonstrable effects on Catholics' views of public policies, their civic participation, and their work.

On Being Catholic and Ecumenical in a Pluralistic World

The *Catechism of the Catholic Church* states that "[t]he sole Church of Christ...constituted and organized as a society in the present world, subsists in (*subsitit in*) the Catholic Church" (816). Vatican II stresses that "it is through Christ's Catholic Church alone, which is the universal help toward salvation, that the fullness of the means of salvation can be obtained" (Vatican II, Decree on Ecumenism). While maintaining that the Catholic Church has a greater share of religious truth than other faiths, the Council and the *Catechism* acknowledge that "'many elements of sanctification and of truth' are found outside the visible confines of the Catholic Church" (CCC, 819).

Some observers fear U.S. Catholics no longer agree with this point of view. They argue that Catholics have succumbed to America's postmodern or relativistic culture, which portrays all faiths as essentially equal and viable pathways to the same God. Catholics now have a "denominational mentality" and believe that the Catholic Church as "just another denomination."[1]

The 2003 national survey Dean Hoge and I conducted for the University of Notre Dame points to a different interpretation. First, Catholics like being Catholic and are not very likely to leave the Church for other religious groups. Eighty-one percent of Catholics said that "being Catholic is a very important part of who I am," and two-thirds said they "cannot imagine…being anything other than Catholic." Eighty-two percent said the "Catholic Church is very important to me personally," and 71 percent said they "would never leave the Catholic Church." Sixty-three percent said that there "is something very special about being Catholic that you can't find in other religions," and 53 percent said that the "Catholic religion contains a greater share of the truth than other religions do." A majority of Catholics also embrace distinctively Catholic teachings. They affirm the importance of charitable efforts toward helping the poor (82 percent), the belief that Jesus is really present in the Eucharist (81 percent), devotion to Mary, the Mother of God (72 percent), and belief that God is present in a special way in the poor (71 percent).

However, there also are elements of relativism in Catholics' responses to other items in our survey. Eighty-six percent said, "If you believe in God, it doesn't really matter which religion you belong to." Seventy-six percent said, "Individuals should seek out religious truth for themselves and not automatically conform to the doctrines of any church." Seventy-four percent said, "The major world religions are equally good ways of finding ultimate truth." Fifty-two percent said that they "could be just as happy in some other church—it wouldn't have to be Catholic." The same percentage said, "The Catholic religion has no more spiritual truth than other major religions."

Thus, Catholics continue to believe in the distinctiveness of their Church, but they also have a high level of appreciation and acceptance of other faiths. They are trying hard to be both Catholic and respectful of other faiths in a highly pluralistic world.

Pre-Vatican II Catholics are the most likely to endorse the *Catechism*'s view and least likely to express the view that all faiths are equally true. There are no noteworthy differences between members of the Vatican II, post-Vatican II, and millennial generations on these issues. Registered parishioners also feel a stronger Catholic identity than nonparishioners, but on the questions about the validity of other faiths, differences between registered parishioners and others are small. The nonparishioners are slightly more affirming of the equal truth in other religions, but not much.

As Catholics strive to be both Catholic and respectful of other faiths, they encounter some boundary issues that need to be addressed. Laypeople need to explain to theologians and other experts how it is they are trying to being both Catholic and ecumenical. Theologians and other experts need to appreciate the sociological dimensions of this struggle, avoiding the temptation to simply write it off as a logical impossibility. At the same time, theologians and other experts need to clarify the Church's view of itself, its commitment to ecumenism and interfaith dialogue, and the points at which relativism is problematic.[2]

Catholic Identity Not the Same as Commitment

Catholic identity is a broad concept referring to people's identification with the Catholic *faith*. It has to do with the importance people attach to being Catholic. Commitment to the Church is a narrower concept having to do with people's attachment to the Catholic *Church*. It has to do with their investment in the institutional life of the Church.

Certainly the two are related. The more one identifies with the Catholic faith, the more one is likely to be involved in the Church; and the more loyal one is to the Church, the more one is likely to identify with the faith.

But, the two are not the same. The difference is evident in my 1995 survey of American Catholics.[3] A clear majority of Catholics identify with the Catholic faith. Eighty-one percent say being a Catholic is a very important part of who they are. Eighty-one percent also say the people who know them know they are Catholic. Seventy-nine percent say it is important that younger generations of their families grow up Catholic. Fewer Catholics are highly committed to the Church. Only 57 percent say they would never leave the Catholic Church. Only 44 percent say the Catholic Church is the most important part or among the most important parts of their life. And, only 37 percent say they attend Mass on a weekly basis. Clearly, many Catholics identify as being Catholic but are not highly committed to the Church.

TABLE 8.1 Catholic Identity and Commitment to the Church by Generation

	All Catholics	Generation		
		Pre-Vatican II	Vatican II	Post-Vatican II
Catholic Identity				
Being a Catholic is a very important part of who you are.	81	90	80	78
People who know you know you are a Catholic.	81	88	84	76
It is important to you that younger generations of your family grow up as Catholics.	79	85	77	77
Commitment to the Church				
Would never leave the Church	57	76	60	47
The Catholic Church is the most important part, or among the most important parts, of your life.	44	66	46	38
Attend Mass weekly	37	57	39	20

The study also points to two other findings, both of which involve comparisons between three generations of Catholics: pre-Vatican II Catholics (born in 1940 or before), Vatican II Catholics (born between 1941 and 1960), and post-Vatican II Catholics (born between 1961 and 1982).

First, there is some decline in Catholic identity. Whereas 90 percent of the pre-Vatican II generation say that being Catholic is an important part of who they are, only 80 percent of the Vatican II generation and only 78 percent of the post-Vatican II generation say that. While 88 percent of pre-Vatican II Catholics say the people who know them know they are Catholic, only 84 percent of Vatican II Catholics and only 76 percent of post-Vatican II Catholics say that. Although 85 percent of pre-Vatican II Catholics say it is important that future generations in their families grow up Catholic, only 77 percent of Vatican II and post-Vatican II Catholics say that.

There is a sharper decline in commitment to the Church. While 76 percent of pre-Vatican II Catholics say they would never leave the Church, only 60 percent of Vatican II Catholics, and only 47 percent of post-Vatican II Catholics say that. Although 66 percent of pre-Vatican II Catholics say the Church is among the most important parts of their life, only 46 percent of Vatican II Catholics, and only 38 percent of post-Vatican II Catholics say that. Whereas 57 percent of pre-Vatican II Catholics attend Mass weekly, only 39 percent of Vatican II Catholics, and only 20 percent of post-Vatican II Catholics do.

In short, generational differences are larger on the three commitment items than they are on the three Catholic identity items. Thus, there is good reason to be concerned about declines in Catholic identity, but there is even more reason to be concerned about declines in commitment to the Church.

What It Means to Be Catholic

The following examines two questions about what it means to be Catholic, as that is understood by laypeople. First, what do American Catholics consider to be at the core of their identity as Catholics? What do they think are the most, and least, important elements of their faith? Second, have Catholics' views on these issues remained stable, or changed over time? Is Catholic identity changing?

Studies consistently show that Catholics attach the most importance to three things: "pan-Vatican II" beliefs (official Church teachings which were important before the Council and remain important after the Council) that are grounded in the Nicene Creed, the importance of sacraments such as Eucharist, and the Church's social teachings about peace and social justice.[4] Evidence consistently shows that Catholics consider beliefs such as Incarnation, Resurrection, Trinity, Mary as the Mother of God, and the Real Presence to be the core of their faith. Catholics also attach importance to God's presence in the sacraments. They also report that concern for the poor is a core element in their view of what it means to be Catholic.

While laypeople believe these beliefs and practices are at the heart of their Catholic identity, they attach less importance to matters such as devotional practices, ordination policies, and sexual-reproductive ethics. A 1995 study shows that on a weekly basis Catholics are more likely to attend Mass (43 percent) and receive holy Communion (36 percent) than they are to pray the rosary (20 percent), read the Bible (19 percent), or participate in prayer groups (5 percent). According to a 1997 study, 65 percent of young-adult

Catholics say it is important to believe that God is present in the sacraments, and 58 percent say charitable efforts toward the poor are essential. On the other hand, only 31 percent say it is important to agree with the Church's view that abortion is morally wrong, and only 17 percent say it is important to believe that only men can be priests.

A 1999 survey also indicates that Catholics differentiate between what they consider core and peripheral elements of Catholic identity. For example, only 23 percent of Catholic laypeople believe one can be a good Catholic without believing that Jesus rose physically from the dead. Only 38 percent say one can be a good Catholic without believing that at Mass bread and wine actually become the Body and Blood of Christ. On the other hand, 67 percent say one can be a good Catholic without marrying in the Church, and 72 percent say one can be a good Catholic without agreeing with in the Church about birth control.

Have Catholics' views on these issues remained stable, or changed over time? There is stability in what laypeople consider the core elements of their faith, but a growing gap between Church teachings and the beliefs of the laity on other matters. For example, in 1987 only 39 percent of laypeople said one can be a good Catholic without obeying the Church's teaching about abortion. By 1999, 53 percent of Catholics felt that way.

As laypeople think about what it means to be Catholic, they distinguish between elements they consider more important (such as the Nicene Creed, sacraments, and some social teachings) and those which they consider less important (such as sexual and reproductive ethics). There is stability in what they consider to be the core of being Catholic, but important changes are taking place in the way they view other matters. These changes are producing a growing gap between official Church teachings and what laypeople think it takes to be a good Catholic. As Catholics enter the new millennium, we should celebrate our agreement on matters such as the Nicene Creed and social teachings. We also need to be charitable toward one another as we clarify what it means to be Catholic in areas where there is less agreement.

The Importance of Commitment to the Church

If Catholics are to pass the faith on to future generations, they cannot do it simply by nurturing Christian identity or a sense of personal spirituality. They also need to foster commitment to the Catholic Church.

Commitment has two interrelated components: self-concept and self-interest. Self-concept refers to a person's identification with the Church. It has to do with salience—the importance a person attaches to the Church. Self-interest has more to do with a person's stake in the Church. It indicates the extent to which people feel they get something out of being part of the Church.

You can tell the extent of people's identification with the Church by listening to them talk. Someone who says she cannot imagine being anything but Catholic has a strong Catholic identity. A man who says the Church is not an important part of his daily life is not as closely attached to the Church. Neither is a person who says she could be just as happy in some other religious group.

Words also indicate the extent to which people have a stake in the Church. People who say the Church has given them a strong moral foundation have some investment in the Church. So do people who say there is something special about being Catholic that one cannot find in other religions. Their stake in the Church is greater than that of people who say they get little or nothing out of attending Mass.

Self-concept and self-interest tend to go hand in hand. People who think the Church is an important part of their life also tend to get the most out of being part of it. Those who feel there are significant benefits to being Catholic also tend to identify with the Church.

Together, self-concept and self-interest increase Catholics' readiness to embrace Church teachings about faith and morals. Researchers have shown that the more people are committed to the Church the more likely they are to value the Church's core teachings about matters such as Incarnation, Resurrection, and Real Presence.[5] They also are more likely to attend Mass and receive holy Communion. They are more active in devotional practices such as the rosary and Bible study. Those who are highly committed also are most inclined to accept the Church's views on sexual and reproductive issues, such as premarital sex and abortion. They also tend to agree with the Church's social teachings related to peace and justice. They are not as likely to accept ideas that are inconsistent with Church teachings, such as the view that one can be a good Catholic without going to Mass on a regular basis.

These results have important implications for Catholic parents and Church leaders. For one thing, they point to the importance of building strong identification with the Church. Christian identity is necessary and good, but specifically Catholic identity also is important if future generations are to value the teachings of the Catholic Church. The data on commitment also indicate the value of explaining the benefits one can derive from being part of the Church. Rather than being shy about it, parents and parish leaders should boldly communicate the many ways people gain from being involved in the Church. The more they stress Catholic identity and the advantages of being Catholic, the more successful they will be in passing Catholic faith and morals on to future generations.

Religious Commitment and Public Policy: Is There a Connection?

One certainly would hope there is a connection between Catholics' religious commitment and their views on public-policy issues. But, is there any such connection?

One aspect of religious commitment is the extent of Catholics' identification with the Catholic faith. About 80 percent of Catholics say being a Catholic is a very important part of who they are. About two-thirds say they cannot imagine being anything but Catholic. Two out of three also say there is something special about being Catholic that one cannot find in other religions. Fifty to 60 percent say Catholicism contains a greater share of the truth than other religions.

Another dimension of commitment is Catholics' attachment to the institutional Church. Sixty to 70 percent say they would never leave the Church. Two-thirds are registered parishioners. Just over 40 percent say the Church is the most important part, or among the most important parts, of their lives, and a similar percent attend Mass at least once a week.

Now, let's turn to public policy. A majority of Catholics embrace the broad principles of the Church's social teachings and the Church's stance on many specific issues. For example, most Catholics say helping the needy is an important part of their religious beliefs. About three-quarters say economic decisions that increase poverty are immoral. Similar numbers of Catholics believe poverty results from social conditions such as the lack of jobs and low wages (only one in five blame it on the poor themselves). Catholics are more divided on other social issues. About half say one cannot be a good Catholic without donating time or money to help the poor. Half also believe that Catholics have a duty to try to close the gap between the rich and the poor. Catholics tend to disagree with the Church on capital punishment, with a majority favoring stiffer enforcement of the death penalty.

The Massachusetts Supreme Court's recent ruling in favor of gay marriage and the California Supreme Court's ruling that Catholic Charities must provide birth-control benefits for its employees indicate that sexual and reproductive issues are not just matters of personal morality. They also are matters of public policy. What are Catholics' views on these issues?

Catholics are sharply divided on homosexuality. About half of Catholics believe homosexual behavior is always immoral; the other half say it is completely up to the individual to decide. About one-third say abortion is always wrong, one-third say it is usually wrong but acceptable under certain circumstances, and one-third say it is strictly up to the individual. Only one-quarter say premarital sex is always wrong, and even fewer (about 10 percent) say artificial birth control is wrong.

Finally, there is a clear connection between religious commitment and agreement with Church teachings on public-policy matters. The more highly committed Catholics are, the more their views on both social issues and sexual-reproductive issues coincide with official Church teachings. Highly committed Catholics are about ten times as likely as those who are low in commitment to agree with Church teachings on sexual and reproductive issues. They are about twice as likely to accept the Church's social teachings as are Catholics who are low in commitment. Disagreement is greatest among people who tend not to identify with the faith and are least attached to the Church.

The good news for Church leaders is that the Church makes a difference in Catholics' lives. It affects the way laypeople think about matters of public policy. The bad news is that this connection is not as tight as many Church leaders would like it to be. If leaders want a closer alignment between church teachings and the views of the laity, they need to promote Catholic identity and attachment to the Church.

What Effect Does the Church Have on Civic Participation?

Does involvement in the Catholic Church stifle or contribute to other forms of civic involvement? Do parishioners withdraw from community life or become more active in their communities? Are highly committed Catholics any more involved in civic organizations than Catholics who are not as committed to the Church?

I explored these issues using data from my 1999 national survey of American Catholics.[6] In that survey, colleagues and I asked Catholics if they belong to any religious and/or civic organizations. Sixty-two percent said they belong to no such groups, 21 percent named one group, and 17 percent mentioned two or more groups.

Those who listed one or more groups were asked to describe these groups, which I put into two categories. The "religious/Catholic" category includes a wide variety of groups, such as the Knights of Columbus, Altar Society, Right to Life, Legion of Mary, and RENEW. The "other" category is made up of fraternal/sororal, sports/fitness, education/cultural, political/volunteer, business, and other groups.

I then compared the responses of registered parishioners with those of people who identify as Catholic but are not registered in a parish. I also compared people who scored high, medium, and low on a three-item index of religious commitment (measuring the importance people attach to the Church, their unwillingness to ever leave the Church, and their frequency of Mass attendance). Here's what I found.

Not surprisingly, parishioners and highly committed Catholics are much more likely to belong to religious/Catholic organizations. Fifteen percent of parishioners but only 1 percent of nonparishioners belong to a religious/Catholic organization. Thirty-one percent of highly committed Catholics belong to a religious/Catholic organization, compared to only 4 percent of people who score low in commitment.

What about Catholics' involvement in other civic organizations? Are parishioners and highly committed Catholics also more involved in these groups? Overall, the answer is "yes." Thirty-one percent of parishioners, compared to 25 percent of nonparishioners, and 30 percent of highly committed Catholics, compared to 27 percent of Catholics who are low in commitment are involved in other civic groups.

Parishioners and highly committed Catholics are considerably more involved in fraternal/sororal groups than are nonparishioners and less-committed Catholics. Nine percent of parishioners, compared to only 4 percent of nonparishioners belong to groups such as the Elks, the Women's Guild, singles' groups, and women's clubs. Eleven percent of highly committed Catholics belonged to such groups, compared to none of the less-committed Catholics.

Parishioners and highly committed Catholics are not much different from nonparishioners and less-committed Catholics in terms of education/cultural groups, political/volunteer groups, and business groups. Being a parishioner or highly committed to the Church does not foster these activities as much as it fosters membership in fraternal/sororal groups.

There is one area where parishioners and highly committed Catholics are noticeably *less* involved: sports/fitness groups. Nonparishioners and people who score low in religious commitment are more likely to belong to sports/fitness groups than are parishioners and highly committed Catholics.

These findings raise a number of questions that Church leaders might want to explore with laypeople. For example, what is it about being a parishioner and being committed to the Church that fosters participation in fraternal/sororal groups? Why are parishioners and less-committed Catholics less inclined to participate in sports/fitness groups? What more could the Church do to strengthen the connection between Church participation and other forms of civic engagement?

The Meaning of Your Work: Is It Job, Career, or Calling?

How do you think of your work? What does work mean to you? Let me give you three choices.

First, do you think of your work as a job? You are paid to perform a service. You probably have been paid to do other things at other times, and you are quite willing to do other types of work if the pay and job security are better.

Second, do you think of your work as a career? You chose a particular field, which you plan to pursue for most of your life. You might change where you work, but you are not likely to change the kind of work you do.

Or, third, do you think of your work as a calling? Your work has special meaning because you've been called by God to do what you are doing, regardless of how much time it takes or how little money you earn. You feel you have been put on this earth to do what you are doing.

Have you picked one? Having done so, other questions might naturally arise. Why do some people think of their work as a job, while others see it as a career, and still others believe it is a calling? Do family situations and working conditions affect the way people approach their work? Does religion have anything to do with it?

David Caddell and I uncovered some answers to these questions in a recent study of Protestants and Catholics who belonged to thirty-one affluent congregations.[7] While the members of these congregations had a full range of educational backgrounds, work situations, and family incomes, they were above the national average in terms of social and economic resources.

Half of these churchgoers thought of their work as a career, 29 percent said it was a job, and 15 percent thought of their work as a calling. The people who thought of the work as a job tended to have less education, tended to be in blue-collar occupations (often part time), worked with things more than people, had comparatively low-family incomes, and had relatively little job security. People who thought of their work as either a career or calling, on the other hand, had more education, were in full-time, white-collar occupations, worked with people more than things, had higher incomes, and had considerable job security. In other words, the more work-related benefits people enjoyed, the more likely they were to see their work as a career and not a job. Religious beliefs and practices had little or no effect.

However, when we compared people who thought of the work as a calling (not as a career or job), secular influences, such as educational background and job security, became inconsequential, though working with people continued to be important.

Several religion variables continued to have little or no effect. Belonging to a church with Calvinist theology (for example, Presbyterian, Baptist, United Methodist) did not inspire attitudes that were any different from ones found among people who belonged to other churches, including Catholic. Simply being exposed to homilies about the importance of expressing one's faith in good works also did not make much difference. Nor did interactions with pastors who stressed the goals of charity and justice.

However, several other religious influences became very important. The more important religion was to people, and the more religiously active they were, the more likely they were to think of their work as a calling. Also, the more they believed that building a just and equal world was an integral part of their personal faith, the more they thought of work as a calling.

In short, the key factor that separated people who saw their work as a calling was religious commitment—the tendency to think of religion as an important part of one's life, and to act accordingly, both in church and in the world. When a person takes faith seriously, it provides a framework within which one can think of work as having a sacred significance. When religion is internalized, people who are already inclined to think of their work as important often go one step further, seeing their work as a calling or ministry. Religious commitment provides a context in which some people, especially people with rewarding jobs, come to think of their work in sacred, not just secular, terms.

Questions for Reflection

1. How do you assess the *Catechism*'s claim that the Catholic Church possesses a greater share of truth over other religious traditions with respect to sanctification? What bearing does that view have on your perceptions of and respect for other faiths?

2. Do you find it useful to distinguish between Catholics' identification with the Catholic faith and their attachment to the Catholic Church? If so, in what way is this distinction useful? If not, explain why it is not helpful?

3. What do you make of data showing that a majority of Catholics still identify with the faith, but that there has been some overall decline in Catholic identity? To what extent should we be pleased by the persistence of Catholic identity, and how concerned should we be about its decline?

4. How do you explain the fact that the decline in Catholic identity has not been as pronounced as the decline in commitment to the Church? In your view, what accounts for the more precipitous decline in attachment to the Church?

5. Are you disturbed, or pleased, that Catholics distinguish between matters they consider essential or ones they consider nonessential? Is this a positive development, or one that Church leaders should be concerned about?

6. In what ways does your Catholic identity and/or your commitment to the Catholic Church affect your views of public-policy issues, your involvement in civic organizations, and your work?

7. Since commitment has important impacts on people's lives, what do you believe should be done to increase Catholics' commitment to the Church?

Chapter 9

Catholics' Beliefs and Practices

This chapter opens with a question: What do Catholics mean when they talk about "tradition"? It, then, examines trends related to a number of beliefs and practices within that tradition. Only about two-thirds of Americans who think of themselves as Catholic are registered parishioners. Although Catholics believe God is present in their lives, their participation in the sacraments has declined in recent years. This trend is documented in sections indicating lower rates of Mass attendance, less frequent confession, and an increased tendency to marry outside the Church. Other parts of the chapter show that the Church teachings that Catholics consider essential (and tend to agree with) are grounded in the Nicene Creed and the Church's social teachings. The ones they consider peripheral (and tend not to agree with) have to do with ecclesiastical norms and moral teachings related to sexuality and reproduction.

What Does "Tradition" Mean to You?

Tradition is important to Catholics. Listen to any group of Catholics as they talk about their faith, and it will not be long before you hear the word *tradition.*

It also will not take long to realize they have very different views of tradition. Some think fondly of tradition, while others think of it as largely antiquated ideas and rituals that no longer apply to our world. Some say tradition has to do with religious practices; others say it consists of Church teachings that must be passed on to future generations.

So what does the Catholic Tradition mean to you? As you reflect on this question, I invite you to consider the contributions of two scholars who have influenced my understanding of the Catholic Tradition.

Yale University historian Jaroslav Pelikan observes that "[t]radition is the living faith of the dead; traditionalism is the dead faith of the living."[1] Thus, according to Pelikan, tradition refers to aspects of our Catholic heritage that mean as much to us today as they did to our Catholic ancestors. It refers to beliefs and practices that made sense to our ancestors and continue to make sense to us today. There are ideas and behaviors that were the essence of our ancestors' faith and still express our profoundest needs and aspirations. There are aspects of the Catholic faith that our ancestors created and which continue to inspire us. These beliefs and practices are the living faith of the dead.

There are also beliefs and practices that meant a lot to our ancestors, but do not have as much meaning in today's world. There are parts of our Catholic heritage that were appropriate in historical times and circumstances, but do not seem as appropriate now. There are ways of thinking and acting that were very meaningful to our parents, grandparents, and earlier generations, but which no longer make as much sense to today's Catholics. There are things that our ancestors did with great care, but when we do them today, we simply go through the motions. These beliefs and practices are the dead faith of the living.

University of Dayton theologian Terrence Tilley says that Tradition is a way of life consisting of two components: *traditio* and *tradita*. *Traditio* has to do with "knowing how to live in and live out a tradition."[2] It refers to "the actual process or practice of handing on the tradition." It has to do with the interaction between "an agent handing something on" and "an agent or agents receiving what is being handed on." *Traditio* includes parents' efforts to raise their children in the faith, and the children's willingness to do what their parents ask them to do. It includes catechists' and youth ministers' attempts to pass the faith along to the next generation, and their students' willingness to learn. It includes the homilies at Mass, and the laity's response to what is said.

Tradita are the content of the tradition that is being handed on. They are "attitudes, doctrines, visions, skills, practices, virtues, etc." Examples include Church teachings about the Trinity; God's decision to become incarnate in the person of our Lord Jesus Christ; Mary's role as the Mother of God; Christ's death and resurrection; and the Lord's continued presence in the Eucharist. Other examples include the practices such as attending Mass, receiving holy Communion, and caring for one another. Still others include the Church's emphases on life and social justice.

Tilley argues that *traditio* and *tradita* are inseparable. Tradition is not just a matter of content, or just a matter of practice; it is both. The content (*tradita*) of the Catholic Tradition cannot be separated from the process of handing it on and receiving it (*traditio*). Catholic Tradition is not "reified 'things' that can be known apart from practice." It is the "doctrine or creedal beliefs…that Catholics learn *as they participate in the practices that constitute the tradition*" [my emphasis].

To the extent that the context of learning remains constant, the content of tradition does not change much. However, to the extent that circumstances vary from place to place or change from time to time, so do the expressions of Church teachings and the laity's understanding of them. The Catholic Tradition is practiced and understood differently in different parts of the world. Moreover, in Tilley's words, "as practices change, the significance of the concepts and beliefs they carry change." Thus, the content of the Catholic Tradition unfolds differently in relation to the variety of circumstances affecting the interaction between the people handing it on and the people receiving it.

A Profile of Parishioners and Nonparishioners

In the 1995 national study that became the basis of *The Search for Common Ground*, colleagues and I were among the first researchers to ask American Catholics whether they were registered members of a parish.[3] We found that 68 percent were registered parishioners; 31 percent were not. In the 1999 national study that is the foundation of *American Catholics: Gender, Generation, and Commitment*, colleagues and I explore this issue once again (partly to see if we could replicate our earlier finding).[4] Sure enough, we got essentially the same result. Sixty-seven percent of Catholics are registered parishioners; 33 percent are not.

In the 1995 study, we identified groups that were especially likely to be on parish rolls. These included women, whites, and Asians. They also included people who had the most religious parents, had parents who frequently talked with them about religion, were highly religious when they were children, had the most Catholic schooling, and had the most religious instruction when they were young. They also included married Catholics, people who had a Catholic spouse, and people whose social network included other religiously active Catholics. Finally, they included people who had more than a college education and high family incomes.

We also located groups that were overrepresented among the Catholics who were not registered. These included men, Hispanics, and African Americans. They also included people whose parents were not especially religious, did not enroll their children in Catholic schools or other forms of religious instruction, and did not encourage their children to be religious when they were young. They also included single people, along with divorced and separated Catholics, and people whose social circles did not include religiously active Catholics. They had a high-school education or less and modest- to low-family incomes.

Our 1999 survey does not permit direct comparisons on all of these factors, but produces a similar profile of parishioners and nonparishioners. Parishioners are more likely to be women, whites and Asians, older Catholics, married people, and highly educated and economically prosperous Catholics. Parishioners also are more likely to include people who have the most years of Catholic schooling, could not imagine leaving the Catholic Church, and attend Mass weekly or more.

TABLE 9.1 Nonregistered Parishioners	
All Catholics	***33%***
Say Church not important	68
Seldom attend Mass	63
Could leave Church	55
Hispanic	46
Young	44
Div/sep/widowed	41
1–6 years of Cath school	40
Men	39
High school or less	37
<$50,000 income	37

Nonparishioners are more likely to be men, Hispanics and African Americans, young adults, divorced, separated, widowed, or single (never married), less educated, and less prosperous. They also are more likely to be people with the fewest years of Catholic schooling, Catholics who say they could imagine circumstances under which they might leave the Church, and people who seldom or never attend Mass.

Together, these findings indicate that people with social advantages, personal religious commitment, and religiously active Catholic relationships tend to become parishioners. In light of their life circumstances, registering in a parish makes sense and is relatively easy to accomplish. On the other hand, people who are less fortunate socially, less attached to the Church, and less likely to interact with active Catholics are not as likely to join a parish. In relation to their upbringing and their current life circumstances, registering in a parish tends to be a low priority and a more difficult thing to do. Certainly there are some fortunate and active Catholics who do not belong to parishes, just as there are some less fortunate and less religious individuals who do belong. These, however, are exceptional cases.

These findings imply at least three main challenges for Church leaders. For one thing, leaders need to understand the social and religious conditions that make it difficult for some Catholics to join parishes. Leaders, especially parishioners who share nonparishioners' social attributes, ought to build relationships with nonparishioners and discern their social and spiritual needs. Finally, leaders need to create conditions in their parishes that would be welcoming to nonparishioners.

Three Keys to a Close Relationship With God

A majority of American Catholics have at least some meaningful relationship with God.[5] Seventy-seven percent say God has forgiven their sins at least several times during their lives. Seventy percent say God has taken care of them several times when they've really needed help. Sixty-four percent say God has answered their prayers at least several times over the course of their lives. Forty-two percent say they have sensed God's presence in a very special way on at least several occasions.

These data also suggest that some Catholics have a closer relationship with God than others do. Some feel God's presence in their lives more often than others do. The next question, quite naturally, is why. Why do some people feel closer to God than others? How is it that some Catholics feel God's presence more often than others? Which Catholics are most likely to experience God's love?

Our research suggests three keys to a close relationship with God. These keys are childhood religiosity, involvement in an adult social network that supports a close relationship with God, and an active prayer life.

1. The more religious Catholics are during childhood, the more likely they are to feel close to God during their adult years. The more religiously active people are as children, the more likely they are to feel God's presence in their adult lives. Catholics who develop a sense of being religious in their youth are likely to feel that God is part of their lives later on. Conversely, Catholics who are not religiously active and do not develop a religious self-concept in their early years are not as likely to feel close

to God later in life. Childhood religiosity, however, does not guarantee that a close personal relationship with God will last forever. Some Catholics who are religiously active as children are not especially close to God later in life. More than childhood religiosity is needed.

2. The more adults are embedded in social networks that include religiously active Catholics, the more likely they are to feel close to God. For example, Catholics who are married to Catholics feel closer to God than those who are married to people of other faiths or no faith. People who include a religiously active Catholic among the people they admire most also feel closer to God than people who lack such a referent. Finally, people who are registered parishioners feel closer to God than Catholics who have no parish. In other words, it helps to be in a social environment that supports experiences of God's love.

While childhood religiosity and a strong Catholic network set the stage for a close relationship with God, the individual also needs to have some sort of prayer life.

TABLE 9.2 Religious Practices (percent)

Weekly or more

Pray privately	77
Start/end day with prayer	65
Attend Mass	43
Practice devotions to Mary/saints	39
Receive holy Communion	36
Pray rosary	20
Read Bible	19

Monthly or more

Prayer group	16
Bible study	7

Yearly or more

Private confession	43
Group penance services	24

3. When we asked Catholics about their prayer lives, we found a real variation in the frequency of different forms of prayer. At least two-thirds of Catholics engage in some sort of private prayer at least once a week. About four in ten attend Mass weekly. A similar number practice devotions to Mary or other saints at least once a week. Just over one-third receive holy Communion weekly. About 20 percent pray the rosary or read the Bible. We also found a strong, positive relationship between participation in these practices and having a close relationship with God. An active prayer life cultivates and sustains a close personal relationship with God.

Developing a sense of personal religiosity early in life is an important step toward a lifelong relationship with God. Being in a social network that includes religiously active Catholics also increases the likelihood of experiencing God's love. Finally, an individual claims personal responsibility for his or her own relationship with God through an active prayer life.

Why Is Mass Attendance Declining?

It is a well-established fact that there has been a dramatic decline in Mass attendance in the last fifty years. In the 1950s, about 75 percent of Catholics attended Mass on a weekly basis. Since then the percentage of Catholics attending Mass each week has slipped to 66 percent in 1970, 53 percent in the mid-1980s, about 40 percent in the mid-1990s, and only 37 percent in 1999. The percentage of Catholics attending Mass each week is now about half of what it was fifty years ago.

How are we to explain this trend? Why has Mass attendance declined so precipitously? There are two leading hypotheses. One is that the decline is largely a function of societal conditions outside the Church. According to this perspective, the decline reflects the increased secularization of American society and/or the cultural revolution of the 1960s, when the culture shifted from an emphasis on compliance with institutional norms and values to an emphasis on personal freedom.

If this hypothesis were true, we might expect church attendance rates to decline for the society as a whole and in other religious groups as well as the Catholic Church. But, neither of these things has occurred.

There has been no major change in church attendance rates for the society as a whole since Gallup began polling on this issue back to the late 1930s. For example, in 1937 and 1939, 41 percent of Americans went to church weekly. In 1972, 40 percent attended weekly. In 1982, 41 percent went to church each week, and in 2001, the figure was still 41 percent.

Also, church attendance rates have not declined for Protestants. In the late 1950s and early 1960s, about 44 percent of Protestants attended church every week. By the mid-1960s, that figure had slipped to 37, 38, or 39 percent (depending on the year of the survey). With only minor fluctuations, it has remained quite stable ever since.

Over this same period, however, Mass attendance has continued to decline. As a result, I lean toward the alternative hypothesis that the decline has more to do with changing conditions in the Church itself. Rather than being the result of any one internal change, the decline is probably due to a combination of Church-related influences.

With the decline of the Catholic ghetto of the 1940s and 1950s, the structure of American Catholicism changed dramatically. Catholics are no longer segregated from the rest of society and no longer as dependent on the Church as they used to be. There also have been enormous cultural changes in American Catholicism. Catholics' image of the Creator as a judgmental God who would condemn people to hell if they missed Mass has given way to an image of God as much more willing to forgive people who do not make it to Mass every week. The fear and guilt that fostered very high rates of Mass attendance (and participation in other sacraments as well) has given way to an emphasis on taking personal responsibility for one's own faith and choosing to attend Mass as often as one can.

There also has been a marked decline in recognition of episcopal authority. Andrew Greeley traces this decline to Pope Paul VI's decision in 1968 to uphold the Church's ban on artificial means of birth control. I contend that it has numerous sources, including the rising levels of education among laypeople. Whatever its origins, the decline in recognition of episcopal authority preceded the recent sex scandal and almost certainly has continued in its wake. As a result, Church leaders are no longer able to command the high levels of religious practice that existed in the 1950s.

Protestants and other Americans have not experienced these changes, and their rates of church attendance have not declined. These changes are peculiar to American Catholicism and, I believe, go a long way toward explaining the decline in Mass attendance among Catholics.

The Latest Data on Participation in the Sacrament of Reconciliation

Reconciliation (also called confession or penance) is one of the Catholic Church's seven sacraments. Although its form has changed from time to time, the sacrament has two essential elements: "the acts of the man who undergoes conversion through the action of the Holy Spirit" and "God's action through the intervention of the Church" (CCC, 1448).

The *Catechism* (1457) also says "after having attained the age of discretion, each of the faithful is bound by an obligation faithfully to confess serious sins at least once a year." The *Catechism* (1458) adds, "Without being strictly necessary, confession of everyday faults (venial sins) is nevertheless strongly recommended by the Church."

In recent years, colleagues and I have had two opportunities to study Catholics' participation in the sacrament of reconciliation. The first was a 1995 national survey of 1,058 American Catholics.[6] The most recent was a 2003 survey of 1,119 U.S. Catholics, which sociologist Dean Hoge of Catholic University and I did for the University of Notre Dame.[7]

The two studies revealed essentially the same rates of participation. In 1995, 43 percent of Catholics went to confession at least once a year; 57 percent did not. In 2003, 46 percent said they go to confession once a year or more; 53 percent said they never or almost never do.

TABLE 9.3 Frequency of Confession (percent)

	Once a Month +	Several per Year	1–2 a Year	Never
1995 Study	8	11	24	57
2003 Study	9	10	27	53
In 2003, Confession:				
Is essential	15	17	33	35
May/not be essential	6	10	38	45
Is not essential	5	4	14	76

The 2003 study indicates that confession is linked to participation in other religious practices. Here are just two examples. Two-thirds of Catholics who go to Mass and receive holy Communion weekly also go to confession at least annually, compared to less than one-fifth of Catholics who seldom if ever go to Mass or Communion. Fifty-three percent of Catholics who pray regularly go to confession once or more each year, compared to only 20 percent of Catholics who seldom or never pray.

Confession also is tied to religious beliefs. Nearly two-thirds of Catholics who believe that Jesus is truly present in the Eucharist go to confession at least annually. Among those who question or disagree with the doctrine of the Real Presence, only one-fifth go to confession. Sixty-two percent of Catholics who believe abortion is always wrong go to confession at least once a year. Among those who say the decision to have an abortion is entirely up to the individual, only one-third go to confession.

An even more direct link has to do with Catholics' beliefs about the importance of confession (see table 9.3). In the 2003 study, only 38 percent of Catholics believe private confession to a priest is "essential to [their] vision of being Catholic." Twenty-four percent say it "may or may not be essential," and 35 percent think it is "not essential."

Responses to this question predict rates of participation. Among Catholics who say confession is essential, 65 percent go to confession at least once a year. Of those who say they are not sure of the sacrament's importance, 54 percent participate. Among Catholics who say confession is not essential, the figure is only 23 percent.

Interfaith Marriage Is Increasing

Research about the 1970s and 1980s points to two conclusions about Catholic marriages. While a majority of Catholics were still marrying Catholics, interfaith marriage was increasing. A national study, which I completed with colleagues William V. D'Antonio, Dean Hoge, and Katherine Meyer in 1999 shows that the trend toward interfaith marriage continues (see table 9.4).[8]

Seventy-one percent of married Catholics are involved in *intrafaith* marriages (that is, they have Catholic spouses). Twenty-nine percent are involved in *interfaith* marriages (they have spouses who belong to other faiths or have no particular faith).

There are two types of intrafaith marriages. Fifty-six percent of married Catholics are in *purely intrafaith* marriages, where someone who was born and raised Catholic (or was a child convert) married another cradle Catholic (or child convert). Fifteen percent are in *currently intrafaith* marriages, meaning a cradle Catholic married a non-Catholic who converted to Catholicism later in life.

There also are two types of interfaith marriages. Twenty-seven percent of married Catholics are in *purely interfaith* marriages, meaning a cradle Catholic married a person who was not raised Catholic. Two percent are in *currently interfaith* marriages, where an adult convert is married to a non-Catholic.

We also examined the marriage patterns of three Catholic generations. The pre-Vatican II generation was born in or before 1940. At the time of our study, its members were fifty-nine years of age or older. The Vatican II generation was born between 1941 and 1960. When we did our study, these baby-boomers were between thirty-nine and fifty-eight years of age. The post-Vatican II generation was born between 1961 and 1981. These so-called Generation Xers were eighteen to thirty-eight years of age when we interviewed them in 1999.

Seventy-six percent of pre-Vatican II Catholics are married to Catholics. While a majority of post-Vatican II Catholics are married to Catholics, the percentage in intrafaith marriages declines to 60 among young adults. While only 24 percent of Catholics in pre-Vatican II generation are in interfaith marriages, 40 percent of post-Vatican II Catholics are.

TABLE 9.4 Catholic Marriage Trends (percent)

	Total	Pre-Vatican II	Vatican II	Post-Vatican II
Intrafaith marriages	71	76	73	60
Purely intrafaith	56	57	58	50
Currently intrafaith	15	19	15	10
Interfaith marriages	29	24	27	40
Purely interfaith	27	21	25	36
Currently interfaith	2	3	2	4

Further analysis indicates that the percentages of Catholics in both purely intrafaith and currently intrafaith marriages are declining. While 57 percent of pre-Vatican II Catholics and 58 percent of Vatican II Catholics are in purely intrafaith marriages, only half of post-Vatican II Catholics are in purely intrafaith marriages. While 19 percent of pre-Vatican II Catholics are in currently intrafaith marriages, that percentage drops to 15 in the Vatican II generation and only 10 percent in the post-Vatican II generation.

Whereas 21 percent of pre-Vatican II Catholics are in purely interfaith marriages, 25 percent of Vatican II Catholics and as many as 36 percent of post-Vatican II Catholics are. The figures for Catholics in currently interfaith marriages are small and do not indicate any clear trend.

These findings indicate that the marriage patterns reported in earlier research continue into the present. A majority of Catholics, including post-Vatican II Catholics, still marry Catholics. However, the percentage of Catholics marrying non-Catholics continues to increase.

Since 93 percent of pre-Vatican II Catholics and 90 percent of Vatican II Catholics are already married, the percentages for these two generations are not likely to change. However, only 51 percent of post-Vatican II Catholics are married, so the percentage of young adults in each type of marriage is subject to change. As more and more post-Vatican II Catholics marry, we expect the percentage involved in interfaith marriages will continue to increase. We will keep our eyes on that in future research.

The Effect of Group Size on Interfaith Marriage Rates

Sociologist Peter Blau has shown that group size affects the relationships between groups.[9] In relationships between a large group and a small one, members of the small group have frequent contacts with members of the large group, while members of the large group have relatively few contacts with members of the small group.

Consider the relationship between racial and ethnic groups. If whites comprise 80 percent of the population in a given area and African Americans are only 20 percent, African Americans will have more contact with whites than whites will have with African Americans. Conversely, when African Americans make up 80 percent of the population and only 20 percent of the population is white, whites will interact with African Americans more often than African Americans will interact with whites.

The same principle applies to relationships between religious groups. In areas where Catholics are the majority and Protestants are the minority, Protestants will have lots of contact with Catholics, but Catholics will not have as much contact with Protestants. When Protestants are the majority and Catholics the minority, Catholics will interact with Protestants more than Protestants will with Catholics.

The effect of group size has important implications for the chances that Catholics in any given diocese will marry Catholics or people who are not Catholic. Catholics are most likely to marry Catholics in dioceses where Catholics are a majority of the population. They are most likely to marry non-Catholics in dioceses where Catholics are only a small percentage of the total population.

Priest-sociologist Father John Thomas first documented this fact in the 1940s and 1950s.[10] Thomas reported that in dioceses such as Raleigh (NC), Charleston (SC), Savannah-Atlanta (GA), Nashville (TN), and Little Rock (AR)—where Catholics were less than 2 percent of the population—over three-quarters of all marriages recognized by the Church involved a Catholic marrying a non-Catholic. On the other hand, Thomas reported, in dioceses such as El Paso (TX), Corpus Christi (TX), Lafayette (LA), Providence (RI), and Santa Fe (NM)—where Catholics were in the majority—intermarriages accounted for less than 10 percent of all the marriages sanctioned by the Church.

In an analysis of interfaith marriage rates since the 1940s and 1950s, Tracy Widman and I have shown that the effect of group size on interfaith marriage rates holds up over time.[11] The very strong connection Thomas found between group size and intermarriage in 1945 and 1955 also occurs in 1960, 1965, 1970, 1975, 1980, 1985, 1990, and 1995. Thus, the impact of group size is not limited to pre-Vatican II Catholicism. It persists to this day.

It also holds up when regional influences are taken into account. Living in a diocese with a small percentage of Catholics increases the chances of marrying a non-Catholic, whether the diocese is in the north, south, east, or west. Intermarriage rates are lower in dioceses with the largest Catholic populations, regardless of the region in which the dioceses are located.

For the first time, Widman and I also have been able to demonstrate that changes in the size of the Catholic population produce changes in intermarriage rates over time.

We identified three dioceses whose geographic boundaries had remained the same between 1960 and 1995 and where the size of the Catholic population had increased by 10 percentage points or more. These included the Archdiocese of New York and the Dioceses of Rockville Centre (NY) and

Reno (NV). As we expected, the interfaith marriage rate decreased in two of these three locations: Reno, where it declined by 16 percentage points, and Rockville Centre, where it dropped by eight points. The exception was the Archdiocese of New York, where it remained unchanged.

We also located five dioceses whose geographic boundaries had remained stable and where the Catholic population had declined by 10 percentage points or more. These dioceses were Helena (MT), Marquette (MI), St. Louis (MO), Honolulu (HA), and Springfield (MA). Again, as expected, the intermarriage rate went up in four of the five dioceses, with an average increase of 6 percentage points. The only exception was Honolulu, where it declined by less than 1 percentage point.

Group size certainly is not the only factor affecting intermarriage rates, but it probably is the most important influence. Thus, Church leaders in dioceses where Catholics are only a small percentage of the total population should not blame themselves when they find that large numbers of Catholics are entering into interfaith marriages. Under such sociological circumstances, high intermarriage rates are very predictable.

Catholics Increasingly Marrying Outside the Church

My 1999 national survey of American Catholics showed that 71 percent of married Catholics were married in the Church; 29 percent were not.[12]

Which Catholics are most likely to marry with the Church's blessing? Which are most likely to marry outside the Church?

To answer these questions, I distinguished between four types of Catholics. One group consists of Catholics who were born and raised in the Church and married a person who also was born and raised Catholic. Fifty-six percent of married Catholics are involved in these "purely intrafaith" marriages. Another group consists of cradle Catholics who married a person who was not Catholic at the time of the wedding but has converted to Catholicism. Fifteen percent of Catholics are involved in these "currently intrafaith" marriages. A third category consists of cradle Catholics who married a person who was not Catholic at the time of the wedding and still is not Catholic. Twenty-seven percent of married Catholics are in these "purely interfaith" marriages. The final group consists of people who were raised in another faith but converted to Catholicism and are married to a non-Catholic. Only 2 percent of Catholics are involved in these "currently interfaith" marriages.

Catholics in intrafaith marriages tend to marry in the Church, while those in interfaith marriages are more likely to marry outside the Church. Eighty-four percent of Catholics involved in purely intrafaith marriages and 78 percent of people in currently intrafaith marriages were married in the Church. Forty-three percent of Catholics in purely interfaith marriages and only 25 percent of those who are in currently interfaith marriages were married in the Church.

Are Catholics marrying in the Church at the same rate that they used to, or is there a trend toward marrying outside the Church?

To address these questions, I distinguished between three generations of American Catholics: pre-Vatican II Catholics (who were born in 1940 or before), Vatican II Catholics (born between 1941 and 1960), and post-Vatican II Catholics (born since 1961).

TABLE 9.5 Percent Married Outside the Church

	Generation		
	Pre-Vatican II	**Vatican II**	**Post-Vatican II**
In purely intrafaith marriages	5	15	27
In currently intrafaith marriages	11	21	40
In purely interfaith marriages	47	57	59

The marriage patterns of the three generations indicate a trend toward marrying outside the Church (see table 9.5). Only 5 percent of pre-Vatican II Catholics in purely intrafaith marriages were married outside the Church, compared to 15 percent of Vatican II Catholics, and 27 percent of post-Vatican II Catholics. The percentage of Catholics in currently intrafaith marriages who married outside the Church rises from 11 percent among pre-Vatican II Catholics to 21 percent among Vatican II Catholics, and 40 percent among post-Vatican II Catholics. Forty-seven percent of pre-Vatican II Catholics in purely interfaith marriages were married outside the Church, compared to 57 percent of Vatican II Catholics, and 59 percent of post-Vatican II Catholics. The number of Catholics in currently interfaith marriages is too small to calculate generational differences.

These results pose some serious challenges. We should be concerned that Catholics involved in both intrafaith and interfaith marriages increasingly are marrying outside the Church. If Church leaders have not done so already, they might look to see if this trend is occurring in their parishes and dioceses, investigate the reasons behind it, and consider ways to respond to it.

Laity Distinguishing Between Core and Periphery

Since Vatican II (1962–65), Catholics have lived through a period of rapid change. Many traditional Church teachings have remained largely unchanged, but some have changed quite dramatically. Many new ideas have been authorized by the Church; others have emerged that are not consistent with official Church teachings.

As Catholics try to make sense of this vast array of beliefs and practices, they are assigning more importance to some than others. They are deciding that some matters are central to the faith. They have differing opinions about other beliefs and practices. They also are deciding that some teachings are not essential to being a good Catholic. In short, they are differentiating between what they think is at the core of the Catholic faith and what they think is on the periphery.

Three studies indicate that Catholics attach the greatest importance to teachings that are grounded in the Nicene Creed and Church's social teachings.[13] These teachings include doctrines such as Incarnation, Resurrection, Mary as the Mother of God, Trinity, Christ's Real Presence in the Eucharist, and the need to love one's neighbor, especially the poor. All three studies indicate that over three-quarters of Catholics believe these are core Church teachings. These beliefs are at the top of Catholics' hierarchy of truth.

There is another set of beliefs and practices that some Catholics consider important but others do not. This cluster includes the Church's opposition to abortion, the need for a pope, the need to donate time or money to help the parish, belief that Christ established the authority of the bishops by choosing Peter, devotions to the saints, and the need to marry in the Church. For every person who attaches importance to each of these ideas, there is another one who does not.

Toward the bottom of the laity's hierarchy of truth is another set of beliefs and practices that a majority of laypeople considers optional. This list includes the obligation to attend Mass weekly, private confession with a priest, the need to agree with the Church's opposition to the death penalty, celibacy among priests, belief that only men can be priests, and the need to support unions.

Whether we like the fact that laypeople are distinguishing between the core and the periphery, and whether we agree with what they consider core and peripheral, it is important to recognize that they are engaged in this process. It is a fact of life in today's Church.

What Catholics Say About the Importance of the Eucharist

I showed above that the percentage of Catholics attending Mass weekly has fallen from about 75 percent in the 1950s to 43 percent in 1995 (see page 151). I also showed that the percentage of Catholics receiving holy Communion weekly has fallen from about 40 percent to 36 percent. Consequently, the weekly Communion rate has actually risen from only 55 percent of the Mass attendance rate in the 1950s to 84 percent of the Mass attendance rate in the 1990s.

While only 43 percent of Catholics now attend Mass weekly, and only 36 percent receive Communion on a weekly basis, a majority still attach a great deal of importance to the belief that the bread and wine actually become the Body and Blood of Christ. Though Catholics do not attend Mass or receive Communion as often as they might, they still say that belief in the Real Presence is more important to them personally than many other religious beliefs and practices.

In a 1995 national survey, colleagues and I asked American Catholics about the importance they attach to a variety of "pan-Vatican II beliefs" which, according to official Church teachings, were important before the Council and remain important after the Council.[14] One of these beliefs concerns the idea that at Mass "the bread and wine actually become the Body and Blood of Christ." Sixty-three percent of Catholics said this belief is "very important" to them personally. Another 14 percent said this belief is "fairly important." Nine percent said "somewhat important." Twelve percent said it is "not very important." In short, the vast majority of Catholics believe that the Real Presence is an important part of their personal faith.

In 1997, a group of young-adult Catholics (20–39) were asked what they considered "essential to the faith."[15] Two of the three items young adults rated most highly were "belief that God is present in the sacraments," and "belief that Christ is really present in the Eucharist." Eighty percent of young adults who attend Mass regularly, and 65 percent of all young Catholics, said that "belief that God is present in the sacraments" is essential. Seventy-four percent of young weekly Mass attenders, and 58 percent of all young adults, said that "belief that Christ is really present in the Eucharist" is an essential part of their faith.

In 1999, William D'Antonio, Dean Hoge, Katherine Meyer and I did a national study of American Catholics.[16] Eighty percent of our respondents said "sacraments such as Eucharist and marriage" are "very important." Another 16 percent said "somewhat important." Only four percent said "not important at all." When we asked Catholics what it takes to be a good Catholic, 60 percent said one cannot be a good Catholic "without believing that in the Mass, the bread and wine actually become the Body and Blood of Jesus."

These studies also indicate that Catholics attach more importance to the Eucharist than they do to many other beliefs and practices. While 60 percent of Catholics say a person cannot be a good Catholic without believing in the Real Presence, only 32 percent say that obeying the Church's teaching on divorce and remarriage is required. Only 31 percent say one cannot be a good Catholic without one's marriage being approved by the Church. Only 25 percent say it is necessary to obey the Church's teaching on artificial birth control. And, only 22 percent say one needs to attend Mass every Sunday.

It would be wonderful if more Catholics attached importance to the Real Presence, and if there were a closer link between the importance they assign to the Real Presence and their views about the importance of attending Mass. There certainly is room for improvement in both areas. However, we also should be impressed by the fact that the vast majority of American Catholics—including young adults—put belief in the Real Presence at the very center of their personal faith. Catholic laypeople have their own hierarchy of truths, and believing that the bread and wine are transformed into the Body and Blood of Christ is right up there at the top.

What Catholics Believe About the Real Presence

Earlier, I reported that, even though today's Catholics do not attend Mass and receive Communion as often as they might, most believe the Eucharist is an important component of their personal faith. Now, I show that most Catholics also agree with the Church's teaching that in Mass, the bread and wine actually become the Body and Blood of Christ.

In 1994, colleagues and I did a statewide survey of Catholic parishioners in Indiana.[17] In a series of questions about their religious beliefs and practices, we asked Indiana Catholics whether they agreed with the statement: "In Mass, the bread and wine actually become the Body and Blood of Christ." Eighty-seven percent agreed. Seven percent were uncertain. Only 6 percent disagreed. In 1997, Dean Hoge, William Dinges, Mary Johnson, and Juan Gonzales used the same item in their national survey of American Catholics.[18] This time, over 80 percent of Catholics agreed. They found no significant differences between age groups. Also in 1997, the Roper polling company found that 82 percent of Catholics believe that the "bread and wine used in Mass are actually transformed into the Body and Blood of Jesus Christ."[19] All three studies point to the same conclusion: the vast majority of Catholics believe that Christ is really present in the Eucharist.

One well-known study suggests otherwise. In the *New York Times*, Peter Steinfels summarized a national survey, in which American Catholics were asked whether the bread and wine are "changed into the Body and Blood of Christ" or are "symbolic reminders of Christ."[20] Steinfels reports that "almost two-thirds of American Catholics believe that during Mass, the central sacred ritual of Catholicism, the bread and wine can best be understood as 'symbolic reminders of Christ' rather than as actually being changed into Christ's Body and Blood." He also says, "Even among the subgroups of Catholics who said they attended Mass every week or almost every week, 51 percent described the rite as strictly symbolic." As further evidence of a "hollowing out" of belief in this vital area, he shows that younger Catholics are most inclined toward a symbolic view of the Eucharist.

What are we to make of the apparent conflict between Steinfels' findings and the results of the other three studies I have summarized? I believe the other three studies accurately portray what Catholics believe about the Real Presence. They describe the Real Presence in language that laypeople understand, and they yield consistent results. Steinfels' analysis is more problematic. He frames the issue of Real Presence as a choice between the bread and wine becoming the Body and Blood of Christ *or* being purely symbolic. This "either-or" formulation overlooks a third possibility: that the bread and wine are symbols of Christ *and* become the Body and Blood of Christ. This "both-and" approach is deeply rooted in Catholic theology (Saint Thomas Aquinas said that "we do not understand that Christ is there only as in a sign, although a sacrament is a kind of sign"). It also is found in songs Catholics sing during Mass ("In the song *We Remember*, Catholics sing, "We bring the bread and wine to share a meal. A sign of grace and mercy, the presence of the Lord."). If Steinfels had offered his respondents a category reflecting this "both-and" point of view, I think most would have chosen it. It would have given them a chance to say what I think they really believe: that the bread and wine are symbolic reminders of Christ, *and* they are transformed into the Body and Blood of Christ. If I am right, their response would be consistent with Church teachings and the other studies I have cited.

Clearly, we need more research before we know for sure what Catholics believe about the Real Presence. Researchers should interview Catholics, asking them to interpret the Real Presence in their own words. We also should design a variety of survey questions that capture a Catholic understanding of Real Presence and allow respondents to express what they really believe. In the meantime, we should assume that the vast majority of American Catholics—including young adults—agree with the Church's teaching that the bread and wine actually become the Body and Blood of Christ in both substance and symbol.[21]

Catholics Generally Agree on Church's Social Teachings

The Catholic Church has a long tradition of caring about the poor. Old Testament prophets Isaiah, Micah, Jeremiah, and Amos condemned the social and economic injustices of their time, especially the exploitation of the poor. The New Testament tells us of Jesus' special concern for the poor. The search for justice and concern for the poor are expressed over and over again in papal encyclicals such as *Rerum Novarum* (1891), *Quadragesimo Anno* (1931), and *Pacem in Terris* (1963). These "social teachings" also are found in pastoral letters, such as the American bishops' 1986 pastoral letter *Economic Justice for All*.[22] Key figures in Catholic history, including Saint Francis of Assisi, Dorothy Day, and Mother Teresa symbolize the Church's "preferential option" for the poor. The Church's commitment to justice and its concern for the poor also are evident in the self-help programs funded by the Catholic Campaign for Human Development.

To what extent do American Catholics agree with these social teachings? Do laypeople share the Church's view that Catholics are to help the needy and close the gap between the rich and the poor? Do they agree with the idea that the Church should address economic and political conditions that harm the poor? Do Catholics agree with the Church's view that poverty is rooted in structural conditions over which the poor have little or no control, or do they think that poverty results mainly from the attitudes and actions of the poor themselves?

Several colleagues and I have examined these issues in three national studies of American Catholics. The results indicate that, while most Catholics have not read the papal encyclicals or the bishops' 1986 pastoral letter on economic justice, a majority believe that Catholics should be concerned about the poor and should do their best to build a more just and equal world. At the same time, they are not convinced that the institutional Church should be involved in economic and political issues.

Here are the results from five items in our 1995 national study.[23] I start with the items where there is most agreement with Church teachings, and end with the one where there is least agreement.

The vast majority of Catholics say that helping the needy is an important part of their personal religious beliefs. Seventy-six percent strongly agree with this idea, 20 percent agree somewhat, and only 3 percent disagree. A second item asks Catholics which of the following comes closer to explaining why there is poverty in the U.S.: poor people's own behavior, such as not managing their money well and lack of effort on their part, or social conditions, such as lack of jobs and low wages? Seventy-one percent of laypeople say social conditions, thereby expressing agreement with Church teachings. Twenty-one percent express the dissenting view that poverty is mainly the result of poor people's own behavior.

There also is considerable agreement with the American bishops' claim that economic decisions increasing poverty are morally wrong. Fifty percent of laypeople strongly agree, 26 percent agree somewhat, 18 percent disagree, and 6 percent are unsure. A majority of laypeople also agree that Catholics have a duty to try to close the gap between the rich and the poor, though there is more variation on this issue. Thirty percent strongly agree, 24 percent agree somewhat, 19 percent disagree somewhat, 21 percent disagree, and 7 percent are unsure.

The fifth item ("The Church should stick to religion and not be involved in economic or political issues.") expresses a view that is contrary to Church teachings. Sixty-two percent of Catholics agree with this statement, thereby disagreeing with Church teaching. Thirty-two percent of Catholics disagree with this statement, indicating agreement with Church teaching. Five percent of Catholics are unsure.

Catholics are not fully informed about the Church's social teachings and question some specific social teachings, especially the Church's role in economic and political issues. Yet, they understand that being Catholic includes a special concern for the poor and a desire for social justice.

Catholics' Views on Abortion: Pro-Life or Pro-Choice?

Let me ask you about your views on abortion. I offer you four choices, and you must choose one. First, abortion should never be permitted. Second, abortion should only be permitted in cases of rape, incest, or danger to the mother's life. Third, abortion should be permitted for reasons other than rape, incest or danger to the mother's life. Fourth, abortion is a matter of the woman's personal choice.

Now, how do you think your response compares with the views of American Catholics in general? Also, how do you think the views of American Catholics compare with those of Protestants, Jews, and people with no religious preference? Are Catholics more pro-life, or more pro-choice, than other Americans?

Some answers to these questions are found in the 2003 edition of political scientist Kenneth Wald's popular text *Religion and Politics in the United States*.[24] In chapter 6, "The Religious Dimension of American Political Behavior," Wald examines the way a national sample of Americans responded to questions about their religious affiliation and their views on a variety of issues, including abortion.

In terms of religious affiliation, Wald divides the sample into six categories: Roman Catholics, Jews, African American Protestants, evangelical Protestants, mainline Protestants and "seculars." The first three categories are pretty self-explanatory. The evangelical Protestant category includes white Protestants who belong to fundamentalist, pentecostal, or holiness groups, such as Assemblies of God, Church of Christ, and Southern Baptist Convention. Mainline Protestants are whites who belong to theologically moderate to liberal denominations, such as Episcopalians, Presbyterians, and United Methodists. The secular group includes "people who neither adopt a religious label nor have any involvement with a recognizable religion." With regard to views on abortion, the sample was asked to select from the very same views I offered you in the first paragraph.

Nine percent of Catholics believe abortion should never be permitted, and 35 percent believe it only should be allowed in cases of rape, incest, and danger to the mother's life. Sixteen percent believe it also ought to be permitted for other reasons, and 40 percent say the decision of whether or not to have an abortion is a woman's personal choice.

TABLE 9.6 Abortion Attitudes by Religious Tradition

Abortion should	Evan Prot	Af-Am Prot	Roman Cath	Main Prot	Secular	Jewish
Never be permitted	22%	22%	9%	9%	6%	3%
Be permitted in cases of rape, incest, or danger to mother's life	38	34	35	28	19	6
Be permitted for reasons other than rape, incest, or danger to mother's life	16	10	16	17	15	18
Be a matter of the woman's personal choice	24	35	40	45	61	74

Comparing the six religious traditions, Wald writes that "the groups divide into three distinct clusters on the abortion issue. A majority of white evangelical and African American Protestants favor what is often known as the 'pro-life' position. They believe abortions should not be permitted under any circumstances or only in cases when the pregnancy is involuntary, incestuous, or threatens the life of the mother. At the other extreme, there is overwhelming support for discretionary abortion among Jews and secular

Americans. That leaves Roman Catholics and mainline Protestants in the middle. In these groups, pluralities favor abortion at the discretion of the mother but almost the same percentage of adherents affirm a much more restricted policy toward abortion. Unlike white evangelicals, African American Protestants, Jews, and seculars, who clearly fall into either the pro-life or pro-choice camp, the two centrist religious traditions are divided internally."

Thus, Catholics are not as pro-life as evangelical Protestants and African American Protestants, and they are not as pro-choice as Jews and people with no religious attachment. There also are important differences among the people in each religious tradition, especially among mainline Protestants and Catholics. Leaders in these two traditions face special pastoral and catechetical challenges as they work with laypeople who hold very different views on this controversial moral issue.

Questions for Reflection

1. In what ways is Catholic Tradition unchanging, and in what ways is to subject to change?

2. What, if anything, can be done to increase the percentage of Catholics who are registered members of a parish?

3. Catholics who were religious as children, have close ties with religiously active Catholics, and participate in spiritual practices are likely to have a close personal relationship with God. What implications do these findings have for you personally, members of your family, and your parish?

4. How do you explain the decline in Mass attendance and participation in other sacraments? In light of that explanation, what, if anything, should be done about this trend?

5. Can anything be done in areas with small Catholic populations to increase Catholics' chances of marrying other Catholics? If so, what is that?

6. Is it, or is it not, your experience that a majority of today's Catholics believe in Christ's Real Presence in the Eucharist? Explain your answer.

7. How do you explain the fact that significant numbers of Catholics disagree with the Church's teachings on abortion? What implications does your explanation have for the Church?

Chapter 10

Generations and Other Influences

Earlier generations of Catholic parents and religious educators taught young people to obey and emphasized the importance of the Catholic Church. More recent generations of parents and catechists stress the importance of thinking for one's self and being good Christians. As a result, there are important differences in the beliefs and practices of pre-Vatican II, Vatican II, post-Vatican II, and millennial Catholics (with older Catholics being more loyal and committed to the Church than younger Catholics). Research also documents differences within each generation, with some members of each generation tending toward a Culture-I approach to faith and others tending toward a Culture-II approach. Although there are some reports of increased orthodoxy among young adults, at least to date, there is no evidence of this trend in national surveys. There also are some noteworthy differences between Anglos and Hispanics, converts and cradle Catholics, and men and women (especially young men and young women). In general, the differences between racial, ethnic, religious, and gender groups are smaller than generational differences.

Catholic Parents Are Teaching Children to Think for Themselves

Have you ever wondered why today's young Catholics feel it is all right to disagree with the Church on issues of faith and morals? Have you ever wondered why they think it is OK to make up their own minds, even when their ideas are at odds with Church teachings?

One answer is that they are simply doing what their parents have taught them to do. According to two studies by University of Michigan sociologist Duane Alwin, Catholic parents are placing less and less emphasis on obedience and more and more emphasis on thinking for one's self.[1]

One study examined answers Protestant and Catholic parents in Detroit

170

gave to the following question: "If you had to choose, which thing on this list would you pick as the most important for a child to learn to prepare him for life?" The possible responses were "to obey, to be well-liked or popular, to think for himself, to work hard, and to help others when they need help." Alwin examined the answers Protestant and Catholic parents gave to this question in 1958, 1971, and 1983.

The results indicated a convergence of Protestant and Catholic parents on this issue. Protestant parents put more emphasis on thinking for oneself than on obedience in all three years. In 1958, Catholic parents put more emphasis on obedience than on thinking for oneself. However, between 1958 and 1983, there was a steady decline in Catholic parents' emphasis on obedience and a corresponding increase in their emphasis on thinking for oneself. Alwin also found that parents' education was the most important influence on their child-rearing values, with highly educated parents emphasizing thinking for oneself and less educated parents emphasizing obedience. Alwin also reported that some of this trend results from "the gradual assimilation of Catholic ethnic groups into American society."

The other study involved seven national samples of Protestant and Catholic parents between 1973 and 1984. This time, Alwin examined responses to the following question: "The qualities listed on this card may all be important, but which three would you say are the most desirable for a child to have?" He grouped three responses ("responsible," "good sense and sound judgment," and "interested in how and why things happen") into a category called "autonomy." He group three other responses ("obey," "good manners," and "neat and clean") into a category called "conformity."

Alwin found that in "every year surveyed since 1973, Catholics and white Protestants are virtually indistinguishable," with both groups putting more emphasis on autonomy than on conformity. He also found that the frequency of parents' religious participation was a stronger influence on their answers than their religious affiliation, with religiously active parents giving higher priority to conformity and less active parents giving higher priority to autonomy.

Together these studies point to convergence in the child-rearing values of Protestant and Catholic parents. Although the values of Protestant parents have remained quite stable over the years, there has been a marked shift away from obedience and toward autonomy among Catholic parents. This shift seems to be tied to higher levels of education, increased social integration, and declining levels of religious participation among Catholic parents.

Thus, older Catholics should not condemn today's young Catholics for making up their own minds on issues of faith and morals. They are simply doing what their parents have taught them to do.

The Religious Education of Baby Boomers and Generation-X Catholics

Baby boomers (or Vatican II Catholics, as I prefer to call them) were born between 1941 and 1960. Gen-Xers (or post-Vatican II Catholics) were born between 1961 and 1982. In a national survey, members of these two generations were asked about their religion teachers and what they learned from them.[2] Their responses point to six important differences in religious education of Vatican II and post-Vatican II Catholics.

TABLE 10.1 Religious Education by Generation (percent)

	Vatican II Catholics	Post-Vatican II Catholics
1. Had either an equal mix of laity and priests/nuns, or mostly lay teachers	39	76
2. Taught that being a good Christian is more important than the denomination one belongs to (vs. Catholic Church is the one true Church)	29	59
3. Taught the importance of one's personal relationship with God (vs. importance of the Church)	43	57
4. Taught importance of being a good Christian (vs. knowing Church teachings)	35	49
5. Taught that morality of our actions depends on circumstances (vs. action always right or wrong)	26	42
6. Taught to think for themselves (vs. obey Church teachings)	13	23

1. *Post-Vatican II Catholics are more likely to have had lay teachers.* Sixty-one percent of Vatican II Catholics say most of their religion instructors were priests or nuns. Thirty percent say they had an equal mix of priests and sisters on the one hand and laypeople on the other. Only 9 percent say they had mostly laypeople. The pattern for post-Vatican II Catholics is very different. Half say they had an equal mix of lay teachers and priests or sisters. Twenty-six percent say they had mostly lay teachers. Only 24 percent say they had mostly priests and sisters.

2. *Post-Vatican II Catholics are more likely to have been taught that being a good Christian is more important than the denomination to which one belongs.* Fifty-eight percent of Vatican II Catholics say they were taught that the Catholic Church is the one, true Church. Only 29 percent say they were taught that being a good Christian is more important than the religion to which one belongs. The pattern is reversed for post-Vatican II Catholics. Fifty-nine percent of the post-Vatican II generation say they were taught that being a good Christian is most important. Only a third say they were taught that the Catholic Church is the one, true Church.

3. *Post-Vatican II Catholics are more likely to have been taught the importance of their personal relationship with God.* A third question asks whether the generations were taught the importance of their personal relationship with God or the importance of the Church. The Vatican II generation is divided, with 45 percent saying they were taught the importance of the Church and 43 percent saying the importance of their relationship with God. Post-Vatican II Catholics, on the other hand, are twice as likely to say the importance of their relationship with God as the importance of the Church.

4. *Post-Vatican II Catholics are more likely to have been taught the importance of being a good Christian.* The next question asks if Catholics were taught the importance of being a good Christian or the importance of knowing what the Catholic Church teaches. Fifty-five percent of Vatican II Catholics say they were taught the importance of knowing what the Church teaches. Only a third say they were taught the importance of being a good Christian. The pattern is reversed among post-Vatican II Catholics. Half say they were taught the importance of being a good Christian. Only 40 percent say they were taught the importance of knowing what the Church teaches.

5. *Post-Vatican II Catholics are more likely to have been taught that the morality of our actions depends on the circumstances.* The fifth question examines two different approaches to morality. One option is that our

actions are intrinsically right or wrong (the natural-law approach). The other is that the morality of our actions depends on the situation (sometimes called consequentialism). Two-thirds of Vatican II Catholics say they were taught that our actions are always right or always wrong. Only 25 percent say they were taught that the morality of our actions depends on the circumstances. Just over half of post-Vatican II Catholics (53 percent) say they were taught the natural-law approach. Forty-two percent say they were taught the consequentialist approach.

6. *Post-Vatican II Catholics are more likely to have been taught to think for themselves.* When asked whether they were taught to obey Church teachings or to think for themselves, a majority of both groups say they were taught to obey. However, while 77 percent of Vatican II Catholics say they were taught to obey, just 64 percent of post-Vatican II Catholics give that response. Though only 13 percent of boomers say they were taught to think for themselves, almost twice as many post-Vatican II Catholics (23 percent) say that.

The Elusive Spirituality of Generation-X Catholics

Older, pre-Vatican II Catholics think of "spirituality" and "religiosity" as one and the same thing. They use the two terms interchangeably. They assume that you cultivate your personal relationship with God by participating in the Church, that you talk to God when you participate in Mass and go to Communion, and that the more you participate in the Church, the more likely God is to answer your prayers.

Young, post-Vatican II Catholics do not think that way. They make a rather clear distinction between being spiritual and being religious. Being spiritual means having a personal relationship with God. Being religious has more to do with participation in the Church. Being spiritual means talking to God and knowing that he will listen. Being religious means going to Mass and receiving holy Communion. Being spiritual means knowing that God will answer your prayers. Being religious means abiding by Church rules, such as getting married in the Church. Being spiritual means knowing that God is with you all the time. Being religious means agreeing with what the Church teaches.

Young people acknowledge that spirituality and religiosity are not mutually exclusive; being spiritual does not prevent you from being religious, and being religious does not mean you cannot be spiritual. However, they insist that you can be one without being the other. They believe that many older Catholics are religious without being spiritual. By this they mean that many older Catholics go to church, participate in the sacraments, and live according to Church rules, but do not necessarily have a personal relationship with God or love their neighbor the way God wants them to. Likewise, young Catholics think they can be spiritual without being religious. They believe they can have a personal relationship with God and love their neighbor without being active in the Church.

Research consistently shows that young Catholics are less religious than older Catholics, in the sense of being less actively involved in the Church. As I have documented many times, and as you probably know from personal experience, today's young Catholics are less likely than previous generations of young adults to attend Mass, receive holy Communion, and participate in parish groups and activities. But are they any less spiritual in the sense of having a personal relationship with God?

My 1995 national survey showed that a clear majority of young adults believe that God is in their lives. Almost as many young adults (78 percent) as older Catholics (82 percent) said that God has forgiven their sins many times.[3] Almost as many young people (60 percent versus 68 percent of older Catholics) said God has answered their prayers many times. Almost as many young adults (66 percent versus 74 percent) said that God has taken care of them when they have really needed help. Almost as many young people (36 percent versus 40 percent) said that they have sensed God's presence in a special way many times.

However, when we asked young adults how they nurture their spirituality, most were unable to specify particular actions. And, when we asked them how often they participate in a variety of spiritual practices, a majority said they "talk to God" regularly, but fewer than one in five said they read the Bible, pray the rosary, participate in prayer groups, or practice devotions to special saints. Gen-X theologian Tom Beaudoin—author of *Virtual Faith*—also has observed that, while young adults "may see their music or dancing or sports or cyberspace as spiritual in some diffused sense," they are not "willing to subject their popular culture to religious analysis."[4]

In short, young adults' spirituality is elusive. They seem to think of it as something that is given to them by God, not as something they intentionally pursue. They seem to think of it as something that happens to them, not as something they bring about through spiritual practices.

One Church, Two Cultures?

In his book *Tomorrow's Catholics, Yesterday's Church*, Eugene Kennedy suggests that American Catholics are divided into two cultures.[5] Culture-I Catholics tend to be older (pre-Vatican II) Catholics who emphasize the importance of external authority (clergy). Culture-II Catholics are younger (post-Vatican II) Catholics who stress the importance of internal authority (personal conscience).

According to Kennedy, Culture-I Catholics emphasize the stability of the institutional Church. They are concerned about the credibility of the Church and its persistence as a social institution. Culture-I Catholics are rooted in the traditional, hierarchical exercise of authority. They stress the importance of private confession, where priests, representing the external authority of the institutional Church, give counsel and absolve sins. Kennedy argues that this cultural orientation is found most often in Catholics who were raised in the pre-Vatican II years of the 1920s, 1930s, and 1940s.

Culture-II Catholics conceive of religious authority as internal, flowing from the exercise of one's conscience. They believe the locus of authority is within the believer—that God speaks through the experiences and reflections of individual Christians. From this perspective, Catholics are to take personal responsibility for their faith, which is intimately related to their daily experience in the world. According to Kennedy, this cultural orientation is most common among Catholics raised in the post-Vatican II years of the 1970s, 1980s, and 1990s.

Father Anthony Pogorelc and I have tested Kennedy's thesis using a national survey of American Catholics.[6] A Culture-I orientation is indicated by frequent participation in the sacrament of reconciliation, belief that one should obey Church teachings even when one doesn't fully understand them, belief that one must attend Mass to be a "good Catholic," and agreement with the Church's teaching that premarital sex is morally wrong. A Culture-II orientation is indicated by infrequent confession, denying the need to obey teachings one does not fully understand, indicating that one can be a "good Catholic" without attending Mass, and belief that it is up to the individual to decide whether premarital sex is right or wrong. Scores on our four-item index ranged from 4 (Culture I) to 16 (Culture II).

TABLE 10.2 Culteral Orientation by Generation (percent)

	Definitely Culture I	Toward Culture I	Toward Culture I	Definitely Culture I	Total
Pre-Vatican II	30	23	26	21	100%
Vatican II	7	18	36	39	100%
Post-Vatican II	7	14	38	41	100%

Overall, our findings indicate much more variation than Kennedy's two-culture model suggests. Rather than being divided into two distinct cultures, American Catholics are found at virtually every point along the continuum. Twelve percent are definitely Culture I, 18 percent tend toward Culture I, 34 percent tend toward Culture II, and 35 percent are definitely Culture II. We do not find a U-shaped curve, with most Catholics located in the two end categories and only few in the middle. Instead, we find that a majority of Catholics (52 percent) are in the middle, only 12 percent are definitely Culture I, and only 35 percent are definitely Culture II.

There is a modest correlation between generation and cultural orientation, with pre-Vatican II Catholics (born in or before 1940) tending toward a Culture-I orientation and post-Vatican II Catholics (born since 1961) tending toward Culture II (see table 10.2). However, there are important variations within as well as between generations. Thirty percent of pre-Vatican II Catholics are definitely Culture I and another 23 percent tend toward Culture I; but 26 percent tend toward Culture II and 21 percent are definitely Culture II. Forty-one percent of post-Vatican II Catholics are clearly Culture II, and 38 percent tend toward Culture II; but 14 percent tend toward Culture I and 7 percent are definitely Culture I. In each cohort, the percentages in the middle categories are larger than percentages at the extremes. In the pre-Vatican II cohort, 49 percent are in the middle categories. In the post-Vatican II cohort, 52 percent are in the middle categories.

American Catholics are not polarized into two distinct cultures. The American Catholic landscape is more complex than Kennedy's book suggests.

Who Are the
Conservative Young Catholics?

Most research shows that young Catholics have "liberal" attitudes about sexual and reproductive issues. Studies indicate the eighteen- to thirty-four-year-old Catholics tend to disagree with the Church's teaching that premarital sex, artificial birth control, homosexual practices, and abortion are morally wrong. Rather than adopting the Church's view that these behaviors violate natural law, young-adult Catholics tend to believe that the rightness or wrongness of these actions should be judged in relation to specific circumstances and the consequences they have for the persons involved. For example, data from my 1995 national survey indicate that 87 percent of young-adult Catholics believe the decision to use condoms or birth control pills to prevent pregnancy is "entirely up to the individual." Seventy-six percent say the same thing regarding premarital sex. Fifty-six percent say that homosexual actions are not intrinsically wrong; instead, they say, the rightness or wrongness of such actions is up to individuals to decide. Thirty-seven percent say that the decision to terminate a pregnancy by having an abortion also is strictly up to the individual.

Not all young adults think this way, however. Thirty-eight percent believe homosexual actions are "always wrong" and another 4 percent say that homosexual activities are "wrong, except under certain circumstances." Twenty-nine percent say abortion is always wrong, with another 34 percent saying it is usually wrong. Twenty-three percent say premarital sex is always or usually wrong. Eleven percent believe the use of condoms or birth control pills to prevent pregnancy is always or usually wrong.

Who are these "conservative" young-adult Catholics who are bucking the "liberal" trends among most of their peers? Why do some young adults agree with the Church on sexual matters, while the majority of their age-mates do not?

According to the research of sociologist Richard Featherstone, there are five conclusions that have important implications for parents, lay leaders, and clergy.[7]

- The more religiously active mothers are when their children are growing up, the more likely their offspring are to accept the Church's sexual and reproductive teachings when they become young adults.
- Young adults with religiously active and traditional Catholic role

models are more likely than other young adults are to have conservative views on sexual and reproductive issues.

- Mother's religiosity and the tendency to look up to religiously active, traditional Catholics have separate effects of their own, but they also contribute to young adults' identity as Catholic (for example, "I cannot imagine being anything other than Catholic").
- The stronger young adults' Catholic identity, the more likely they are to share the Church's views on sexual and reproductive issues.
- Of these three influences, the strength of young adults' Catholic identity has the largest and most direct effect.

Thus, young adults who are most likely to embrace the Church's views on sexual and reproductive issues have grown up in religious environments that nurture a strong Catholic identity. These influences combine to make the Church's teachings plausible. The Church's teachings have little or no plausibility for young adults who are not grounded in religious networks and do not think of the Church as an important part of their lives.

The implications are quite clear. People who want to pass the Church's sexual and reproductive teachings on to the next generation should do three things: nurture religious commitment among Catholic parents, see that young people have religiously active and traditional Catholics to look up to, and cultivate a sense of identification with the Church. Pursuing these goals will not guarantee compliance with Church teachings, but it certainly increases the chances of passing them on.

Are Young Catholics Increasingly Orthodox?

Colleen Carroll is a twentysomething Catholic woman and a journalist with a special interest in the faith of young adults born between 1965 and 1983. She spent a year traveling among and talking with young-adult Christians, including many Catholics. The result of her investigation is a book entitled *The New Faithful: Why Young Adults Are Embracing Christian Orthodoxy.*[8]

Carroll's book is a sympathetic and penetrating look inside the world of young adults who identify themselves as orthodox Christians. She examines their views of the Church and worship, small Christian communities, sexuality and marriage, life on college campuses, politics, and religion's role in society. According to Carroll, the two key experiences of orthodox young adults are "a spiritual search and the resulting commitment to organized religion and traditional morality." In her words, orthodox young adults are "not content to search forever. They want answers." They stress the importance of having a personal relationship with Christ, have an identity that is "centered on their religious beliefs," believe in " time-tested teachings," "embrace challenging faith commitments," adhere to "traditional morality," "yearn for mystery," "seek guidance and formation from legitimate sources of authority and trust these authorities," and "strive for personal holiness." Their beliefs, she says, defy conventional distinctions between liberal and conservative.

These orthodox young adults have a countercultural worldview. They see themselves as standing over against "relativists [who] argue that no belief system or ethical code is superior to another" and postmodernists who, Carroll says, reject the "Enlightenment-era emphasis on reason, science, and progress." Instead, these young adults emphasize the importance of "universal standards and absolute-truth claims." Themes of tradition, authority, surrender, sacrifice, and obedience run throughout the book. Far from retreating from the world around them, however, these young adults intend to transform it. They are distinctly pro-life in their views on abortion and tend to vote Republican.

Despite the book's many insights about the worldview of orthodox young adults, readers need to be aware of two things. For one thing, the young adults Carroll talked with are a very select group, not a representative cross-section of all young adults. They are mostly young professionals and white, upper-middle-class students at private colleges and universities (Harvard, Georgetown, Notre Dame, and Franciscan University of Steubenville are mentioned frequently). In Carroll's words, they "are college students, monks, beauty queens, rocket scientists, and landscape architects...cultural leaders, young adults blessed with talent, intelligence, good looks, wealth, successful careers, impressive educational pedigrees, or charisma—or some dynamic combination thereof." There is no indication that Carroll's findings reflect the life experiences of young adults who are Hispanic, African American, or in blue-collar work.

Second, at numerous places throughout her book, Carroll claims that there is a "trend toward orthodoxy." It is very clear from Carroll's book that these young adults are increasingly organized and will have significant impact on the Church and the culture. However, there is no empirical basis for Carroll's claim that they are part of a trend toward religious orthodoxy and conventional morality. National studies of young-adult Catholics simply do not support this claim. Instead, they consistently show that the majority of young adults are not orthodox, and when researchers compare the youngest young adults with the oldest young adults, they find no evidence that the youngest cohort is more orthodox than the oldest.

Carroll's book is getting considerable attention among Church leaders and favorable treatment in a number of Catholic magazines and newspapers. Although it includes many insights about the beliefs and practices of the young orthodox Christians she studied, the book needs to be approached cautiously and interpreted carefully. The "new faithful" in Carroll's book are an important and highly organized subset of young-adult Catholics, but they are not typical of their generation and, even though Carroll might like them to be, they are not part of an overall trend toward orthodoxy and conventional morality.

Are Millennial Catholics Different?

We know a great deal about the religious beliefs and practices of the pre-Vatican II generation (born in 1940 or before), the Vatican II generation (born between 1941 and 1960), and the post-Vatican II generation (born between 1961 and 1982). We do not know as much about the next, so-called "millennial," generation. The reason is that most millennials are under the age of twenty-one and have not yet completed their formative years.

Even so, many Church leaders are eager to know if the millennial generation is going to be any different from post-Vatican II Catholics. Some leaders think millennials might be more inclined to agree with Church teachings. Others disagree.

Three recent studies are helpful in trying to anticipate what the next generation might be like. In *The Search for Common Ground*, colleagues and I compared older members of the post-Vatican II generation (born between 1961 and 1969) with younger members (born between 1970 and 1977).[9] We did not find any indications of a trend toward orthodoxy in the youngest cohort. On three of the five dimensions we studied, we found no significant differences. On the other two dimensions, we found that the youngest cohort was somewhat less likely to comply with official Church teachings. These results pointed to a continuation of recent trends in Catholics' views on faith and morals.

In the June 2003 issue of *Catholic Education: A Journal of Inquiry and Practice,* Father James Heft and I argued that "the emerging generation of millennial Catholics is likely to reflect many of the same social and religious tendencies that have been found among post-Vatican II, or Generation-X,

Catholics." We predicted that "millennials are likely to be natural extensions of, not radical departures from, their parents' generation."[10]

In fall 2003, Dean Hoge of Catholic University and I had another opportunity to study this issue. In a national survey of American Catholics (sponsored by the University of Notre Dame), we distinguished between respondents who were between twenty-six and forty-two years of age and those who were between eighteen and twenty-five years old (thus, representing the leading edge of the millennial generation). We compared the groups' responses to questions relating to faith and morals, spirituality, and issues facing today's Church.[11]

We could not find any series of questions on which millennials were more orthodox than the older post-Vatican II respondents. More often than not, the eighteen- to twenty-five-year-old respondents were very similar to the twenty-six- to forty-two-year-old respondents. For example, on ten items having to do with the importance of the Catholic faith, the Catholic Church, and views of other religious groups, the responses of post-Vatican II and millennial Catholics were virtually identical. Levels of parish involvement also were virtually the same. Views of core Church teachings and reactions to problems facing the Church also were quite similar.

When there were noteworthy differences, millennials were less traditional than post-Vatican II Catholics. For example, 51 percent of twenty-six- to forty-two-year-olds said their religion is "very important in their daily life"; 40 percent of eighteen- to twenty-five-year-olds gave that response. Although 79 percent of post-Vatican II Catholics said they pray privately once a week or more, 67 percent of millennials said that. While 50 percent of tweny-six- to forty-two-year-olds reported that God has answered their prayers many times, only 37 percent of eighteen- to twenty-five-year-olds gave that response.

Thus, in three recent efforts to discern the central tendencies of post-Vatican II and millennial Catholics, I find no evidence of a trend toward greater compliance with official Church teachings. Certainly, some millennial Catholics are more traditional than their parents, but so far they do not reflect the views of their generation. For the most part, millennial Catholics are likely to think and act in much the same way as post-Vatican II Catholics. If anything, they might be a little bit less orthodox.

Anglo and Hispanic Catholics:
Similarities and Differences

Historically, American Catholics have tended to have European roots, with parents and grandparents coming from places such as Ireland, Italy, Poland, and France. In recent years, there has been a dramatic increase in the number of Catholics whose families have come to this country from places such as Mexico, Puerto Rico, Cuba, and Guatemala. As a result, white Europeans have declined to about 71 percent of all U.S. Catholics, and Hispanics have climbed to about 22 percent (with African, Asian, and Native Americans accounting for the other 7 percent).

These trends present Church leaders with many challenges. Perhaps the biggest task is to understand how Anglos and Hispanics compare socially and culturally. How different are they in terms of demographic characteristics such as education, occupation, and income? In what ways are their religious worldviews different? In what areas of faith and morals are they more similar than different? The more answers Church leaders have to questions such as these, the more successful they are likely to be in their efforts to meet the needs of laypeople in both groups.

To find some answers, I have reviewed findings in three books that I have coauthored with colleagues: *The Search for Common Ground*, *American Catholics*, and *Lay Ministers and Their Spiritual Practices*.[12] I also have examined findings from a 2003 national survey that Dean Hoge and I conducted for the University of Notre Dame.[13]

All studies show there are sizable demographic differences between Anglo and Hispanic Catholics. Anglos are much more likely to live in the East and South, while Hispanics are more likely to reside in the Midwest and Southwest. Anglos rank higher in formal education, are more likely to have white-collar jobs, and have considerably larger incomes. They also are more likely to have attended Catholic grade schools, high schools, and colleges. Hispanics are much younger, have more children, and have more people (such as grandparents and other relatives) living in their households.

Not surprisingly, the two groups also are quite different in terms of many religious beliefs and practices. Anglos are more likely to be registered parishioners, attend Mass and receive holy Communion on a weekly basis, and contribute to the Church financially. On various indices of overall commitment to the Church, Anglos score higher than Hispanics. On the other hand, Hispanics are more likely to attach importance to traditional beliefs (such as belief that Mary is the Mother of God) and participate in traditional devotional practices, many of which are distinctively Hispanic (such as the home *altarito* and family home prayers). They also are more likely to report that God is present in their daily lives and that the Catholic Church has a greater share of the truth than other religious groups.

It would be a mistake, however, to overlook the many ways in which Anglos and Hispanics are similar in religious outlook. The vast majority of both Anglos and Hispanics accept core Church teachings, such as the Incarnation and the Lord's presence in the sacraments. They have similar views on sexual and reproductive issues, with most not accepting the Church's view that premarital sex and birth control are always wrong. Their views on the Church's social teachings also are similar. For example, a majority of people in both groups believe Catholics have a duty to try to close the gap between the rich and poor.

These findings have at least four implications for Church leaders. Given the Church's social teachings, Church leaders need to address the socioeconomic disparity between the two groups. They also need to recognize, understand, and celebrate the cultural differences between the groups. Given the differences between the two groups, leaders also need to respect members' tendencies to interact within their own groups. At the same time, the similarities in their religious beliefs and practices provide Church leaders with opportunities to build bridges between Anglo and Hispanic Catholics.

Converts Are More Active and Traditional Than Cradle Catholics

A recent national study indicates that about 10 percent of American Catholics are converts.[14] It also shows that converts are more religiously active and have more traditional beliefs than "cradle" Catholics, who were born and raised in the Church.

Converts are more likely than cradle Catholics are to believe there is something special about being Catholic. Converts also are more likely to be registered parishioners (87 percent versus 67 percent of cradle Catholics). They are more inclined to say their parishes are an important part of their lives. They are more likely to donate time (49 percent versus 35 percent) and money (67 percent versus 53 percent) to the Church. Compared to persons who were born and raised Catholic, converts are more likely to say their parish meets their spiritual needs (40 percent versus 30 percent) and helps them make daily decisions related to work and family (35 percent versus 21 percent).

TABLE 10.3 Beliefs of Converts and Cradle Catholics (percent)

	Converts	Cradles
Something special about being Catholic	76	59
Parish is important part of life	89	72
Think of self as religious	75	57
Belief that the bread and wine actually become Body and Blood of Christ is important	76	66

They also are more likely to think of themselves as religious, and with good reason. They are more likely to receive holy Communion (50 percent versus 35 percent), read the Bible (51 percent versus 33 percent), attend prayer groups (35 percent versus 22 percent), participate in group reconciliation services (24 percent versus 11 percent), and enroll in Bible study (16 percent versus 7 percent).

Converts also are more informed about religious matters. For example, they are more likely to have heard of Vatican II from the pulpit (76 percent versus 54 percent), read books or articles about it (47 percent versus 34 percent), and talked with others about it (41 percent versus 29 percent).

Converts are somewhat more traditional than cradle Catholics. For example, they are more likely to say that people should obey Church teachings even if they do not understand them (55 percent versus 44 percent). They also are more likely to stress the importance of believing that the bread and wine actually become the Body and Blood of Christ during Mass. Fifty-two percent of converts say you can be a good Catholic without going to Mass, compared to 64 percent of cradle Catholics.

There is little or no difference between converts and cradle Catholics in other areas of faith and morals. For example, the two groups have similar views about the importance of the Trinity, Incarnation, Resurrection, and Mary as the Mother of God. Converts and cradle Catholics also are similar in the frequency with which they attend Mass, pray privately, and observe holy days of obligation. Finally, they are similar in practicing devotions to Mary, praying the rosary, beginning and end each day with prayer, and going to private confession.

Catholic Men and Women
Not From Different Planets

John Gray has built a media empire promoting the view that men and women are from different planets. In books, on tapes, and at conferences, he argues that women are from Venus and men are from Mars. There is no doubt that men and women often approach relationships differently. But, when it comes to religious beliefs and practices, and attitudes about sexual and reproductive issues, Catholic men and women are not from different planets. Evidence from a recent national study indicates they are more similar than different in matters of faith and morals.[15]

A majority of both men and women say that beliefs such as the Trinity, Incarnation, Resurrection, Real Presence, and Mary as the Mother of God are cornerstones of their personal religiosity. For example, 74 percent of women and 67 percent of men believe the Resurrection of Christ is very important to them personally. Seventy-eight percent of women and 65 percent of men stress the importance of Mary as the mother of God. Sixty-eight percent of women and 55 percent of men say it is important to believe that bread and wine are transformed into the Body and Blood of Christ during Mass. While women are somewhat more traditional than men on these important issues, the fact that a majority of both groups embrace these core doctrines indicates that men and women are on the same planet, not different ones.

Though women are a bit more religiously active than men, the sexes are more similar than different when it comes to religious practices. A majority of both groups (86 percent of women, 62 percent of men) pray privately at least once a week. About four of ten men and women celebrate the sacrament of reconciliation at least once a year. Thirty-nine percent of women and 33 percent of men attend Mass weekly. One-third of women and one-fifth of men practice devotions to Mary or a special saint at least once a week. About one-quarter of women and one-fifth of men participate in communal penance at least once a year. Only 18 percent of women and 15 percent of men pray the rosary each week. Even fewer men and women read the Bible or participate in Bible study groups.

Men and women have similar views of the Church. Six of ten men and women say there is something special about being Catholic that one cannot find in other faiths. Similar numbers of men and women say they cannot imagine being anything other than Catholic. Seven of ten men and women believe the pope is the vicar of Christ on earth. Half of men and women say the Church is the one, true Church (the other half disagrees). Forty-seven percent of men and 43 percent of women say it is important to obey Church teachings even if one does not understand them. Yet, 85 percent of both sexes feel laypeople are just as important as the clergy. Sixty-five percent of women and 62 percent of men believe one can be a good Catholic without going to Mass on a regular basis. Fifty-nine percent of men and 57 percent of women say women should be allowed to be priests.

Both groups have mixed feelings about the roles of men and women in society. A majority of women (79 percent) and men (74 percent) agree that there are still laws and customs that discriminate against women. Three out of four Catholic men and women also feel that the sexes are equally suited for political life. Three-quarters of both men and women question the traditional idea of putting the husband's career ahead of the wife's. Yet, 57 percent of men and 59 percent of women think leaders of the women's movement are too radical. Half of men and half of women say that, when children are young, husbands should be the breadwinners with wives staying home with the children. The other half disagrees.

Men and women have similar views of artificial birth control, premarital sex, homosexual activity, and abortion. Eighty-two percent of both men and women say there is nothing intrinsically wrong with artificial means of birth control; in their view, it is completely up to the individual to decide whether to use condoms or birth-control pills to prevent pregnancy. Sixty-four percent of both men and women also think the decision whether or not to engage is premarital sex is completely up to the individual. Half of women and four of every ten men say there is nothing intrinsically wrong with homosexual activity. One-third of both men and women say that abortion is always wrong; one third say it is wrong except under certain circumstances; and one-third say it is completely up to the individual to decide.

Finally, Catholic men and women have similar views of the Church's social teachings. Over three-quarters of both groups say that helping the needy is important to them personally and agree with Catholic bishops in saying that economic decisions that hurt the poor are morally wrong. Half of men and women say Catholics have a special duty to close the gap between the rich and poor.

Though there are some differences in the way Catholic men and women approach matters of faith and morals, they do not seem to be from different planets. When it comes to religious beliefs and practices and attitudes about sexual and reproductive issues, they are more similar than different.

Young Women More Alienated Than Young Men

In two national studies, colleagues and I have concluded that young-adult Catholic women are more alienated from the Church than young-adult Catholic men.

In our 1996 book *Laity: American and Catholic*, we wrote: "Compared to men their age, [young] women have less hierarchical conceptions of authority in the Church and put more emphasis on the importance of lay participation in most facets of Church life, especially matters affecting their parishes and personal lives. Their behaviors indicate they are more highly committed to the Church, yet they feel less committed than five years ago. This sense of alienation seems tied to the gap between their views on birth control and abortion and the views expressed by Church leaders."[16]

Young-adult women were less likely to say they would never leave the Church (46 percent versus 54 percent of young men). When asked if their commitment to the Church had changed in the last five years, 38 percent of young women—compared to only 30 percent of young men—said their commitment had declined.

We also asked about the effects of specific Church teachings. Fifty-three percent of young women (versus 35 percent of young men) said the Church's opposition to artificial means of birth control had weakened their commitment. Thirty-nine percent of young women (versus 20 percent of young men) said the Church's views on abortion had diminished their attachment to the Church. Thirty-one percent of young women (versus 25 percent of young men) said the Church's policy of not ordaining women had adversely affected their commitment.

TABLE 10.4 Percent of Young Men and Women Saying Each Teaching Had Weakened Their Commitment

	Men	Women
Birth control	35	53
Abortion	20	39
Not ordaining women	25	31

When asked if one could be a good Catholic without agreeing with the Church on abortion, 76 percent of young women (versus 61 percent of young men) said yes. Seventy-three percent of young women (versus 63 percent of young men) said one could be a good Catholic without agreeing with the Church's policies on divorce and remarriage. When asked if one could be a good Catholic without marrying in the Church, 73 percent of young women (versus 57 percent of young men) responded in the affirmative.

In our 1997 book *The Search for Common Ground*, we wrote: "young men and young women have rather different approaches to faith and morals. Young women are increasingly inclined to disagree with Church teachings, especially on traditional beliefs and practices and on issues such as the ordination of women, the need to attend Mass, and premarital sex. While this pattern of increased dissent also appears among young men, it is not occurring at the same rate and on some dimensions there is evidence of a rebound effect among young men. Together, these trends produce larger gender differences among post-Vatican II parishioners than among older cohorts."[17]

Let me cite just two of many findings supporting this conclusion. Forty-five percent of pre-Vatican II women and 49 percent of pre-Vatican II men said one can be a good Catholic without attending Mass (only a 4 percent difference). Fifty-seven percent of both Vatican II men and Vatican II women gave this response (no difference). However, 79 percent of post-Vatican II women—compared to 61 percent post-Vatican II men—said one can be a good Catholic without going to Mass (an 18 point difference).

When asked if abortion is always wrong, wrong except under certain circumstances, or entirely up to the individual, 20 percent of pre-Vatican II women and 18 percent of pre-Vatican II men said abortion is entirely up to the individual (only a 2 percent difference). Thirty-four percent of Vatican II women and the same percentage of Vatican II men gave that response. However, 35 percent of post-Vatican II women, compared to 19 percent of post-Vatican II men, said abortion is up to the individual (a 16 percent difference).

Questions for Reflection

1. Apply the distinctions between pre-Vatican II, Vatican II, post-Vatican II, and millennial generations to your own family, asking members of each generation to discuss what they were taught by their parents and religion teachers and to describe their current beliefs and practices. How do your results compare with the national findings reported in this section of the book?

2. Do the generational differences that appear in national data also appear in your parish or diocese? In what ways and with what consequence? In what ways do they enrich the Church, and in what ways do they cause problems?

3. How do you respond to the data on the spirituality of today's young Catholics? Are you encouraged or discouraged by recent findings? Why?

4. National studies show that a majority of post-Vatican II Catholics have a liberal, Culture-II orientation to faith and a minority tend toward a conservative, Culture-I approach. Is that also true in your parish? Are conservative young adults growing in numbers and/or influence in the parish? How well, if at all, do young liberals and young conservatives get along with one another?

5. What can the Church do to celebrate both the similarities and the differences between Anglos and Hispanics?

6. There's an old adage: "Converts are better Catholics." Does the evidence support this claim?

7. Although Catholic men and women seem to be on the same planet, young women are more alienated from the Church than young men. What can be done to address this difference and its potentially ominous implications for the religious formation of the next generation of Catholics?

Notes

Introduction

1. James D. Davidson, Andrea Williams, Richard Lamanna, Jan Stenftenagel, Kathleen Maas Weigert, William Whalen, and Patricia Wittberg S.C., *The Search for Common Ground: What Unites and Divides Catholic Americans* (Huntington, Ind.: Our Sunday Visitor, 1997).
2. William V. D'Antonio, James D. Davidson, Dean Hoge, and Ruth Wallace, *Laity: American and Catholic: Transforming the Church* (Kansas City, Mo.: Sheed and Ward, 1996).
3. William D'Antonio, James D. Davidson, Dean Hoge, and Katherine Meyer, *American Catholics: Gender, Generation, and Commitment* (Walnut Creek, Calif.: AltaMira Press, 2001).
4. James D. Davidson, Thomas Walters, Bede Cisco O.S.B., Katherine Meyer, and Charles Zech, *Lay Ministers and Their Spiritual Practices* (Huntington, Ind.: Our Sunday Visitor, 2003).
5. James D. Davidson and Dean R. Hoge, "Catholics After the Scandal: A New Study's Major Findings," *Commonweal*, November 19, 2004, 13–19.

Chapter One

1. Ralph E. Pyle and James D. Davidson, "The Origins of Religious Stratification in Colonial America," *Journal for the Scientific Study of Religion* 42 (March 2003): 57–75.
2. Robert K. Merton, *Social Theory and Social Structure* (New York: Free Press, 1957): 426–430.
3. Martin E. Marty, *Pilgrims in Their Own Land* (New York: Penguin Books, 1986), 77.
4. Jay P. Dolan, *In Search of an American Catholicism: A History of Religion and Culture in Tension* (New York: Oxford University Press, 2002).
5. James D. Davidson, Ralph E. Pyle, and David V. Reyes, "Persistence and Change in the Protestant Establishment, 1930-1992," *Social Forces* 74 (September 1995): 157–175.
6. *Official Catholic Directory* (New Providence, New Jersey: P.J. Kenedy and Sons, annually).
7. James D. Davidson et al, *The Search for Common Ground*; and William D'Antonio et al., *American Catholics*.
8. Guillermina Jasso, Douglas S. Massey, Mark R. Rosenzweig, and James P. Smith, "Exploring the Religious Preference of Recent Immigrants to the United States: Evidence from the New Immigrant Survey Pilot," in Yvonne Yazbeck Haddad, Jane I. Smith, and John L. Esposito, eds., *Religion and Immigration: Christian, Jewish, and Muslim Experiences in the United States* (Walnut Creek, Calif.: AltaMira Press, 2003), 217–253.

Chapter Two

1. Larry Shriner, "The Concept of Secularization in Empirical Research," *Journal for the Scientific Study of Religion* 6 (June 1967): 207–220. Roger Finke and Rodney Stark, *The Churching of America, 1776–1990* (New Brunswick, N.J.: Rutgers University Press, 1992). R. Stephen Warner, "Work in Progress toward a New Paradigm for the Sociological Study of Religion in the United States," *American Journal of Sociology* 98 (March 1993): 1044–1093.

2. Michael Hout and Claude Fischer, "Explaining the Rise of Americans with No Religious Preference," *American Sociological Review* 67 (April 2002): 165–190.

3. James D. Davidson et al., *The Search for Common Ground.*

4. Wade Clark Roof, *Spiritual Marketplace: Baby Boomers and the Remaking of American Religion* (Princeton, N.J.: Princeton University Press, 1999).

5. Dean Hoge et al., *Young Adult Catholics.*

6. Robert Fuller, *Spiritual but not Religious* (New York: Oxford University Press, 2001).

7. Penny Long Marler and C. Kirk Hadaway, "'Being religious' or 'Being spiritual' in America: A Zero-Sum Proposition?" *Journal of the Scientific Study of Religion* 41 (June 2002): 289–300.

8. Leonard Sweet, *Post-Modern Pilgrims: First Century Passion for the 21st Century Church* (Nashville, Tenn.: Broadman and Holman Publishers, 2000).

9. Miller McPherson, Lynn Smith-Lovin, and James M. Cook, "Birds of a Feather: Homophily in Social Networks," *Annual Review of Sociology* 27 (2001): 415–444.

Chapter Three

1. James D. Davidson, Margaret E. Cole, and Anthony J. Pogorelc, "The Economic Impact of Religious Organizations: Results from Two Recent Studies," *The Changing Social Contract* (Washington D.C.: The Independent Sector, 1997), 93–112.

2. Hugh J. Nolan, editor, *Pastoral Letters of the Catholic Bishops* 5 (Washington, D.C.: National Conference of Catholic Bishops/United States Catholic Conference [now U.S. Conference of Catholic Bishops], 1989): 371–492.

3. Martin N. Marger, *Social Inequality: Patterns and Processes* (Mountain View, Calif.: Mayfield Publishing Company, 1999).

4. Harold Kerbo, *Social Stratification and Inequality: Class Conflict in Historical, Comparative, and Global Perspective* (Boston: McGraw Hill, 2000), 30.

5. Hugh J. Nolan, editor, *Pastoral Letters of the Catholic Bishops* 5 (Washington, D.C.: National Conference of Catholic Bishops/United States Catholic Conference [now U.S. Conference of Catholic Bishops], 1989), 431.

6. Christopher Kauffman, *Patriotism and Fraternalism in the Knights of Columbus* (New York: Crossroad, 2001).

7. Stephen J. Whitfield, *The Culture of the Cold War* (Baltimore, Maryland: Johns Hopkins University Press, 1996), 89.

8. See the *Congressional Record: Proceeding and Debates of the United States Congress* 100 (1954): 6077–6078, 7757–7766.

9. Christopher Kauffman, *Patriotism and Fraternalism in the Knights of Columbus* (New York: Crossroad, 2001), 124, 163.

10. See U.S. Treasury website: http://www.treas.gov/education/fact-sheets/currency/in-god-we-trust.shtml.

11. James D. Davidson, "Why Churches Cannot Endorse or Oppose Political Candidates," *Review of Religious Research* 40 (September 1998): 16–34.

12. James D. Davidson, Rachel Kraus, and Scott Morrissey, "Presidential Appointments and Religious Stratification in the U.S., 1789–2003," *Journal for the Scientific Study of Religion* 44 (December 2005).

13. James D. Davidson, Rachel Kraus, and Scott Morrissey, "Presidential Appointments and Religious Stratification in the U.S., 1789–2003," *Journal for the Scientific Study of Religion* 44 (December 2005).

14. Mark D. Brewer, *Relevant No More? The Protestant/Catholic Divide in American Electoral Politics* (Lanham, Maryland: Lexington Books), 2003.

15. William B. Prendergast, *The Catholic Voter in American Politics: The Passing of the Democratic Monolith* (Washington, D.C.: Georgetown University Press), 1999.

16. See National Election Studies at http://www.umich.edu/~nes/.

17. Thomas B. Edsall, "Bush Aims to Strengthen Catholic Base," *Washington Post*, April 16, 2001, A2.

18. Barry Kosmin, Egon Mayer, and Ariela Keysar, *American Religious Identification Survey* (New York: Graduate Center of the City University of New York), 2001. Also available at http://www.gc.cuny.edu/faculty/research_studies/aris.pdf.

Chapter Four

1. Lee Bolman and Terrence Deal, *Reframing Organizations: Artistry, Choice, and Leadership* (San Francisco: Jossey-Bass, 1997).

2. James D. Davidson et al., *The Search for Common Ground*, 61.

3. Kevin J. Dougherty, "How Monochromatic is Church Membership? Racial-Ethnic Diversity in Religious Community," *Sociology of Religion* 64 (Spring 2003): 65–85.

4. Anthony Stevens-Arroyo, et al., *The National Survey of Leadership in Latino Parishes and Congregations* (Brooklyn, New York: Program for the Analysis of Religion among Latinas/os, 2003).

5. Alan Mock, James D. Davidson, and C. Lincoln Johnson, "Threading the Needle: Faith and Works in Affluent Churches," in Carl S. Dudley, Jackson W. Carroll, and James P. Wind (editors), *Carriers of Faith* (Louisville, Kent.: Westminster John Knox Press, 1991), 86–103.

6. James D. Davidson, Alan Mock, and C. Lincoln Johnson, "Through the Eye of a Needle: Social Ministry in Affluent Churches," *Review of Religious Research* 38 (March 1997): 247–262.

7. Charles E. Zech, *Why Catholics Don't Give, And What Can Be Done About It* (Huntington, Ind.: Our Sunday Visitor, 2000).

Chapter Five

1. James D. Davidson and Dean R. Hoge, "Catholics After the Scandal," 13–19.

2. William D'Antonio et al., *American Catholics*.

3. Ibid.

4. Andrew M. Greeley, *The American Catholic: A Social Portrait* (New York: Basic Books, 1977), 159.

5. William D'Antonio et al., *American Catholics*.

6. Garry Wills, *Papal Sin* (London: Darton, Longman & Todd Ltd, 2000).

7. Peter Steinfels, "The Church's Sexual Abuse Scandal," *Commonweal*, April 19, 2002, 13–19.

8. William V. D'Antonio et al., *Laity: American and Catholic*, 79–80.

9. James D. Davidson and Dean R. Hoge, "Catholics After the Scandal," 13–19.

10. United States Conference of Catholic Bishops, *Charter for the Protection of Children and Young People* (Washington, D.C.: United States Conference of Catholic Bishops, 2003).

11. All three reports are available online at http://www.usccb.org/nrb. Also see "A Report on the Implementation of the 'Charter for the Protection of Children and Young People,'" [the Gavin Report] (Washington, D.C.: United States Conference of Catholic Bishops, 2004). "The Nature and Scope of the Problem of Sexual Abuse of Minors by Catholic Priests and Deacons in the United States 1950–2002," [John Jay College Report] (Washington, D.C.: United States Conference of Catholic Bishops, 2004). "A Report on the Crisis in the Catholic Church in the United States," [National Review Board Report] (Washington, D.C.: United States Conference of Catholic Bishops, 2004).

12. See Lee Bolman and Terrence Deal, *Reframing Organizations: Artistry, Choice, and Leadership* (San Francisco: Jossey-Bass, 1997).

13. Max Weber, *The Theory of Social and Economic Organization* (New York: Oxford University Press, 1947).

14. FADICA, *2003 Catholic Donor Attitude Survey* (Washington, D.C.: Foundations and Donors Interested in Catholic Activities, Inc., 2003).

15. See Joseph Claude Harris, "Did Catholic Giving to Parishes or Dioceses Decline in 2002?" as reported in http://www.catholiccitizens.org/platform/platformview.asp?c=9732 and *CARA Report* 9 (Spring 2004): 4.
16. See James D. Davidson and Dean R. Hoge, "Catholics After the Scandal," 13–19.

Chapter Six

1. Bryan Froehle and Mary Gautier, *Global Catholicism: Portrait of a World Church* (Maryknoll, New York: Orbis Books, 2003).
2. Sandi Brunette-Hill and Roger Finke, "A Time for Every Purpose Under Heaven: Updating and Extending Blizzard's Survey of Time Allocation," *Review of Religious Research* 41 (Fall 1999): 48–64.
3. Dean Hoge and Jacqueline Wenger, *Evolving Visions of the Priesthood: Changes from Vatican II to the Turn of the New Century* (Collegeville, Minn.: Liturgical Press, 2003).
4. Bryan Froehle and Mary Gautier, *Catholicism USA* (Maryknoll, New York: Orbis Books, 2000), 112.
5. Rodney Stark and Roger Finke, "Catholic Religious Vocations: Decline and Revival," *Review of Religious Research* 42 (December 2000): 125–145.
6. Dean Hoge, *The First Five Years of the Priesthood: A Study of Newly Ordained Catholic Priests* (Collegeville, Minn.: Liturgical Press, 2002).
7. William D'Antonio et al., *American Catholics*.
8. Eileen W. Linder, editor, *Yearbook of American and Canadian Churches* Nashville, Tenn.: Abingdon Press, annually.
9. For a more complete analysis of the clergy shortage, see James Davidson, "Fewer and Fewer: Is the Clergy Shortage Unique to the Catholic Church?" *America* 189 (December 1, 2003), 10–13.
10. Frank R. DeRego Jr. and James D. Davidson, "Catholic Deacons: A Lesson in Role Conflict and Ambiguity," in Madeleine Cousineau, ed., *Religion in a Changing World* (Westport, Conn.: Praeger, 1998), 89–98.
11. Philip Murnion, *New Parish Ministers: Laity and Religious on Parish Staffs* (New York: National Pastoral Life Center, 1992).
12. Philip Murnion and David DeLambo, *Parishes and Parish Ministries* (New York: National Pastoral Life Center, 1999).
13. James D. Davidson et al., *Lay Ministers and Their Spiritual Practices*.

Chapter Seven

1. See David G. Myers, "Faith and Action: A Seamless Tapestry," *Christianity Today* 24 (November 21, 1980): 16–19.

Chapter Eight

1. See David Carlin, *The Decline and Fall of the Catholic Church in America* (Manchester, New Hampshire: Sophia Institute Press, 2003), 163–170.
2. For more on these issues, see James D. Davidson and Dean R. Hoge, "Catholics After the Scandal," 13–19.
3. James D. Davidson et al., *The Search for Common Ground*.
4. This conclusion is based on William V. D'Antonio et al., *American Catholic Laity in a Changing Church* (Kansas City, Mo.: Sheed & Ward, 1989); William V. D'Antonio et al., *Laity: American and Catholic*; James D. Davidson, et al., *The Search for Common Ground*; William Dinges, Dean R. Hoge, Mary Johnson, and Juan L. Gonzales Jr., "A Faith Loosely Held: The Institutional Allegiances of Young Catholics," *Commonweal*, July 17, 1998, 13–18; and Dean R. Hoge, "What Is Most Central to Being a Catholic?" *National Catholic Reporter*, October 29, 1999), 13, 15.
5. James D. Davidson, et al., *The Search for Common Ground*, 57–71.

6. James D. Davidson, "Civic Engagement among American Catholics, Especially the Post-Vatican II Generation," at http://www.catholicsinpublicsquare.org/papeers/winter2001commonweal/davidson/davidson6.htm. Also see Margaret O'Brien Steinfels, "American Catholics in the Public Square," *Commonweal*, July 16, 2004, 1–16.

7. James D. Davidson and David Caddell, "Religion and the Meaning of Work," *Journal for the Scientific Study of Religion* 33 (June 1994): 135–147.

Chapter Nine

1. Jaroslav Pelikan, *The Christian Tradition: A History of the Development of Doctrine, Volume I:The Emergence of the Catholic Tradition (100–600)* (Chicago: University of Chicago Press, 1975), 9.

2. Terrence Tilley, *Inventing Catholic Tradition* (Maryknoll, New York: Orbis Books, 2000), 13–65.

3. James D. Davidson et al., *The Search for Common Ground*, 177–197

4. William D'Antonio et al., *American Catholics*, 157–158.

5. The percentage is even higher for Catholics who are registered parishioners. See James D. Davidson et al., *The Search for Common Ground*, 80–81.

6. James D. Davidson et al., *The Search for Common Ground*, 44–45.

7. James D. Davidson and Dean R. Hoge "Catholics After the Scandal," 13–19.

8. William D'Antonio et al., *American Catholics*, 55–57.

9. Peter M. Blau, *Inequality and Heterogeneity* (New York: Free Press, 1977); Peter M. Blau and Joseph E. Schwartz, *Crosscutting Social Circles* (New York: Academic Press, 1984).

10. John Thomas, "The Factor of Religion in the Selection of Marriage Mates, *American Sociological Review* 16 (August 1951): 487–491.

11. James D. Davidson and Tracy Widman, "The Effect of Group Size on Interfaith Marriage Among Catholics," *Journal for the Scientific Study of Religion* 41 (September 2002): 397–404.

12. William D'Antonio et al., *American Catholics*, 55–57. Also, James D. Davidson, "Outside the Church: Whom Catholics Marry and Where," *Commonweal*, September 11, 1999, 14–16, and James D. Davidson, "Marriage Trends Signal Declining Role of Church," *National Catholic Reporter*, October 29, 1999, 20.

13. James D. Davidson et al., *The Search for Common Ground*; William D'Antonio et al., *American Catholics*; and Dean Hoge et al., *Young Adult Catholics*.

14. James D. Davidson et al., *The Search for Common Ground*, 41–56.

15. Dean R. Hoge et al, *Young Adult Catholics*.

16. William D'Antonio et al., *American Catholics*.

17. James D. Davidson, "Yes, Jesus is Really There: Most Catholics Still Agree" in *Commonweal*, October 12, 2001, 14–16. Also see James D. Davidson et al., *The Search for Common Ground*.

18. Dean R. Hoge et al, *Young Adult Catholics*.

19. Also reported in James D. Davidson, "Yes, Jesus Is Really There: Most Catholics Still Agree" in *Commonweal*, October 12, 2001, 14–16.

20. Peter Steinfels, "Future of Faith Worries Catholic Leaders" *New York Times,* June 1, 1994, A1, B8.

21. For an even more comprehensive review of studies of the Real Presence, see James D. Davidson, "Yes, Jesus is Really There: Most Catholics Still Agree" in *Commonweal*, October 12, 2001, 14–16.

22. U.S. Catholic Bishops, *Economic Justice for All*. (Washington, D.C.: National Conference of Catholic Bishops, 1986).

23. James D. Davidson et al., *The Search for Common Ground*.

24. Kenneth Wald, *Religion and Politics in the United States* (Lanham, Md.: Rowman and Littlefield, 2004), 171.

Chapter Ten

1. For more details, see Duane F. Alwin, "Trends in Parental Socialization Values: Detroit, 1958–1983," *American Journal of Sociology* 90 (September 1984): 359–382; "Religion and Parental Child-Rearing Orientations: Evidence of a Catholic-Protestant Convergence," *American Journal of Sociology* 92 (September 1986): 412–440.
2. James D. Davidson, "American Catholics: Three Generations, One Church," *Liguorian*, January 2000, 12–16.
3. For data on registered parishioners, see James D. Davidson et al., *The Search for Common Ground*.
4. Arthur Jones, "The Gen X Theologian," *National Catholic Reporter*, February 16, 2001, at www.natcath.com/NCR_Online/archives/021601/021601/.htm.
5. Eugene Kennedy, *Tomorrow's Catholics, Yesterday's Church* (New York: Harper and Row, 1988).
6. Anthony J. Pogorelc and James D. Davidson, "One Church, Two Cultures?" *Review of Religious Research* 42 (December 2000): 146–158.
7. Richard Featherstone, "Compliance as Dissidence: Young Catholics and Sexual Ethics," *Sociological Focus* 34 (May 2001): 139–154.
8. Colleen Carroll, *The New Faithful: Why Young Adults are Embracing Christian Orthodoxy* (Chicago: Loyola Press, 2002).
9. James D. Davidson et al., *The Search for Common Ground*, 111–139.
10. James L. Heft S.M. and James D. Davidson, "The Mission of Catholic High Schools and Today's Millennials," *Catholic Education: A Journal of Inquiry and Practice* 6 (June 2003): 410–422.
11. James D. Davidson and Dean R. Hoge, "Catholics After the Scandal," 13–19.
12. James D. Davidson et al., *The Search for Common Ground*; William D'Antonio et al., *American Catholics*; James D. Davidson et al., *Lay Ministers and Their Spiritual Practices*.
13. James D. Davidson and Dean R. Hoge, "Catholics After the Scandal," 13–19.
14. James D. Davidson et al., *The Search for Common Ground*.
15. James D. Davidson et al., *The Search for Common Ground*.
16. William V. D'Antonio et al., *Laity: American and Catholic*, 99.
17. James D. Davidson, *The Search for Common Ground*, 153–154.

Index

abortion 24, 46, 54, 138, 139, 141, 155, 161, 167–169, 178, 180, 187–189
Abraham Lincoln 49, 52
abuse 81, 89, 91
accountability
    91, 93, 98; financial 81, 94
Adams
    John Quincy 6, 48; Samuel 6
adults
    compared to youth 150; older 28, 29, 131; social network 150, 151; younger 26, 28, 29, 35, 80, 82, 87, 88, 96, 97, 105, 131, 149, 156, 157, 162–63, 170, 175, 178–181
Africa/African 100, 101, 180, 183
African Americans 16–18, 42, 69, 117, 126, 148, 149, 157, 167–169
age
    differences 105, 120; homophily and 32–33; of Latinos 71; of pre-Vatican II Catholics 90 (see also *Vatican II*); priest vs. laypeople 104; relationships and 32
AIDS 71
Alabama 20, 30
Alaska 21, 56
Allen, Woody 30
Altar Society 142
altarito 184
Alwin, Duane 170, 171
America
    colonial 3; cultural history 9; global Catholicism 100, 101; integration of parishes 69; models of Catholicism 9; other churches 112; pledge of allegiance 43; postmodern culture 23, 133; poverty 42, 58; priest shortage 110; priests, deacons, and lay ministers 99; Protestant Establishment 36; status of Catholics 11, 13, 31, 40; stratification 5; voting 54; vs. communism 45
American Baptists 33, 34, 112, 113
American Catholics
    national surveys of 141, 159, 164, 176, 182; practices of 126, 128, 130, 132, 134, 136, 138, 140, 142, 144, 148, 150, 152, 154, 156
American
    culture 10, 23, 88; families 40; households 17, 56
American Legion 43
American
    life 3, 13; model of 3, 10, 21; people 10–12, 15, 16, 22–25, 27, 39–42, 45, 46, 54, 69, 126,

146, 152, 153, 167; population 14, 70; society 9, 12, 13, 19, 21, 25, 152, 171
American Sociological Association 18
Amos, Old Testament Prophet 165
Anglicanism 5
Anglos 183, 184
annual appeals 94
anti-Catholicism 6, 10, 11, 43, 89, 90
Aquinas, Saint Thomas 165
Archdiocese
    Boston 95; Indianapolis 116; Milwaukee 37; New York 158, 159; St. Louis (MO) 159
ARIS survey 56
Arizona 20, 57, 58, 158
Arkansas 21, 45
Asia 12, 100, 101
Asians 16–18, 42, 117, 126, 148, 149, 183
Assemblies of God 33, 34, 69, 78, 101, 112, 113, 167
Atlanta 158
Australia 100
authority
    of bishops/clergy 176; orthodox Catholics 180; personal conscience 88, 176; traditional vs. legal-rational 92–94; types of 92, 93; women and 188
autonomy 171

baby-boomers 172
Bacik, James 103
Beaudoin, Tom 175
ban
    artificial birth 88; electioneering 47
baptism 66, 67
Baptists 5, 8, 12, 13, 30, 39, 47, 48, 50, 51, 113, 144
Beaudoin, Tom 175
behavior
    ancestors and 147; and Catholics 125; attitudes and 130, 132; criteria 15; homophily 32; in-group and out-group 7, 8; learning theory and 126; of Church leaders 91; of conservatives 178; of laity 188; of the poor 166; patterns 126; understanding change 125
Bellamy, Francis 43
Bells of St. Mary's 65
benedictions 119
benefactors 79

197